· OMNIUM LUX CIVIUM ·

BOSTON
PUBLIC LIBRARY
A Centennial History

By WALTER MUIR WHITEHILL

Director and Librarian, Boston Athenæum

Illustrations by RUDOLPH RUZICKA

Cambridge, Massachusetts

HARVARD UNIVERSITY PRESS

1956

© Copyright, 1956,
by the President and Fellows of Harvard College

Distributed in Great Britain by Geoffrey Cumberlege,
Oxford University Press, London

Library of Congress Catalog Card Number 56–6528
PRINTED IN THE UNITED STATES OF AMERICA

Preface

Justin Winsor, who became Superintendent of the Boston Public Library in 1868 after one year as a Trustee (and a dozen years of literary work), once remarked, in the idiom of his native Duxbury: "It was by much the same process as in the New England seaboard towns, in old times, a young man sometimes attained command of a ship without apprenticeship before the mast, by 'crawling in through the cabin windows', that I got so conspicuous a place in the librarian's calling."

When I became Librarian of the Boston Athenæum in 1946, with two decades of *using* libraries in the pursuit of history as my chief experience, I similarly attained command without apprenticeship before the mast. I cannot claim to have "crawled in through the cabin windows" for in a sense I had begun my adult life inside, as a cabin-boy. From 1918 to 1920 I passed two dreary years in the Boston Latin School, which were chiefly bearable because twice daily, on my way to and from the gloomy red brick monster at the corner of Warren Avenue and Dartmouth Street, I passed the Boston Public Library and, on most afternoons, went in. I had known and loved the building for at least ten years, for the visits to Dr. Geoffrey Brackett in Newbury Street that had punctuated my earliest years invariably concluded with a climb up the Siena marble staircase of the library to visit the dignified lions that guard the landing while bearing witness to the Civil War valor of the Second and Twentieth Massachusetts Volunteer Infantry regiments. Dr. Brackett had assured me that if I pulled the lions' tails, they *might* roar, and I never failed to try. At about this same period, my future wife, escaping from a maid who had escorted her to the dentist, hauled herself up by the paint-brush and attempted to sit in the lap of Bela Pratt's bronze personification of Art, outside on the terrace, only to be reprimanded by a frock-coated and helmeted policeman with ginger colored whiskers, who had abandoned the direction of traffic at Huntington Avenue and Dartmouth Street for the purpose. We did not meet, however, for another fifteen years.

The Boston Latin School thirty-five years ago suited my temperament so poorly that I welcomed the daily opportunity to escape to the third floor of the Public Library, where I could wallow to my heart's content in architectural accounts of the palaces of Versailles. I recall vividly poring over Arnott and Wilson's measured drawings of the Petit Trianon; the freedom with which similar folios were delivered to a small boy in his early teens seems, in retrospect, to show remarkable sympathy and faith on the part of the attendants in the Fine Arts Department.

One day in the winter of 1919 I fell into conversation with the late Frank A. Bourne, who had temporarily deserted his architectural practice to bring about some changes in the Fine Arts Department of the Library. We became good friends, as can so readily happen when an older person has the imagination to treat a small boy like a contemporary who knows what he is about, and when Mr. Bourne one day offered me a job I jumped at the chance. There was the slight formality of an entrance examination, but, as that could easily have been passed by anyone able to read and write, I was soon a very junior member of the Boston Public Library staff, hunting for mislaid books and doing odd chores in the Fine Arts Department after school. It is extraordinarily pleasant to do what you most enjoy and have other people not only consider it work, but pay you for it! That thought has often crossed my mind during the last eight years in the Athenæum, and as I look back to my brief employment in the Boston Public Library I view it in the same terms, even though my weekly wages ranged from a high of $2.50 to a low of eighty-one cents! Moreover, that period did give me the professional respectability of at least *beginning* in a library.

Three years' service on the Examining Committee always gave me the sensation of revisiting an old friend, and the amiable request of the Trustees that I prepare a centennial history of the Public Library has furnished me a welcome excuse to explore the family history and background of that old friend. That request is also typical of the harmonious relations that exist between Boston institutions. The Boston Athenæum will be a century and a half old in 1957. Twice in its forties it declined offers of marriage from the infant Public Library, yet though the infant has grown into a veritable

Herakles, with more arms than the god Siva, there have never been any hard feelings. The two libraries have gone their separate ways, yet it is characteristic that the Director of the Athenæum should be given the privilege of recording the history of the Public Library.

This book is purely an institutional history that does not attempt to reflect the development of the public library movement. In very recent years Jesse H. Shera's *Foundations of the Public Library: The Origins of the Public Library Movement in New England, 1629–1855* and C. Seymour Thompson's *Evolution of the American Public Library, 1653–1876* have dealt with the background, while Sidney Ditzion's *Arsenals of a Democratic Culture* has explored the social circumstances of the public library movement from 1850 to 1900. I am indebted to Francis Gilman Collier for permission to read his unpublished Harvard Ph.D. thesis of 1951, entitled *A History of the American Public Library Movement through 1880.* The investigations of these four scholars makes winnowing of their fields superfluous. Moreover, the numerous and full quotations from public documents in Horace G. Wadlin's *The Public Library of the City of Boston, a History,* published in 1911, hardly require repetition in their entirety. As my chief sources have been the reports and other official records of the library itself, supplemented by the manuscript (T.R. 25.59) "Annals of the Public Library of the City of Boston from the year 1848 to its removal to the new edifice in Copley Square" by William Whitwell Greenough, a Trustee from 1856 to 1888, it has not seemed necessary to indulge in a wealth of citation, and I have contented myself with simple bibliographical references to other sources at the ends of certain chapters.

WALTER MUIR WHITEHILL

Boston Athenæum
1 July 1954

CONTENTS

LIST OF ILLUSTRATIONS

CHAPTER I

"Out of Small Beginnings"

> The City of Boston is hereby authorized to establish and maintain a public library, for the use of the inhabitants of the said city . . . provided, however, that no appropriation for the said library shall exceed the sum of five thousand dollars in any one year.
> —Act of Massachusetts Legislature, 1848

SINCE the Massachusetts Bay Colony Tercentenary in 1930, similar observances have crowded upon each other. Three-hundredth anniversaries of the foundation of towns, churches, and educational institutions have become so numerous that it is hard to realize that a simple centenary marks the true age of one of the most completely accepted and characteristic features of our daily life. In the United States of today a public library, supported by citizens through their own taxes, is by common consent as usual and necessary a part of an established community as a church or a school, yet the Boston Public Library—the pioneer in this movement—first opened its doors to readers in the spring of 1854.

To understand the rarity of libraries in the American scene in the mid-nineteenth century, one must turn, as is so often necessary, to a singularly dreary-looking government document—*Notices of Public Libraries in the United States of America* by Charles C. Jewett, Librarian of the Smithsonian Institution, published in 1851 as an appendix to the *Fourth Annual Report of the Board of Regents of the Smithsonian Institution*. Working from answers received from broadcast circular letters and from published accounts, Jewett prepared a description, state by state, of those libraries that he considered *public* in that they "are accessible—either without restriction, or upon conditions with which all can easily comply—to every person who wishes to use them for their appropriate purposes." The whole number of such libraries in the United States, exclusive of those of the public schools, was, according to Jewett's calculation, 694, with an aggregate of 2,201,632 volumes. Of the 694, 271 libraries contained less than a thousand volumes each, while only five in the entire country reached a total of 50,000 volumes each. Of these five, two were in greater Boston—Harvard University (84,200) and the Boston Athenæum (50,000)—while Yale College possessed 50,481 volumes, the Philadelphia Library Company 60,000, and the Library of Congress 50,000. Numerically the resources of Boston libraries exceeded those of any other city, for the fifteen collections that Jewett recorded within the city proper, plus the Harvard University Library across the river in Cambridge, totalled 198,009 volumes, while New York City showed 186,567, Philadelphia 162,433 and the District of Columbia 111,573. Moreover Jewett commended Boston quality as well as quantity, for he observed of the Athenæum: "The library is hardly surpassed, either in size or in value, by any other in the country; and its regulations are framed with the design that it shall answer the highest purposes of a public library. Practically it is such."

From Jewett's picture, Boston was singularly fortunate, yet, as in the parable of the talents—"for unto every one that hath shall be given, and he shall have abundance"—there had been for twenty-five years intermittent agitation for more books and better libraries. The arch-agitator, who in the end superbly accomplished his purpose, was George Ticknor (1791–1871), Smith Professor of the French and Spanish Languages in Harvard College and historian of Spanish literature. Elected a Trustee of the Athenæum in 1823, Ticknor not only gave both time and money to the advancement of the library, but evolved a plan for uniting all Boston libraries into one. Writing to Daniel Webster on 2 February 1826 he confided his hopes:

> We are making quite a movement about libraries, lecture-rooms, Athenæum, etc. I have a project, which may or may not succeed; but I hope it will. The project is, to unite into one establishment, viz. the Athenæum, all the public libraries in town; such as the

Arch Library, the Medical Library, the new Scientific Library, and so on, and then let the whole circulate, Athenæum and all. In this way, there will be an end of buying duplicates, paying double rents, double librarians, etc.; the whole money raised will go to books, and all the books will be made useful. To this great establishment I would attach all the lectures wanted, whether fashionable, popular, scientific—for the mechanics or their employers; and have the whole made a Capitol of the knowledge of the town, with its uses, which I would open to the public, according to the admirable direction in the Charter of the University of Göttingen. *Quam commodissimè quamque latissimè.* Mr. Prescott, Judge Jackson, Dr. Bowditch, and a few young men are much in earnest about it.

The project did not succeed, but Ticknor continued to support the Athenæum, serving as a Trustee until 1832 and as Vice President for the year 1833. Soon after the death of a beloved son in 1834, Ticknor resigned the Smith Professorship—in which he was succeeded by Longfellow—and for several years lived abroad, travelling in England and on the continent. When he came home in 1838, Ticknor did not return to a place on the Athenæum board, but his good will seemingly continued, for in 1848 he was among the subscribers who bought from Henry Stevens of Vermont a major portion of George Washington's library and gave it to the Athenæum.

The next proposal for unifying Boston libraries came from a very different and less responsible source, Alexandre Vattemare, a native of Lisieux who, after achieving international distinction as a ventriloquist under the stage name of Monsieur Alexandre, had quite surprisingly become obsessed with a grandiose scheme for the international exchange of books and the building of public libraries. The occupations seem hardly in character, but one can only suppose that, having achieved wide notice on the stage, Vattemare longed for less ephemeral recognition of his talents, much as Hollywood artists today set up as art collectors and popular novelists hanker after the trades of the historian and the editor. Two more different characters could hardly be imagined than the scholarly Ticknor, commodiously installed in the dignified red brick house that still survives, sadly mutilated by excrescent shop windows, at the corner of Park and Beacon Streets in the shadow of the State House, and the volatile little French ventriloquist, touring Europe and collecting in an "Album Cosmopolite" tributes to his theatrical prowess from the Emperors of Austria and Russia, Queen Victoria, Beethoven, Victor Hugo, Landseer, and ten thousand others. When Vattemare arrived in New York in October 1839 he filled the Park Theatre and carried to another continent the powers of mimicry that had won him applause in most of the countries of western Europe. But his travels in the United States and Canada from 1839 to 1841 were chiefly devoted to furthering his self-invented and seemingly disinterested "system" that was "designed to give the intellectual treasures of the cultivated world the same dissemination and equalization which commerce has already given to its material ones" and that would lead, so he hoped, to "the establishment in every quarter of the world of free libraries and museums ever open to the use of the people." Had he but lived a few decades later, Vattemare's promotional instincts would have met their proper outlet in a chamber of commerce or an advertising agency, for there were few limits to the expansiveness of his imagination or his ready adaptation to any opening that presented itself. International exchanges of books and works of art were to lead to free institutions that would sooner or later bring about a kind of high-minded millennium. It was all so simple! Even in a rude frontier, lacking books for exchange, one need not be excluded from his happy and improving enterprise. In this vein Vattemare wrote to the Mercantile Library of San Francisco in 1854:

> It is therefore your natural curiosities, the strangest productions of your soils, the beautiful inhabitants of your forests and waters, and your monstrous and extraordinary fossil remains that Europe expects in return. Give us a bullfrog or a rattlesnake for the best moral and philosophical works, an alligator for a cast of the Venus de Milo, etc.

Buildings, adapted to a variety of municipal and benevolent purposes, would spring up. A visit to Montreal produced in Vattemare's fertile mind the pattern of a "suitable and elegant" structure, comprising the following elements:

FIRST,—   The basement, on a slope of a hill if possible, would furnish a lecture room and for other purposes.

SECONDLY,— The ground floor would furnish rooms for the Museum Keeper, or other Officers connected with the Institution.

THIRDLY,— The first floor would contain—a Merchant's Exchange, a Post Office, and a room for the Trinity House.

FOURTHLY,—On the second floor there would be a City Hall, of good dimensions, Treasurer's, Surveyor's and Town Clerk's Offices and Committee Rooms.

FIFTHLY,— On the third floor would be placed the Public Library, Chamber of Arts and other Offices.

SIXTHLY,— In the attic would be a Museum, lit by means of a lantern in a dome.

When this whirlwind descended upon Boston in the spring of 1841, he began a campaign to unite the dozen or more existing libraries of the city into a single institution. The merchants' clerks and other aspiring youths who frequented the Boston Mercantile Library—an estimable institution founded in 1820 to incite self-improvement among what were then called "the younger members of the commercial classes"—provided an audience ripe for the harvest. At a meeting in their rooms on Saturday evening, 24 April 1841, Vattemare bared his soul at considerable length to such effect that his audience was inspired to move a set of extended and turgid resolutions, the drift of which will be sufficiently clear from the following extracts:

> RESOLVED, That we have listened with great delight to Mr. Vattemare's plan of forming a great public Literary and Scientific Institution in this city, by uniting our various Libraries and collections in Science and the Fine Arts; and we think such an institution would benefit the great body of the people, by opening to all the treasures of Science, Literature and Art, by breaking down the factitious distinctions which separate class from class, by disseminating knowledge and taste through every portion of our population, and by the influence it would have in the promotion of universal education.

RESOLVED, That we regard the system of National Interchange suggested by Mr. Vattemare, as one which will tend to remove national and sectional prejudices, will promote the great cause of peace, and the first principle of religion, by uniting all nations in intellectual brotherhood; as one which by making each state and nation a participant in the other's productions, will bring about a kind of mental commerce which cannot fail to promote universal civilization; and we think that the glorious success which has so far attended Mr. Vattemare's labors in this department of his comprehensive plan, and the general favor with which the system has been received by eminent men in all countries, affords us sufficient assurances that it can be achieved in this City, if the public mind be awakened to a sense of its importance . . .

RESOLVED, That as Boston has the reputation of being the first literary city in the Union, it behooves her citizens not to jeopardize that reputation by refusing to do what other cities with less pretensions have triumphantly achieved.

RESOLVED, That Mr. Vattemare's plan having received the encouragement, and been stamped with the approbation of the most eminent sovereigns, statesmen, and literary men of Europe, from the Sultan of Turkey to La Fayette and La Martine—of the President, Chief Justice, and both Houses of Congress of our own country—and moreover as it is a plan, to carry out which all parties, and religions, and sects, cheerfully unite—we may be pardoned in saying—as all the eminent men in this city and vicinity who have examined its claims, have said—that the plan is practicable, is worthy the attention of every man who has a faculty to educate, or a child whom he desires should grow to the intellectual stature of manhood, is replete with advantages to every person in the community, however humble his station, and should stimulate the zealous, energetic, and persevering exertions of the great body of the people.

RESOLVED, That a Committee of twelve be appointed from this meeting, to correspond with the influential men in this community, for the purpose of soliciting them to call a meeting of the citizens at Faneuil Hall, to consider the subject in all its bearings . . .

The result of this happy occasion was a meeting on 5 May at the Masonic Temple, rather than Faneuil Hall, presided over by Mayor Jonathan Chapman. Vattemare once again outlined his proposals, "the whole thing going off with immensely greater effect than I could have conceived possible," as the not easily aroused Charles Francis Adams entered in his diary. Vattemare had, incidentally, obliged by an entertainment of ventriloquism at Mr. Adams's house the previous evening, holding the attention of the company until nearly midnight. At the close of the Masonic Temple meeting, Vattemare was thanked "for his interesting, instructive, and eloquent exposition of his noble project" and a committee consisting of Mr. Adams, Dr. Walter Channing, Josiah Quincy, Jr., the Reverend Ezra S. Gannett, and the Reverend George Washington Blagden was appointed to consider the practicability of the plan. The committee met on several occasions, but without major accomplishment. After the second meeting Adams noted in his diary: "Vattemare admitted that everything had been commenced everywhere, but nothing had been done."

A circular letter was sent by the committee to fifteen Boston institutions to inquire whether they would be disposed to cooperate

. . . if a union of the principal literary associations, and those for the promotion of the arts and sciences, could be effected under a single roof with suitable accommodations to make their various collections as available to the public of Boston as can be, consistently with their safety.

A tentative plan, accompanying this letter, proposed a building to be "erected directly by the citizens, or by the government of the City" that would house a library, collections of natural history and the arts, and provide a hall for public lectures and rooms for the meetings of societies. In this building, which was to "be the property of the people," it was proposed that existing literary, scientific and artistic institutions should not only place their collections, but surrender title to them. Future support was to come from annual subscriptions for "the use of the institution as a circulating library," from "the interest of such property as the several institutions may surrender," from fines for the late return of books, rents from the lecture hall, and a tax levy by the city "on the same principle which now induces the citizens to tax themselves for the support of public schools." It is a tribute to the almost hypnotic power of Vattemare's eloquence that five hard-headed New England individualists—including an Adams—even imagined that their friends and neighbors might so far succumb to emotion as to surrender property painfully accumulated for specific learned purposes over many decades to a promotional scheme of this kind.

William T. Andrews, Edward Wigglesworth, and N. I. Bowditch, who were appointed by the Boston Athenæum to consider the proposal, reported on 12 July 1841 that they were

> . . . unanimously of opinion that there are insuperable objections to the adoption of this measure by the Boston Athenæum. These various objections they do not think it necessary to state in detail. While the Committee would be happy to extend somewhat more widely than at present the benefits of the Institution, they believe that even now much fewer instances occur than might be supposed of deserving individuals who are desirous of obtaining access to the Athenæum and are unable to do so. Regarding our institution as a moderate sized circulating library, the Committee believe that it is only by a limited number of proprietors that its advantages can be conveniently and fully enjoyed. Should it be thrown open, as a circulating library, to the public or to all who should pay an annual sum, and without possessing any duplicates, it would in the opinion of your committee be of far less value than at present.

> A public library, open to all our citizens, would undoubtedly be highly desirable. Such a one may with propriety be established without absorbing all similar private institutions. The advantages of each are in a great degree separate and distinct. On the whole, therefore, the Committee are decidedly of opinion that it is not expedient to adopt the proposed measure, either in view of the interests of the proprietors or of the public.

The Boston Society of Natural History, through its president, George B. Emerson, expressed cautiously qualified approval in November. They strongly stated the opinion that the building must be "erected by means independent of the societies."

> We hold that six hundred dollars a year devoted to the increase of our library and scientific collections, though they must be kept in the poorest rooms, provided they are accessible and capacious enough to contain and exhibit them, would be better than half that

sum devoted to a library and museum in halls that should cost half a million. We maintain that the proposition which is often laid down, that if large and noble buildings be provided, generous men will easily be found to furnish them with books, instruments and the other apparatus for knowledge, is refuted by the uniform and universal experience of the whole country.

Although there would be advantages to a common building erected at the public expense, and great merit in a single responsible librarian or keeper—"a good librarian is the soul of a library"—nevertheless special restrictions would have to govern the use of scientific specimens and books.

The Mechanic Apprentices Library Association, having less at stake, cheerfully climbed aboard the bandwagon, while the Boston Marine Society and the Society for Medical Improvement courteously explained their inability to give corporate support. It is significant that the other ten recipients, including the American Academy of Arts and Sciences, the Massachusetts Historical Society, the American Antiquarian Society and the Lowell Institute, did not even bother to reply. In view of this tepid response, the committee discharged itself from further consideration of the subject, and Charles Francis Adams moved that its report be deposited with the Mercantile Library Association, which had instigated the commotion in the first place, to "bring the subject before the community whenever favorable circumstances shall occur."

Alas for personal magnetism, the enthusiasm generated by Vattemare's eloquence subsided with his return to Europe, and although in 1843 he transmitted some fifty volumes as a gift from the City of Paris to Boston, little happened until his second visit to the United States (1847–1849). Vattemare inspired such contradictory sentiments in his contemporaries that it is uncommonly difficult to assess the significance of the Frenchman's activities in Boston. Even the more conservative Bostonians have been occasionally aroused by the arrival of versatile Europeans who pressed intellectual projects with evangelical fervor; witness the remarkable accomplishments of Louis Agassiz in creating the Museum of Comparative Zoology out of nothing in the late fifties and early sixties. While Agassiz swept all, even the General Court, before him—there is the story of the state legislator sadly observing, "Agassiz is going to speak to us tomorrow. I wish he wouldn't. We can't afford to give him anything now, but after we have heard him we will!"—Vattemare aroused both devotees and detractors. Josiah Quincy, Jr., who served as Mayor of Boston from December 1845 to January 1849, believed in Vattemare's plan so thoroughly as to offer personal support. This enthusiasm carried over into the next generation, for his son, Josiah P. Quincy, writing in the *Proceedings* of the Massachusetts Historical Society for November 1884 about Vattemare, who had died twenty years earlier, observed:

> The idea of establishing a free library in this City seemed to pervade him to his fingers' ends. He followed it up with a vehemence which might well startle the guardians of the sluggish proprieties. He pursued the Mayor with visits and by correspondence; he wrought upon that functionary to make a conditional offer of $5,000 towards providing books for the library, and to see that a petition was sent to the Legislature for permission to levy taxes for its support.

On the other hand, Robert C. Winthrop, reminiscing about the foundation of the library in a letter of 17 November 1871 to Justin Winsor, wrote:

> Our friend Mr. Ticknor was not a little unwilling to have Vattemare's name connected with the Library, regarding him as a Charlatan, as, indeed, we all did. I cannot forget how Mr. T. winced when I read to him my allusion to Vattemare on the 23d page of the Cornerstone Proceedings, and how earnestly he said "I would not say a word about him."

Henry Stevens, who was then purchasing Americana abroad for John Carter Brown and James Lenox, flatly denounced one aspect of Vattemare's system of international exchanges as "an insignificant humbug." Stevens, who knew his books and whose Vermont origins endowed him with a resistance to sales appeal, minced no words when he wrote:

> In Paris Mr. Alexandre has long time been considered a charlatan and his system of international exchange is thought to be only a substitute for his worn-out voice for ventriloquism.

Nevertheless, it was Vattemare's activity, resulting in a second gift of books from Paris to Boston, that provided the next step. The receipt of this second collection, "consisting of rare and useful works relating to internal police, general and local statistics and history, illustrated with engravings, and making a collection of nearly one hundred volumes," led the Boston City Council in August 1847 to appoint a Joint Special Committee, consisting of Mayor Quincy, Aldermen Wetmore and Parker, and Councilmen Hillard, Carter, Thayer and Eaton, to "consider and report what acknowledgment and return should be made to the City of Paris for its gift of books and provide a place for the same." This group, reporting in October 1847, recommended the installation of the Paris gifts, and others that might be received, in a room on the third floor of City Hall— the granite structure in Court Square built in 1835 as a Court House, and occupied as a City Hall from 1841 until the building of the present one was begun upon the same site in 1862. The first concrete proposal backed by cash—Mayor Quincy's anonymous offer —for the establishment of a public library in Boston appeared in this report.

> The Committee cannot close their report without recommending to the City Council a consideration of the propriety of commencing a public library. Many of the citizens would, they believe, be happy to contribute both in books and money to such an object and the Committee are informed that a citizen, who wishes that his name may be concealed, has offered the sum of $5,000 for the purpose of making the commencement, on condition only that $10,000 are raised at large for the same purpose and that the library should be as fully used by all, as may be consistent with the safe-keeping of the property.

By order of 18 October 1847, Mayor Quincy was authorized to acknowledge the gift of the City of Paris, and to solicit and transmit books as a gift in return, while the City Council appointed a Joint Special Committee on the Public Library, consisting of the Mayor, two Aldermen and five Councilmen. The Council further ordered, on 22 November 1847,

> That the joint special committee on the public library be directed to inquire into the expediency of applying to the legislature for the

power to establish, regulate, and control a library for the free use of every citizen, with power to appropriate any sum not exceeding......dollars, whenever a like sum shall be secured and placed in the hands of the city government by private subscription. The said committee to fill the blank with such sum as they deem expedient.

The Joint Special Committee reported favorably on 6 December 1847 regarding the usefulness of establishing a public library, but were not so rash as to propose spending any city money for it.

At all events the establishment of public libraries, and a free exchange of works of science, literature and art will be productive of great good and is well deserving an attempt to obtain it. The Committee do not recommend that the City should make any appropriation for the purchase of books, or hold out any encouragement that it should be done hereafter. They only propose that they should receive and take care of any volume that may be contributed for the purpose, and agree that when the library is of sufficient importance to justify the expense, to provide means that should enable all the citizens to use it with as little restriction as is consistent with the safety and preservation of the property.

Mayor Quincy wished to *bind* the City to provide proper quarters for the library whenever the books contributed reached the value of thirty thousand dollars, but his fellow-committeemen were only disposed to agree that it would be *expedient* to do so. The harmless and economical nature of the proposal at least avoided frightening the City Council, which was about to go out of office, and on 6 December it was resolved:

That this City Council heartily approves of a proper effort on the part of the city government to establish a public library, and recommends that enterprise to the favourable consideration of the next City Council.

Quincy, undiscouraged by the failure of private citizens or public authority to come forward with the $10,000 that was needed to insure his personal contribution of $5,000, brought the proposed public library into his inaugural address when entering upon his new term as Mayor on 3 January 1848. The new City Council heeded his plea, and on 24 January 1848 directed him "to apply to the Legislature for power to enable the City to establish and maintain a public library." Thus it came about that the Legislature passed, and Governor Briggs signed, on 18 March 1848, the first legislation authorizing the plan that was so close to Quincy's heart.

CITY OF BOSTON
AUTHORIZATION TO ESTABLISH A PUBLIC LIBRARY

Be it enacted by the Senate and House of Representatives, in General Court assembled, and by the authority of the same, as follows:

SECTION 1. The City of Boston is hereby authorized to establish and maintain a public library, for the use of the inhabitants of the said city; and the city council of the said city may, from time to time, make such rules and regulations, for the care and maintenance thereof, as they may deem proper; provided, however, that no appropriation for the said library shall exceed the sum of five thousand dollars in any one year.

SECTION 2. This act shall be null and void unless it shall be accepted by the city council of the said city of Boston, within sixty days of its passage.

When it was accepted within sixteen days, on 3 April 1848 (notwithstanding the cautious restriction of funds that it contained), a real step had been taken. One swallow maketh not summer, neither does an act even of the Great and General Court of the Commonwealth of Massachusetts cause a library to spring instantly into being. Otherwise the library's centenary would have been observed in 1948. Nevertheless, this brief piece of legislation was of historic import, for, as Mr. Wadlin pointed out in his history of 1911:

It was the first statute ever passed authorizing the establishment and maintenance of a public library as a municipal institution supported by taxation. It antedated by 16 months the general law in New Hampshire, and preceded by 38 months the first general law in Massachusetts. It was referred to in the discussion preceding the first English statute, authorizing the establishment of libraries and museums in municipal boroughs in England, which received royal assent, August 14, 1850.

With the Boston Athenæum already in substantial existence as one of the leading libraries of the country, Mayor Quincy's eye naturally turned in that direction. He had been Treasurer of the Athenæum since 1837; his father, Josiah Quincy, the second Mayor of Boston (1822–1828), had been its President from 1822 until his migration to Cambridge as President of Harvard College in 1829. Here was an opportunity to graft the future public library upon a stock that had grown wisely and robustly for forty-one years. Moreover, as Treasurer Quincy had reason to know, at this particular moment the Athenæum was thinking very hard about new sources of income. The house in Pearl Street that James Perkins had given it in 1822 had been outgrown within two decades, and in April 1847 the cornerstone of the present Athenæum, at 10½ Beacon Street, overlooking the Granary Burying Ground, had been laid. The design selected in competition was the work of Edward Clarke Cabot, a Boston gentleman engaged in raising sheep in Vermont, who like Thomas Jefferson turned his natural abilities to architecture without previous formal training. Considering many of the horrors and high-shouldered architectural dullnesses of the eighteen forties, Cabot's building was, and still is, extraordinarily pleasant, but it had turned out to be a great deal more expensive than had been anticipated. Consequently when President Thomas G. Cary and Vice President John Amory Lowell of the Athenæum wrote the Mayor on 29 July with a tentative plan for "uniting the interests of the City with those of the Athenæum in order to extend the usefulness of the library," Quincy was entirely in accord. The Trustees of the Athenæum voted on 14 August to recommend to the Proprietors—the 500 share-holders who through their stock actually owned the institution—a proposal "that they should give to the public the use of the Library in as full a manner as it now is, or hereafter may be, enjoyed by the share-holders" in return for the payment of $50,000 by the City of Boston on 1 December 1848, and an annual subsidy of $5,000. The management of the Athenæum, under this new plan, was to be in the hands of ten directors, six of whom were to be chosen by the Athenæum Trustees and four by the City Council. This arrangement, although agreeable to the Athenæum Trustees, and approved by the Joint Standing Commit-

tee on the Public Library on 22 September, was rejected by the
Athenæum Proprietors, who, after hearing a discussion of the plan
at a special meeting on 24 October 1848, voted for indefinite post-
ponement. The decision was in no way surprising. Boston trustees,
as a race, have always combined conservatism with a considerable
proportion of imaginative daring, but meetings at which five hundred New England individualists have the right to vote are seldom
rapidly convinced. It is easy to see the reluctance of the Proprietors
to attempt the adaptation of a building, designed for one quantity
and type of use, to another for which it would certainly have proved
inadequate, before it had even been occupied. Moreover, with no
precedent for municipal support of libraries, they may well be pardoned a reasonable scepticism about the continuing interest of the
City Council. It would have required keener powers of divination
than Bostonians of 1848 possessed to foresee the millions of dollars
that American cities were to devote to the cause of books in the century ahead. The difficulties were recognized at the time, for, as
William W. Greenough remarked in his *Annals* for 1848:

> Later in this year, an unsuccessful effort was made for the union
> with the Boston Athenæum, a result which, in the case of success,
> would have proved unfortunate and injurious to both institutions.
> Each library had its own limitations, the one to the stockholders
> who owned the property, the other to the City of Boston for the
> benefit of whose inhabitants it had been founded.

Signs of rival enterprise in New York City became apparent when
the Trustees of the Astor Library were incorporated on 18 January
1849. John Jacob Astor, who had died on 29 March 1848, only a
few days after the passage of the act to authorize the establishment
of a public library in Boston, had left $400,000 for building a
public library in New York, equipping it with books and maintaining it. Soon after the incorporation of the Trustees, plans were announced for an impressive building "in the Byzantine style, or rather
in the style of the royal palaces of Florence" (as the *Literary World*
rather hesitatingly phrased it) costing $75,000. Joseph Green Cogs-
well, LL.D., who was appointed Librarian, had already by the fall
of 1849 assembled some twenty thousand volumes in England and

on the continent, yet in Boston there were only happy thoughts and another appearance of the irrepressible Monsieur Vattemare.

That gentleman, on 16 April 1849, presented the City of Boston with a third gift from the City of Paris, this time of some fifty volumes, including the following:

> Accounts of the Public Pawn-Brokers, from 1841 to 1844. 2 volumes.
>
> Reports on the Progress and Effects of the Cholera Morbus in the City of Paris and the Department of the Seine, in 1832, by a Committee appointed by the Prefects of the Seine and Police. Paris, 1844. 4to.
>
> Reports made to the Municipal Council by the Special Committee appointed for the Organization of Slaughter-Houses, and the Regulations of Butcheries, 1843.
>
> Regulations concerning the Sale of Spiritous Drinks. 1837. Large folio.
>
> Statistical Map of the Sewers of the City of Paris, showing the Introduction of Water, Cisspools, etc. 1839.

Although it might have seemed that the City of Paris, with true Gallic frugality, had simply allowed Monsieur Vattemare to help himself from a surplus stock of public documents in the attic of the Hôtel de Ville, the gift was gratefully hailed by the Boston City Council and steps were taken to reciprocate. A committee was appointed to solicit donations; by September a tidy number had been assembled, and the full list was proudly printed as City Document No. 46. Emerson, Longfellow, Parkman, Prescott and Whittier contributed their latest works; the American Academy of Arts and Sciences and the Massachusetts Horticultural Society their publications. Publishers parted with copies of their current best-sellers, and in one way and another a fairly representative collection was obtained. One wonders, however, what use the Parisians made of the first Burmese edition of L. Stilson's *Introduction to Plane Trigonometry,* the *New Testament* in Siamese, or *The Basa Hymn Book,* prepared for the Baptist Mission at Cape Palmas, West Africa, and similar works contributed in generous numbers by the American Baptist Missionary Union. It is intriguing to speculate whether anyone really enjoyed the numerous offerings of the Massachusetts Sabbath School Society, of which *Louisa Ralston, or what can I do for the heathen?* (Boston, 1839) is a typical example. Probably they were at least as useful as the *Accounts of the Public Pawn-Brokers, from 1841 to 1844.*

This exchange of international civilities marks the end of Vattemare's prologue to the founding of the Boston Public Library. It is easy to smile at his solemn enthusiasms over anything and everything; it is hard to share his faith in the millennial benefits that were to accrue from exchanging public documents. Tangibly he contributed little, but emotionally he moved many Bostonians, including Josiah Quincy, Jr., whose acts as Mayor undoubtedly speeded a process that might have lagged even more than it did. Justin Winsor summed the matter up rather neatly in his *Memorial History of Boston* when he wrote:

> Whatever we think of Vattemare, whether we call him an enthusiast, or something worse or better, we must recognize his contagious energy, which induced State after State to succumb to his representations, so that by 1853 he had brought one hundred and thirty libraries and institutions within his operations; and between 1847 and 1851 had brought from France for American libraries 30,655 volumes, besides maps, engravings, etc.

SOURCES

Details concerning Vattemare's activity in Boston come largely from a collection of manuscript notes and letters labelled "MSS. relating to Vattemare in Boston" that he gave to the Boston Public Library (T.R. 25.29) in 1855, and from a larger group of documents (T.R. 25.29a) assembled and presented by his devoted admirer Josiah Quincy, Jr., in 1877. Another miscellaneous volume in the Trustees' Room of the library (T.R. 15.10), assembled by Justin Winsor, contains Robert C. Winthrop's letter of 17 November 1871 and other valuable documents on the foundation of the library. The most extensive study of Vattemare is in an unpublished Columbia University thesis for the degree of Master of Science in 1934 by Elizabeth M. Richards, *Alexandre Vattemare and His System of International Exchanges,* generously made available to me on inter-library loan by the Columbia University Library. An abstract of Miss Richard's work was published in the *Bulletin of the Medical Library Association,* XXXII (1944), 413–448. Vattemare was amusingly described in Gertrude Barnes Fiertz, "Charley McCarthy's Grandfather, The Wild Oats of a Boston Benefactor," *New England Quarterly,* XI (1938), 698–708. The references to him in Justin Winsor's "Libraries in Boston," *The Memorial History of Boston* (Boston, 1883), IV, 279–294, are, like everything that Winsor wrote, worth reading. Zoltán Haraszti, "Alexander Vattemare," *More Books,* II (1927), 257–272, published from the Quincy documents (T.R. 25.29a) a letter of 14 April 1841 from President Josiah Quincy to Josiah Quincy, Jr., expressing his interest in Vattemare's proposals. *City Document No. 46. Report of the Committee on the Library, in relation to the donations received from the City of Paris . . .* (Boston, 1849) gives full particulars of the books exchanged through Vattemare's efforts.

Ticknor's activity is well described in George S. Hillard, *Life, Letters and Journals of George Ticknor* (London, 1876).

CHAPTER II

The Founding of the Library

Now what seems to me to be wanted in Boston
is an apparatus that shall carry this taste for reading as deep as possible into society.
—GEORGE TICKNOR, 1851

JOHN PRESCOTT BIGELOW, who had succeeded Josiah
Quincy, Jr., as Mayor of Boston in 1849, conducted himself with
such energy during an epidemic of Asiatic cholera that swept the
city during that summer that certain citizens raised a subscription
fund for a testimonial gift to him. Rather than see this token of
appreciation squandered upon a silver vase, Mayor Bigelow proposed that the sum of $1,000 be contributed to a fund for the pro-
jected public library, which thus, on 5 August 1850, received its
first gift of money. Private individuals had, in the meantime, been
adding books to the scarcely scintillating collection received through
Vattemare's efforts that was housed in an upper room of City Hall.
Robert C. Winthrop, in the autumn of 1849, gave certain bound
volumes of public documents that he had used during his terms in
the national House of Representatives. Ezra Weston, the substantial
shipbuilder and merchant of Duxbury, the Honorable S. A. Eliot,
Dr. J. Mason Warren, J. D. W. Williams and the Reverend J. B.
McMahan followed suit, while the versatile Edward Everett made
an offer of his collection of public documents and State papers that
was, to his expressed annoyance, not acknowledged with great
promptness.

Everett, who later played a major part in the development of the
library, was at this moment—and almost for the first time in his
fifty-five years—without public or academic duties. A Harvard
Master of Arts and Minister of the Brattle Street Church in Boston

at nineteen, Professor of Greek Literature in Harvard College at twenty-one, Everett was, at thirty, elected to the House of Representatives. After nine years in Congress, four terms as Governor of Massachusetts, and four years as Minister at the Court of St. James's, he had, in 1846, become President of Harvard College only to find the turbulence of undergraduates rather too much for his peace of mind. "I am fighting wild beasts in this my new Ephesus; where, however, I shall stay till all are satisfied that I can stay no longer," Everett wrote his brother. By January 1849, he at least was satisfied, and resigned the presidency, entering an interlude of unaccustomed leisure that continued until he succeeded his dear friend Daniel Webster as Secretary of State in November 1852. This interlude occurred at a fortunate moment for Boston, for it was largely through the interplay of Edward Everett's and George Ticknor's divergent thoughts that a reasonable concept of the Boston Public Library evolved. On 22 January 1850 Everett wrote Mayor Bigelow offering his collection of public documents "whenever you think it will be convenient for the City to receive them." Thus he renewed an offer made the previous year, for Mayor Bigelow, in acknowledging on 31 October 1849 Robert C. Winthrop's gift of public documents, had mentioned Everett's previously promised gift, "so that with you and him the enterprise is already in successful progress." When the news of Bigelow's gift of $1,000 appeared in the newspapers, Everett, in some vexation, wrote the mayor on 7 August 1850:

> You are aware that I have more than once intimated to you, orally and in writing, that I should be happy to give my collection of public documents and State papers to the City. Perceiving that a commencement is likely to be made toward the establishment of a public library, I will thank you to inform the city government that this collection is at their service, whenever it will suit their convenience to receive it. I have for nearly thirty years devoted a great deal of time and labor and considerable expense to its formation. It amounts at present to about one thousand volumes. From the foundation of the government up to the year 1825, when I first went to Congress, it contains nearly everything material. While I was in Congress I took great pains to preserve and bind up everything published by either house; and from that time to the year 1840, when I went abroad, the collection is tolerably complete. It is my intention to add to it, as far as they can be pro-

cured, the documents since published, and I omit no opportunity of supplying the deficiencies in other parts of the series.

In addition to State papers and public documents the collection contains other works connected with the civil and political History of the country.

I hope it will not be thought intrusive in me to express the opinion, that, if the city government would provide a suitable building for a public library, it would be so amply supplied from time to time by donations, that only a moderate annual appropriation for books would be wanted . . .

If a building were commenced, on a lot of public land, aiming at nothing but convenience and neatness (and all attempts to go farther in architecture, are almost sure to fail), and so planned as to admit future enlargement, the first expense need not exceed that of one of those numerous school-houses, of which the city does not hesitate to erect one every two or three years. The more retired the situation the better. The library ought not to be a show place for strangers, nor a lounge for idlers; but a quiet retreat for persons of both sexes who desire earnestly to improve their minds.

Such a library would put the finishing hand to that system of public education that lies at the basis of the prosperity of Boston and with her benevolent institutions gives her so much of her name and praise in the land.

The City Council within the week pledged itself to receive Everett's collection "whenever a suitable place shall be provided in which they can be deposited," and expressed appropriate thanks, but Everett obviously felt that his proffered generosity had been crowded into second place by the Mayor's thousand dollars, for on 30 October 1854—when the library was actually in being—he wrote in his journal:

The first important step toward the establishment of this library was the donation of my collection of public documents and State papers. More than a year before the donation took place, I had requested Mr. Bigelow, the Mayor, to inform the City Council that I would make the donation if they would make any provision for the reception of the books. I am not aware that Mr. B. took any notice of this suggestion. Being led to think that this omission was not accidental, I addressed a note to him in January, 1850 (I think), making the same tender in writing. Even this, I believe was not communicated to the City Government. In August of that year, it was announced that Mayor Bigelow intended to appropriate to founding a city library the sum of $1000 which had been subscribed to procure some testimonial of gratitude to him for his services in suppressing the cholera: and paragraphs appeared in the public papers to the effect that in consideration of the *munificent* donation the library was to be called the Bigelow library.

This last rumor, if indeed it had a foundation, never came to anything, although the Mayor, in his inaugural address on 6 January 1851, commended the future library so effectively that the City Council appropriated $1,000 for library purposes. Everett transmitted a catalogue of the collection that he proposed to give, with a letter, dated 7 June 1851, in which he reiterated that "the cost of a suitable building need not exceed that of one of the larger School Houses," and developed his belief that a public library represented "the completion of that noble system of Public Instruction, which reflects so much honor upon the City and does so much to promote its prosperity."

> The first principles of popular government require that the means of education should, as far as possible, be equally within the reach of the whole population . . . This however is the case only up to the age when School education is at an end. We provide our children with the elements of learning and science, and put it in their power by independent study and research to make further acquisitions of useful knowledge from books—but where are they to find the books in which it is contained? Here the noble principle of equality sadly fails. The sons of the wealthy alone have access to well-stored libraries; while those whose means do not allow them to purchase books are too often debarred from them at the moment when they would be most useful. We give them an elementary education, impart to them a taste and inspire them with an earnest desire for further attainment,—which unite in making books a necessary of intellectual life,—and then make no provision for supplying them . . .

> For these reasons I cannot but think that a Public Library, well supplied with books in the various departments of art and science, and open at all times for consultation and study to the citizens at large, is absolutely needed to make our admirable system of Public

Education complete; and to continue in some good degree through life that happy equality of intellectual privileges, which now exists in our Schools, but terminates with them . . .

In transmitting this letter to the City Council on 19 June, Mayor Bigelow observed that two thousand volumes had already been assembled and that, further:

The Committee on the Library have funds at their control which will probably enable them to increase the number to four thousand volumes before the expiration of the year; and if the example of the public spirited citizens who have been named [Everett, Winthrop, Vattemare, Weston and others], should exert its proper influence in the community, the City will, within a short period, possess the largest and most valuable Municipal Library in the country.

The greatest value of Everett's gift lay in its success in arousing the enthusiasm of George Ticknor. A quarter of a century before Ticknor had dreamed of uniting all Boston libraries on the foundation of the Athenæum, but had met with no particular response. Now, having completed his *History of Spanish Literature* in 1849, he once more had the leisure to resume his former interests, and on 14 July 1851 wrote to Edward Everett:

I have seen with much gratification from time to time, within the last year, and particularly in your last letter on the subject, that you interest yourself in the establishment of a public library in Boston;—I mean a library open to all the citizens, and from which all, under proper restrictions, can take out books. Such, at least, I understand to be your plan; and I have thought, more than once, that I would like to talk with you about it, but accident has prevented it. However, perhaps a letter is as good on all accounts, and better as a distinct memorandum of what I mean.

It has seemed to me, for many years, that such a free public library, if adapted to the wants of our people, would be the crowning glory of our public schools. But I think it important that it should be adapted to our peculiar character; that is, that it should come in at the end of our system of free instruction, and be fitted to continue and increase the effects of that system by the self-culture that results from reading.

The great obstacle to this with us is not—as it is in Prussia and elsewhere—a low condition of the mass of the people, condemning them, as soon as they escape from school, and often before it, to such severe labour, in order to procure the coarsest means of physical subsistence, that they have no leisure for intellectual culture, and soon lose all taste for it. Our difficulty is, to furnish means specially fitted to encourage a love of reading, to create an appetite for it, which the schools often fail to do, and then to adapt these means to its gratification. That an appetite for reading can be very widely excited is plain, from what the cheap publications of the last twenty years have accomplished, gradually raising the taste from such poor trash as the novels with which they began, up to the excellent and valuable works of all sorts which now flood the country, and are read by the middling classes everywhere, and in New England, I think, even by a majority of the people.

Now what seems to me to be wanted in Boston is, an apparatus that shall carry this taste for reading as deep as possible into society, assuming, what I believe to be true, that it can be carried deeper in our society than in any other in the world, because we are better fitted for it. To do this I would establish a library which, in its *main* department and purpose, should differ from all free libraries yet attempted; I mean one in which any popular books, tending to moral and intellectual improvement, should be furnished in such numbers of copies that many persons, if they desired it, could be reading the same work at the same time; in short, that not only the best books of all sorts, but the pleasant literature of the day, should be made accessible to the whole people at the only time when they care for it, i.e. when it is fresh and new. I would, therefore, continue to buy additional copies of any book of this class, almost as long as they should continue to be asked for, and thus, by following the popular taste,—unless it should demand something injurious,—create a real appetite for healthy general reading. This appetite, once formed, will take care of itself. It will in the great majority of cases, demand better and better books; and can, I believe, by a little judicious help, rather than by any direct control or restraint, be carried much higher than is generally thought possible . . .

Nor would I, on this plan, neglect the establishment of a department for consultation, and for all the common purposes of public libraries, some of whose books, like encyclopedias and dictionaries, should never be lent out, while others could be permitted to circulate; all on the shelves being accessible for reference as many hours in the day as possible, and always in the evening. This part of the library, I should hope would be much increased by donations from public-spirited individuals, and individuals inter-

ested in the progress of knowledge, while, I think, the public treasury should provide for the more popular department . . .

The notion of a circulating library was new to Everett, for on 26
July he replied:

> The extensive circulation of new and popular works is a feature
> of a public library which I have not hitherto much contemplated.
> It deserves to be well weighed, and I shall be happy hereafter to
> confer with you on the subject. I cannot deny that my views have,
> since my younger days, undergone some change as to the practica-
> bility of freely loaning books at home from large public libraries.
> Those who have been connected with the administration of such
> libraries are apt to get discouraged, by the loss and damage result-
> ing from the loan of books. My present impressions are in favour
> of making the amplest provision in the library for the use of books
> there.
>
> Your plan, however, is intended to apply only to a particular
> class of books, and does not contemplate the unrestrained circula-
> tion of those of which the loss could not be easily replaced.

Although Everett's and Ticknor's conviction that a library "would
help to make our system of Public Education complete" was echoed
in the report of the Joint Standing Committee on the Public Library, presented to the City Council on 1 January 1852 and printed
as City Document No. 79, hopeful words were not augmented by
concrete proposals until February 1852 when Benjamin Seaver, who
had succeeded John P. Bigelow as Mayor, made the following request of the City Council:

> In order to carry this Institution into successful operation, I
> respectfully suggest that a Librarian be appointed, and a large room
> or rooms easy of access in a central portion of the City be secured,
> as the one now occupied has always been regarded more as a place
> for the deposit of books, than a suitable situation for a perma-
> nent Library. I would also respectfully suggest for your considera-
> tion the propriety of appointing, from our citizens at large, five or
> six gentlemen who feel interested in the subject, who, together
> with the Joint Standing Committee, shall form a Board of Directors
> or Trustees for the Public Library. These gentlemen, being annu-
> ally elected by the City Government to act with the Committee
> on the Library in the management of its affairs, would, I think,

essentially aid in giving permanence to the Institution, and in securing the confidence and cooperation of our citizens.

The Mayor's recommendations were adopted on 3 May 1852, and on the thirteenth the City Council, without waiting for the election of a Board of Trustees, which took place on the twenty-fourth, appointed a Librarian. When the word of Mayor Seaver's proposal got abroad in February, William Frederick Poole, a graduate of Yale who had eleven months' experience in a temporary job at the Boston Athenæum behind him, let his friends become aware that he wished the librarian's appointment in the new institution "provided it is to be established on as extensive and liberal a scale as its most ardent advocates anticipate." The City Council looked with greater favor upon a Harvard man, who had a considerably less distinguished career ahead of him, and appointed Edward Capen, A.M. 1842, who, after several years' duty as a clergyman, following his graduation from the Harvard Divinity School in 1845, had recently become Secretary of the Boston School Committee.

Edward Everett and George Ticknor were obvious choices for the Board of Trustees, although Ticknor made it plain that he would not serve unless the library freely circulated the majority of its books and aimed its chief effort at the lower classes of the community. Everett remained unconvinced upon these points, but, seeing that Ticknor would cooperate only in building a popular institution of the freest kind, acquiesced. Fifteen years later in 1867 Charles C. Jewett recalled to Ticknor:

> Few persons alive know as well as you and I do, that with regard to the great features of the plan,—the free circulation of books, and the paramount importance attached to the popular department,—Mr. Everett had from the beginning, serious misgivings, and that he yielded his doubts only to your urgency. He repeated to me within, I think, a week previous to his death, the doubts which he said he had always entertained on these points, and said he did not think he should have yielded his assent, but for your determination not to put your hand to the work unless these features of the plan were adopted in all their prominence.

With this clear understanding, the two friends accepted their appointments, and Everett was designated as President. The other three citizens were equally appropriate choices: ex-Mayor Bigelow, Nathaniel Bradstreet Shurtleff, a physician of historical competence who was in the future to edit the colonial records of the Massachusetts Bay and Plymouth colonies and serve three terms as Mayor of Boston, and Thomas Gold Appleton, the coiner of "cold roast Boston" and many of the other witty phrases of his day. These five, with Mayor Seaver, Aldermen Sampson Reed and Lyman Perry, and Councilmen James Lawrence, Edward S. Erving, James B. Allen, George W. Warren and George Wilson, were declared a Board of Trustees for 1852. At their first meeting of 31 May, Everett, Ticknor, Shurtleff and Reed were appointed a committee to consider and report upon "the objects to be obtained by the establishment of a public library, and the best mode of effecting them."

The result was a masterly performance, largely by Ticknor, which marked the future course not only for Boston but for the public library movement in general. This remarkable document, dated 6 July 1852, in which specific proposals for the library of the future were evolved from Ticknor's head, was printed as *City Document No. 37—Report of the Trustees of the Public Library of the City of Boston, July 1852*. An annotated copy in the Boston Public Library and a statement by Ticknor's biographer make it clear that he alone was responsible for pages 9 to 21, which set forth the details of his concept of the popular circulating library. The earlier pages, apparently drafted by Everett, set forth the significance of printing as a means of multiplying writing—the most useful and important of the human arts—and the consequent multiplication of libraries. "In proportion as books have become more abundant, they have become the principal instrument of instruction in places of education," but, as was forcefully stated in Everett's earlier letters, "although the school and even the college and university are, as all thoughtful persons are well aware, but the first stages in education, the public makes no provision for carrying on the great work." Ticknor, after summarizing the evolution of privately owned circulating libraries and social libraries, then warmed to his dominant theme.

> Strong intimations, therefore, are already given, that ampler means and means better adapted to our peculiar condition and wants, are demanded, in order to diffuse through our society that

knowledge without which we have no right to hope, that the condition of those who are to come after us will be as happy and prosperous as our own. The old roads, so to speak, are admitted to be no longer sufficient. Even the more modern turnpikes do not satisfy our wants. We ask for rail-cars and steamboats, in which many more persons—even multitudes—may advance together to the great end of life, and go faster, farther and better, by the means thus furnished to them, than they have ever been able to do before.

Nowhere are the intimations of this demand more decisive than in our own city, nor, it is believed, is there any city of equal size in the world, where added means for general popular instruction and self-culture,—if wisely adapted to their great ends,—will be so promptly seized upon or so effectively used, as they will be here. One plain proof of this is, the large number of good libraries we already possess, which are constantly resorted to by those who have the right, and which yet—it is well known—fail to supply the demand for popular reading. For we have respectable libraries of almost every class, beginning with those of the Athenæum, of the American Academy, of the Historical Society, and of the General Court,—the Social Library of 1792, the Mercantile Library, the Mechanics Apprentices' Library, the Libraries of the Natural History Society, of the Bar, of the Statistical Association, of the Genealogical Society, of the Medical Society, and of other collective and corporate bodies; and coming down to the "Circulating Libraries" strictly so called; the Sunday School Libraries, and the collections of children's books found occasionally in our Primary Schools. Now all these are important and excellent means for the diffusion of knowledge. They are felt to be such, and they are used as such, and the trustees would be careful not to diminish the resources or the influence of any one of them. They are sure that no public library can do it. But it is admitted,—or else another and more general library would not now be urged,—that these valuable libraries do not, either individually or in the aggregate, reach the great want of this city, considered as a body politic bound to train up its members in the knowledge which will best fit them for the positions in life to which they may have been born, or any others to which they may justly aspire through increased intelligence and personal worthiness. For multitudes among us have no right of access to any one of the more considerable and important of these libraries; and, except in rare instances, no library among us seeks to keep more than a single copy of any book on its shelves, so that no one of them, nor indeed all of them taken together, can do even a tolerable amount of what ought to be done towards satisfying the demands for healthy, nourishing reading made by the great masses of our people, who cannot be expected to purchase such reading for themselves.

And yet there can be no doubt that such reading ought to be furnished to all, as a matter of public policy and duty, on the same principle that we furnish free education, and in fact, as a part, and a most important part, of the education of all. For it has been rightly judged that,—under political, social and religious institutions like ours,—it is of paramount importance that the means of general information should be so diffused that the largest possible number of persons should be induced to read and understand questions of social order, which are constantly presenting themselves, and which we, as a people, are constantly required to decide, and do decide, either ignorantly or wisely. That this *can* be done,— that is, that such libraries *can* be collected, and that they will be used to a much wider extent than libraries have ever been used before, and with much more important results, there can be no doubt; and if it can be done *anywhere,* it can be done *here* in Boston; for no population of one hundred and fifty thousand souls, lying so compactly together as to be able, with tolerable convenience, to resort to one library, was ever before so well fitted to become a reading, self-cultivating population, as the population of our own city at this moment.

To accomplish this object, however,—which has never yet been attempted,—we must use means which have never before been used; otherwise the library we propose to establish, will not be adjusted to its especial purposes. Above all, while the rightful claims of no class,—however highly educated already,—should be overlooked, the first regard should be shown, as in the case of our Free Schools, to the wants of those, who can, in no other way supply themselves with the interesting and healthy reading necessary for their farther education. What precise plan should be adopted for such a library, it is not, perhaps, possible to settle beforehand. It is a new thing, a new step forward in general education; and we must feel our way as we advance. Still, certain points seem to rise up with so much prominence, that without deciding on any formal arrangement, until experience shall show what is practically useful—we may perhaps foresee that such a library as is contemplated would naturally fall into four classes, viz:

I. *Books that cannot be taken out of the Library,* such as Cyclopedias, Dictionaries, important public documents, and books, which, from their rarity or costliness, cannot be easily replaced. Perhaps others should be specifically added to this list, but after all, the Trustees would be sorry to exclude any book whatever so absolutely from circulation that, by permission of the highest authority having control of the library, it could not, in special cases, and with sufficient pledges for its safe and proper return, be taken out. For a book, it should be remembered, is never so much in the way of its duty as it is when it is in the hand to be read or consulted.

II. *Books that few persons will wish to read,* and of which, therefore, only one copy will be kept, but which should be permitted to circulate freely, and if this copy should, contrary to expectation, be so often asked for, as to be rarely on the shelves, another copy should then be bought,—or if needful, more than one other copy,—so as to keep one generally at home, especially if it be such a book as is often wanted for use there.

III. *Books that will be often asked for,* (we mean, the more respectable of the popular works of the time,) of which copies should be provided in such numbers that *many* persons, if they desire it, can be reading the same work at the same moment, and so render the pleasant and healthy literature of the day accessible to the whole people at the only time they care for it,—that is, when it is living, fresh and new. Additional copies, therefore, of any book of this class should continue to be bought almost as long as they are urgently demanded, and thus, by following the popular taste,—unless it should ask for something unhealthy,—we may hope to create a real desire for general reading; and, by permitting the freest circulation of the books that is consistent with their safety, cultivate this desire among the young, and in the families and at the fireside of the greatest possible number of persons in the city.

An appetite like this, when formed, will, we fully believe, provide wisely and well for its own wants. The popular, current literature of the day can occupy but a small portion of the leisure even of the more laborious parts of our population, provided there should exist among them a love for reading as great, for instance, as the love for public lecturing, or for the public schools; and when such a taste for books has once been formed by these lighter publications, then the older and more settled works in Biography, in History, and in the graver departments of knowledge will be demanded. That such a taste can be excited by such means, is proved from the course taken in obedience to the dictates of their own interests, by the publishers of the popular literature of the time during the last twenty or thirty years. The Harpers and others began chiefly with new novels and other books of little value. What they printed, however, was eagerly bought and read, because it was cheap and agreeable, if nothing else. A habit of reading was thus formed. Better books were soon demanded, and gradually the general taste has risen in its requisitions, until now the country abounds with respectable works of all sorts,—such as compose the three hundred volumes of the Harpers' School Library and the two hundred of their Family Library—which are read by great numbers of our people everywhere, especially in New England and in the Middle States. This taste, therefore, once excited will, we are persuaded, go on itself from year to year, demanding better and better books, and, can as we believe, by a little judicious help in the selections for a Free City Library, rather than by any direct control, restraint, or solicitation, be carried much higher than has been commonly deemed possible; preventing at the same time, a great deal of the mischievous, poor reading now indulged in, which is bought and *paid* for, by offering good reading, *without pay,* which will be attractive.

Nor would the process by which this result is to be reached [be] a costly one; certainly not costly compared with its benefits. Nearly all the most popular books are, from the circumstances of their popularity, cheap,—most of them very cheap,—because large editions of them are printed that are suited to the wants of those who cannot afford to buy dear books. It may, indeed, sometimes be necessary to purchase many copies of one of these books, and so the first outlay, in some cases may seem considerable. But such a passion for any given book does not last long, and, as it subsides, the extra copies may be sold for something, until only a few are left in the library, or perhaps, only a single one, while the money received from the sale of the rest,—which, at a reduced price, would, no doubt often be bought of the Librarian by those who had been most interested in reading them,—will serve to increase the general means for purchasing others of the same sort. The plan, therefore, it is believed, is a practicable one, so far as expense is concerned, and will, we think, be found on trial, much cheaper and easier of execution than at the first suggestion, it may seem to be.

IV. The last class of books to be kept in such a library, consists, we suppose, of *periodical publications,* probably excluding newspapers, except such as may be given by their proprietors. Like the first class, they should not be taken out at all, or only in rare and peculiar cases, but they should be kept in a Reading Room accessible to everybody; open as many hours of the day as possible, and always in the evening; and in which all the books on the shelves of every part of the Library should be furnished for perusal or for consultation to all who may ask for them, except to such persons as may, from their disorderly conduct or unseemly condition, interfere with the occupations and comfort of others who may be in the room.

In the establishment of such a library, a beginning should be made, we think, without any sharply defined or settled plan, so as to be governed by circumstances as they may arise. The commencement should be made, of preference, in a very unpretending manner; erecting no new building and making no show; but spending such moneys as may be appropriated for the purpose, chiefly on books that are known to be really wanted, rather than on such as will make an imposing, a scientific or a learned collection; trusting, however, most confidently, that such a library, in the long run, will contain all that anybody can reasonably ask of it. For, to begin by making it a really useful library; by awakening a general interest in it as a City Institution, important to the whole people, a part of their education, and an element of their happiness and prosperity, is the surest way to make it at last, a great and rich library for men of science, statesmen and scholars, as well as for the great body of the people, many of whom are always successfully struggling up to honorable distinctions and all of whom should be encouraged and helped to do it. Certainly this has proved to be the case with some of the best libraries yet formed in the United States, and especially with the Philadelphia Library, whose means were at first extremely humble and trifling, compared with those we can command at the outset. Such libraries have in fact enjoyed the public favor, and become large, learned, and scientific collections of books, exactly in proportion as they have been found generally useful.

As to the terms on which access should be had to a City library, the Trustees can only say, that they would place no restrictions on its use, except such as the nature of individual books, or their safety may demand; regarding it as a great matter to carry as many of them as possible into the home of the young; into poor families; into cheap boarding houses; in short, wherever they will be most likely to affect life and raise personal character and condition. To many classes of persons the doors of such a library may, we conceive be at once opened wide. All officers of the City Government, therefore, including the police, all clergymen settled among us, all city missionaries, all teachers of our public schools, all members of normal schools, all young persons who may have received medals or other honorary distinctions on leaving our Grammar and higher schools, and, in fact, as many classes, as can safely be entrusted with it *as classes* might enjoy, on the mere names and personal responsibility of the individuals composing them, the right of taking out freely all books that are permitted to circulate, receiving one volume at a time. To all other persons,—women as well as men—living in the City, the same privilege might be granted on depositing the value of the volume or of the set to which it may belong; believing that the pledge of a single dollar or even less, may thus insure pleasant and profitable reading to any family among us.

In this way the Trustees would endeavor to make the Public Library of the City, as far as possible, the crowning glory of our system of City Schools; or in other words, they would make it an institution, fitted to continue and increase the best effects of that system, by opening to all the means of self culture through books, for which these schools have been specially qualifying them.

Thus ended the part of the report that Ticknor drafted himself, and which Edward Everett generously accepted, even though still unconvinced of the practicability of a popular circulating library. The remaining three pages are devoted to the steps that should be adopted to accomplish the design.

If it were probable that the City Council would deem it expedient at once to make a large appropriation for the erection of a building and the purchase of an ample library, and that the citizens at large would approve such expenditure, the Trustees would of course feel great satisfaction in the prompt achievement of an object of such high public utility. But in the present state of the finances of the city, and in reference to an object on which the public mind is not yet enlightened by experience, the Trustees regard any such appropriation and expenditure as entirely out of the question. They conceive even that there are advantages to a more gradual course of measures. They look, therefore, only to the continuance of such moderate and frugal expenditure, on the part of the city, as has been already authorized and commenced, for the purchase of books and the compensation of the librarian; and for the assignment of a room or rooms in some one of the public buildings belonging to the city for the reception of the books already on hand, or which the Trustees have the means of procuring.

With aid to this extent on the part of the city, the Trustees believe that all else may be left to the public spirit and liberality of individuals.

Thus, it was confidently believed, not only large collections but small would be attracted, while authors, editors and publishers "would unquestionably show themselves efficient friends and benefactors." Specifically, the Trustees requested the use of the ground floor of the Adams schoolhouse in Mason Street, where at slight expense four or five thousand volumes might be housed and a reading room opened in the predictable future.

Faith in a sound idea is often rewarded from unexpected quarters, and by means that a mere schemer would never anticipate. Ticknor believed so firmly in the possibility and utility of a popular circulating library under public auspices that he persuaded his only partially convinced colleagues to accept it as a basic principle of the proposed institution. In the report just quoted he translated this mental concept into a specific plan so effective that it kindled the "public spirit and liberality" of an entirely unforeseen individual in London. As William W. Greenough described the event in his *Annals,*

> One result which followed from the publication and distribution of this report was as vitally important as it was unexpected.
>
> At this period the City Government was negotiating the Water Loan with the house of Baring Brothers and Co., and among the documents sent for their information as to the status of the City of Boston was a copy of the report of which an extract appears above, and which attracted the notice of Mr. Joshua Bates, the senior partner of the great banking house. It produced so strong an impression upon him as to its opportunities of usefulness to young men, that he addressed to the Mayor the following letter:
>
> LONDON, Oct. 1, 1852
>
> DEAR SIR:
>
> I am indebted to you for a copy of the Report of the Trustees of the Public Library for the City of Boston, which I have perused with great interest, being impressed with the importance to rising and future generations of such a Library as is recommended; and while I am sure that, in a liberal and wealthy community like that of Boston, there will be no want of funds to carry out the recommendations of the Trustees, it may accelerate its accomplishment

and establish the Library at once, on a scale to do credit to the City, if I am allowed to pay for the books required, which I am quite willing to do,—leaving to the City to provide the building and take care of the expenses.

The only condition that I ask is, that the building shall be such as to be an ornament to the City, that there shall be a room for one hundred to one hundred and fifty persons to sit at reading-tables,—that it shall be perfectly free to all, with no other restrictions than may be necessary for the preservation of the books. What the building may cost, I am unable to estimate, but the books, counting additions during my life time, I estimate at $50,000, which I shall gladly contribute, and consider it but a small return for the many acts of confidence and kindness which I have received from my many friends in your City.

> Believe me, Dear Sir, very truly yours,
> JOSHUA BATES

This simple and magnanimous letter, so completely in keeping with the disinterested faith of Ticknor's proposal, was sent by Mr. Bates to his friend, Thomas Wren Ward, a China trade merchant and former Treasurer of the Boston Athenæum, with a private letter in which the inspiration of the gift—Bates's craving for books as a poor boy in Boston half a century before—was set forth.

I enclose a letter to the Mayor, which please to peruse, and then go to Mr. Everett and Mr. Ticknor and explain to them my ideas, which are that my own experience as a poor boy convinced me of the great advantage of such a library. Having no money to spend and no place to go to, not being able to pay for a fire in my own room, I could not pay for books, and the best way I could pass my evenings was to sit in Hastings, Etheridge & Bliss's bookstore, and read what they kindly permitted me to; and I am confident that had there been good, warm, and well-lighted rooms to which we could have resorted, with proper books, nearly all the youth of my acquaintance would have spent their evenings there, to the improvement of their minds and morals.

Now it strikes me, that it will not do to have the rooms in the proposed library much inferior to the rooms occupied for the same object by the upper classes. Let the virtuous and industrious of the middle and mechanic class feel that there is not so much difference between them. Few but worthy young men will frequent the library at first; they may draw others from vice to tread in the same paths; and with large, well-lighted rooms, well-warmed in winter, I feel sure that the moral effect will keep pace with mental improvement, and it will be carrying out the school system of Boston, as it ought to be carried out.

My friends may think differently, or that my proposal is improper, or in the wrong form; but if you all agree that it is right and proper, the trustees may go to work and provide such books as they find cheapest in the United States, drawing on me for the cost, sending me a list of such as can best be procured here or in France, and I will have them purchased without delay. If this conclusion is come to, then my letter to the Mayor may be delivered, if it is thought a proper one. I rely on you, Mr. Everett and Mr. Ticknor, to put the matter right.

The evenings in Hastings, Etheridge & Bliss's bookstore had followed long days in the counting house of William R. Gray, which Joshua Bates—born in Weymouth, Massachusetts, in 1788—had entered at fifteen. Following the War of 1812, this enterprising young man went to Europe as general agent for the elder William Gray, who was then one of the largest Massachusetts ship owners and merchants. A chance encounter with Peter Cæsar Labouchère, senior member of the Amsterdam house of Hope and Company, and a relative by marriage of the Baring family, decisively affected young Bates's future, for it led to immediate financial support, an eventual partnership in Baring Brothers and Company, and finally a great personal fortune. The modesty and good feeling of his letter to Mayor Seaver tell much of the character of Joshua Bates. Having reached an eminent pinnacle of worldly success with energy, imagination, and integrity as his only resources, he welcomed the opportunity to encourage other young men like himself, and did so with a simplicity and an absence of fine words that was hardly typical of his time. Thus within four months of the year 1852 Ticknor had phrased a plan and Bates had provided the means of carrying it out.

The offer was enthusiastically accepted, and Joshua Bates readily acquiesced in the City Council's request to fund the gift, and to use the income only for the purchase of books. Thus, in the ample days when even conservative investment produced at least six per cent, an annual sum of three thousand dollars became available for books.

Gifts in June of $500 from James Brown and in September of $1,000 from Samuel Appleton were spent for immediate additions to the collections then in hand.

The quarters requested in the Mason Street schoolhouse were admittedly temporary, and the problem of a suitable building remained unsolved. In the expectation that steps would soon be taken, Joshua Bates informally passed his thoughts along to Thomas Wren Ward in November 1852, soon after the formal acceptance of his gift by the City Council:

I have received your valued letter with the newspaper account of the proceedings of the Board of Aldermen on my letter offering to furnish the books for the City Library. These proceedings are

MASON STREET SCHOOLHOUSE

very gratifying to me personally and give me confidence that the Library will be established on a footing that will make it extensively useful, and that it will grow into one of the most important institutions in the United States. My ideas are that the building should contain lofty apartments to serve for placing the books and also for reading tables, as the holding of books in the hand damages them very soon. The architecture should be such that a student on entering it will be impressed and elevated, and feel a pride that such a place is free to him. There should be niches and places for a few marble statues, as these will from time to time be contributed by those who may be benefitted by the institution. When on their travels in Italy they see the originals they will be pretty sure to order something. By these means the reading rooms will be made more attractive, and the rising generation will be able to contemplate familiarity with the best works of the celebrated masters. There should be an entrance hall, a room for cloaks and umbrellas, and a room for washing hands, with soap, hot water and towels provided. The rooms should be well-warmed in winter, and well lighted. If you will only provide the building,—and you can hardy have it too large,—I can assure the Committee that all the rest will come as a matter of course. These reading arrangements will not prevent parties who may find it more convenient to read at home from taking books,—giving proper security.

My experience convinces me that there are a large number of young men who make a decent appearance, but living in boarding houses or with poor parents, cannot afford to have fire in their rooms. Such persons in past times having no place of resort have often loitered about the streets in the evenings and got into bad company, which would have been avoided, had such a library as is now proposed been in existence. The moral and intellectual improvement such a library would produce is incalculable. I wish to see the institution a model for other towns and cities. There should be a book of directions for reading in every branch of knowledge, that the young men may know where to begin. In future times when it is desired to know something of a young man, the question will be asked, "Does he frequent the library?" I have no doubt the Committee understand the matter much better than I do, or that it will be carried out in the best possible manner.

Late in February 1853 the City bought the Caleb G. Loring estate in Somerset Street at the top of Beacon Hill, around the corner from the new Athenæum, as a site for the proposed building, and almost immediately there were varied opinions about its appropriateness. An anonymous "Shareholder in the Boston Athenæum," writing in the *Boston Daily Advertiser* of 1 March 1853, once again raised the question of a merger, suggesting that, if the Public Library could be accommodated in the Athenæum's new building, $150,000 that would otherwise be required for bricks and mortar could be put into additional books. George Ticknor, therefore, wrote to that paper a fortnight later, under the pseudonym "An Old Proprietor of the

Athenæum" (which indeed he was, having owned a share since 1822), in support of the union. His letter, printed in the 14 March 1853 issue, reviewed the Athenæum's financial history, indicated the inappropriateness of having two separate libraries within a stone's throw of one another, and pointed out that "four-fifths of the proprietors of the Athenæum, it is confidently believed, regard and always have regarded, their interest in it *as a public rather than a private one,* and, like its other benefactors, they have contributed to it mainly because they have felt the importance of having something in Boston as near to a *Public* Library, as their combined means could furnish." Ticknor alleged that many proprietors were ready immediately to give their shares to the City, provided the remainder would sell theirs at the current market value. But, he continued,

> I do not know a single person among the present proprietors, who would wish to transfer the Athenæum to the City, even in order to make it the foundation of a great and beneficent Public Institution, unless it can be done by the cordial approbation and act of a large majority of our number, and in a manner generous, honorable and useful to all; unless, indeed, it can be done in the same liberal spirit, and for the same general purpose, of advancing the education and the welfare of the community, which have marked its character from the beginning, and which—whatever may be its fate—will, I am persuaded, mark its character to the end.

Ticknor's letter, with an endorsement from seventy-seven highly respected proprietors of the Athenæum, was promptly reprinted and widely circulated in a pamphlet entitled *Union of the Boston Athenæum and the Public Library.* But, alas for Ticknor's hopes, his fellow-trustee of the Public Library, George W. Warren, waggled his tongue irresponsibly in the City Council. Councilman Warren, in answer to criticism of the purchase of land in Somerset Street, said, or at least was reported to have said by the newspapers:

> . . . that the *effect of the purchase* has been most salutary with regard to the proposed purchase of the Athenæum. Before the Loring Estate was selected, the proprietors of the Athenæum were strongly opposed to the sale of the institution to the city. The city, having purchased a lot near the Athenæum building, have now the advantage, and the proprietors are willing to sell. *The Athe-*

næum must soon play second to the Boston Free Library, and the owners are *perfectly willing* now to sell out at *half* what they charged at first.

This suggestion of political chicanery on the part of the City Government instantly undid the reasonableness of Ticknor's arguments, and the opponents rallied around the venerable Josiah Quincy, who, signing himself "The Sole Survivor of the First Five Subscribers to the Athenæum," published on 24 March *An Appeal in Behalf of the Boston Athenæum Addressed to the Proprietors.* Quincy, now in his eighty-second year, was a man of open mind and large ideas. During his term as Mayor of Boston from 1823 to 1828 he had reformed the sanitary condition of the city, built the present Quincy Market, reorganized the fire department, and generally concerned himself with municipal improvement. On 14 April 1841, while President of Harvard College, he had, in a letter to his son, Josiah, Jr., responded to Vattemare's contagious enthusiasm to the point of considering feasible a building in which the Athenæum, the American Academy of Arts and Sciences, the Massachusetts Historical Society and other institutions might house their several libraries in common, yet his own experience of city governments combined with Councilman Warren's indiscretion, convinced him that it would be "unjust, unwise, and unprincipled" to deliver over the care of the Athenæum to "a political body, annually shifting its members, and changing principles and policy with every turn of party or passion." Quincy's vigorous opposition proved so effective that at a meeting of the Athenæum proprietors on 28 March 1853 Ticknor's proposal was resoundingly defeated.

Possible union with the Athenæum was now eliminated from discussion, but there seemed little enthusiasm for Somerset Street as the location of the future library. In March the notion of a new City Hall, in emulation of the Farnese Palace in Rome, with municipal offices on two floors and the library on the third, was investigated by the Joint Committees on Public Library and Public Buildings. Although the majority found this proposal "impracticable and inexpedient," a minority of the committee reported favorably. The land on Somerset Street was soon resold without loss, and, after the possibility of building in the Public Garden was rejected, a new site was purchased on Boylston Street, near the corner of Tremont Street, overlooking the Common, "which secures to it unobstructed light and air, and as fine a prospect as can be enjoyed in any city in the world."

The Trustees, reporting to the City Council on 10 November 1853, as was required by the ordinance of 14 October 1852 by which the library was regulated, requested the appointment of a commission to prepare plans for the proposed building, which "will necessarily occupy two or three years." They had hoped to open the library in its temporary Mason Street quarters by 1 October, but that had not proved possible. In the course of 1853 the Honorable Jonathan Phillips had given $10,000, which, being funded, would add $600 annually for the purchase of books. Gifts of $100 from James Nightingale and $300 from J. I. Bowditch had been spent currently for books, so that the number on hand and "in good order" in November, according to the committee of citizens appointed under the municipal ordinance to examine the library, amounted to 9,688 volumes.

Nathaniel I. Bowditch, having exercised without charge his celebrated talents as a conveyancer in searching the title of the Boylston Street property, was credited with a gift of $200 in kind.

For the new institution 1852 had proved on *annus mirabilis;* 1853 had merely shown slow and somewhat circuitous progress.

SOURCES

The principles upon which the library was founded are contained in *City Document No. 37. Report of the Trustees of the Public Library of the City of Boston, July 1852* (Boston, 1852), a copy of which, reaching London by accident, inspired Joshua Bates's great gifts. Jesse H. Shera reproduced as Appendix V (pp. 267–290) of his *Foundations of the Public Library* a copy of this report with annotations by Charles C. Jewett that establish the sections written by George Ticknor. In subsequent chapters, reference to the printed annual reports of the Trustees of the Boston Public Library is to be assumed without further citation.

Ticknor's and Everett's roles are described in Hillard's previously cited life of Ticknor and in Paul Revere Frothingham's *Edward Everett, Orator and Statesman* (Boston: Houghton Mifflin Company, 1925). The original draft of C. C. Jewett's letter of 15 May 1867 to Ticknor concerning Everett's and Ticknor's views on the free circulation of books is in the Boston Public Library Trustees' Room miscellaneous volume (T.R. 15.10). Poole's aspirations to the librarianship are discussed in Carl B. Roden "The Boston Days of Dr. W. F. Poole," *Essays offered to Herbert Putnam* (New Haven: Yale University Press, 1929).

CHAPTER III

Narrow Premises in Mason Street

It is desirable and important to render this free public library *at once* extensively useful as a large collection of books in as many departments of human knowledge as possible.

—JOSHUA BATES

THE two promised rooms in the Mason Street schoolhouse at last became available, and on 20 March 1854 the outer one, designated as the Reading Room, was opened for public use. Here were kept 138 periodicals, and here, for want of a better place, books were delivered to a daily average of three hundred readers after the circulation department was opened, on 2 May. The Examining Committee found the room "noisy, uncomfortable and unfit for its peculiar purposes as a place for quiet reading," just as the interior room, or library proper, was "small, ill-lighted, ill-ventilated, cold in winter, and so nearly filled with books that it will soon be impossible to find places for more." But all this was known to be temporary, and the library was at last in operation.

By the rules and regulations drawn up by Dr. Shurtleff and Alderman Reed, and adopted by the Trustees on 8 November 1853, the Reading Room was open daily, save on Sundays and holidays, from 9:00 a.m. to 9.30 p.m. All inhabitants of Boston over sixteen had access to it, where not only the periodicals but all books in the library might be consulted. For home use, one volume at a time might, with no formality beyond signing a promise to observe all library rules, be withdrawn for fourteen days, with privilege of renewal for a similar period, by officers and employees of the city government, ordained ministers, teachers in private schools, members of the Normal School, medal scholars annually graduated from the public schools, and benefactors of the library who had given at least $100. Any other inhabitant of Boston might withdraw a book upon depositing its full value with the Librarian, while anyone over twenty-one introduced by "some respectable and responsible citizen, who will thus make himself liable for any loss the Library may sustain in consequence," might have the privilege without deposit. *All* books were to be returned fourteen days before the annual examination in October, for which purpose the library was closed. Readers were particularly requested to suggest titles of books not in the library.

The Librarian maintained a catalogue of accessions, in which every book, with its cost, was entered on receipt, an alphabetical card catalogue, a shelf catalogue, showing the location of books upon the shelves—all for the use of the staff—and a printed alphabetical catalogue in book form—interleaved for the entry of new accessions—copies of which were placed on tables in the Reading Room for consultation by the public.

Even with its crowded quarters, the experiment was encouraging, for in the five and a half months between the opening and the 17 October closing for the annual examination, 6,590 persons used the library and 35,389 books were borrowed for home use. No single book was "wantonly or unreasonably injured," while the 1854 annual examination showed that of the 16,221 books and 3950 pamphlets on hand only twenty were missing from their places on the shelves. These were likely to turn up, but if they did not, the $87.30 received in fines for late return would more than pay for their replacement! The Trustees, in their purchases, had aimed at "useful books, in the English language, in plain, good bindings."

> Works in the learned and foreign tongues, books or editions of books which owe their value to their rarity, works of luxury as they are called, splendidly illustrated publications, and sumptuous and costly bindings have wholly been avoided. The Trustees do not undervalue works of this kind, when surplus funds exist for their purchase. They look forward to the time when, the more immediate wants of the institution having been supplied, there

will be a propriety in making the acquisition, to a reasonable extent, of works of this class; which they also have no doubt will, from time to time, be added to the Library by private liberality. But for the present they are under the impression, that works intended for substantial use, rather than for curiosity and show, are what the public need and have a right to expect.

The last impression is sound enough to have been shared by the majority of their successors ever since, particularly as "private liberality" showed itself early. During 1855, 153 persons made gifts which included the largest size of Audubon's *Birds of America* from Thomas G. Appleton, two hundred volumes from the Royal Commissioners of Patents in Great Britain, the monumental French government work on Egypt from Edward Austin, and $1,000 from Mrs. Sally Inman Kast Shepard. The same year also saw the first definite steps toward the provision of adequate quarters for the library.

From Robert C. Winthrop's letter of 17 April 1855 to J. P. Kennedy, in which he wrote,

I am building a Public Library, setting up a statue of Franklin, presiding over the great charitable association of the city, superintending with others the course of things at Cambridge, helping along the affairs of Trinity Church, presiding over the Historical . . .

one might incorrectly infer that the slow progress was due to an attempt of this former member of Congress to construct the library single-handed. After unsuccessful candidacy for the governorship of Massachusetts and the United States Senate, Winthrop had turned his attention to local problems, although with the patronizing admission that "the gatherings of our Historical Society, of the vestry of Trinity Church and other local bodies are perhaps a little tame to one who has passed so many years at work on the affairs of the Nation." He was, however, simply the president of a board of Commissioners on the erection of a building for the Public Library, elected by the City Council on 11 December 1854, that included Samuel Gray Ward, George Ticknor, Dr. Nathaniel B. Shurtleff and Alderman George Odiorne. Although the Mason Street quarters were obviously inadequate from the day the doors were opened, there had been a good deal of backing and filling about the idea of placing the library in the Public Garden, and it was not until 28 December 1854 that the Commissioners were authorized "to locate the building upon the lot upon Boylston Street, if, in their opinion,

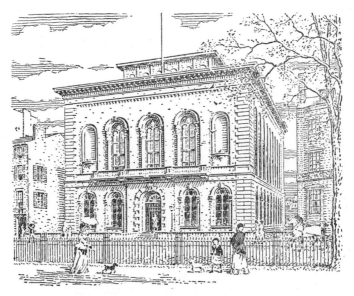

BOYLSTON STREET EXTERIOR

it be deemed expedient." They deemed it so, and on 26 January 1855 issued a public invitation to submit designs for a building on that site.

The requirements for the building were, in brief, a library hall with alcoves capable of containing on fixed shelves at least 200,000 volumes, a general reading room, with ample accommodations at tables for at least 150 readers, a ladies' reading room seating fifty, a room for delivery of books sufficient for at least 200 persons, an adjacent library room for the arrangement of 20,000 books "most constantly demanded for circulation," and quarters for the Trustees and Librarian. The façade was to "be of brick, with stone dressing"; iron was to be used where required, and the general aim was for "a simple but substantial structure, ample in its dimensions, just in its proportions, absolutely fire-proof, and depending for its effect rather upon its adaptation to the use for which it is designed, than upon any ornamental architecture or costly materials."

An amendment of the ordinance establishing the Commissioners, passed on 29 March 1855, empowered them not only to select plans but to let contracts and superintend construction, and provided for the annual election of two commissioners each from the Board of Aldermen and the Common Council to serve with Messrs. Winthrop, Ward, Ticknor and Shurtleff, who were to hold office until the completion of the building. Twenty-four designs had been received and opened on 23 March, and, after a dozen meetings, the Commissioners selected on 27 April the plans submitted by Mr. Charles Kirk Kirby. Competitive bids were invited and on 14 June a contract was signed with Nathan Drake for the masonry. The library in Mason Street had become so thoroughly congested that two small rooms in the Quincy schoolhouse in Tyler Street were made available for storage of books, while in August, with a prudent eye to expansion, additional land in Van Rensaleer Place, adjacent to the Boylston Street site, was purchased.

The laying of the cornerstone on 17 September 1855, at which Robert C. Winthrop delivered graceful compliments to the benefactors of the library and all engaged in its construction, was duly reported to Joshua Bates, who expressed great satisfaction and came forward with a further offer of support. Writing to Mayor Jerome V. C. Smith, Bates said:

> It is, I understand, certain that within two years a building will be completed of dimensions amply sufficient for the reception at once of a large number of books, and for the regular future increase of the library . . . It is desirable and important to render this free public library *at once* extensively useful as a large collection of books in as many departments of human knowledge as possible. For this purpose I now propose, in addition to the fund of fifty thousand dollars already constituted, to purchase and present to the City, a considerable number of books in trust, that the same shall always be accessible, in a convenient and becoming library building, to the inhabitants of Boston generally, under such regulations as may be deemed needful by the persons to whom the government of the institution may, from time to time, be confided.

This generous offer, which was promptly accepted by the City Council, with the request that Mr. Bates sit for a bust to be placed in the library, was not wholly unexpected, for on 6 July, after receiving plans of the building, Bates had written Ticknor:

> Nothing now remains but to provide a sufficient number of books for the opening. I had anticipated this difficulty, as Mr. Ward and Mr. Everett will no doubt have informed you. I see no other way but that the Committee should make out a catalogue of French, German and Italian books, and such English works as are most needed, the whole not to exceed $20,000 or $30,000. I will supply what money your funds will not pay for, but you must tell me how this additional sum can be so bestowed as to secure the application of the Library in future time to the people as originally intended.

The prospect of such large immediate additions of books caused the Trustees to become acutely aware of their lack both of space and of staff, and on 18 October they petitioned the City Council

> . . . for a further appropriation, to be expended in hiring suitable premises where shelves may be immediately erected, and the books be opened, aired, catalogued and arranged; in paying for the services of the persons who will, necessarily, be employed in this work; and in meeting the incidental expenses so that the books can be put upon the shelves of the new building as soon as that structure shall be completed. Otherwise, a year or more will be lost before the books can be prepared, in the new building, for public use.

As the Mason Street rooms and the Tyler Street overflow were already filled, the Trustees rented a house at 13 Boylston Place, and were fortunate enough to persuade Charles Coffin Jewett to install himself there to receive the books sent by Joshua Bates.

A better choice could not have been made, for Jewett had already had more than ordinary experience. As Librarian of Brown University from 1841 to 1848, he had visited Europe to buy books. Becoming Assistant Secretary and Librarian of the Smithsonian Institution in 1848, he prepared the earliest general survey of American libraries—referred to in Chapter I—proposed a system of national cataloguing, and energetically strove to build a national library in the Smithsonian Institution. A controversy over the interpretation of Smithson's will led to Jewett's resignation and the transfer of the books that he had gathered to the Library of Congress. Consequently he was both free and disposed to turn his considerable talents to the benefit of the new Boston Public Library.

George Ticknor had, all along the way, been concerned with every detail of the library, and spent many hours of each week perusing publishers' announcements, booksellers' and auction catalogues. During Edward Everett's absence in Washington as Secretary of State and Senator from the autumn of 1852 to the spring of 1854, Ticknor had carried the chief burden, although always preventing Everett—who alleged that he was simply a "parade officer" —from resigning the presidency of the Trustees. At the first intimation of Bates's second gift, Ticknor began to collect from men distinguished in various branches of learning—such as Professors Agassiz, Felton, Holmes, Lovering, Pierce and many others—lists of books on their specialized fields. Upon Jewett's arrival in Boston, he spent an eight hour day for some two months in Ticknor's library, before installing himself in 13 Boylston Place, preparing and revising lists of desirable acquisitions that were transmitted to Joshua Bates's agents in London, Paris, Leipzig and Florence. The first shipment of books arrived in May 1856, and a month later Ticknor sailed for Europe, with a credit of $1,000 of library funds —subsequently increased—at his disposal, to make further selections on the spot.

The intimation in June 1855 of Bates's second gift had suggested to Edward Everett the need of sending not "an agent but an Envoy Extraordinary to Europe" on the ground—as he wrote Ticknor on 25 July—that "Joshua Bates's purposes are liberal,—munificent,— but he does not know, on the present occasion, what he ought to do to carry his own views into effect." Ticknor had urged Everett to go, but the latter proposed to reverse the situation, alleging with modest rhetoric,

> But if I could go, it is no affected diffidence which make me say that you would accomplish the object much better. I have no particular aptitude for the kind of executive operations which this errand requires,—I mean purchasing books with discrimination

in large masses. Perhaps I am rather deficient in it. You possess it
in an uncommon degree. I think you would buy as many books for
thirty thousand dollars as I should for fifty thousand,—certainly
for forty thousand dollars.

In the end Ticknor acquiesced, spending fifteen months abroad
from June 1856 to September 1857, travelling with his family at his
own expense, on behalf of the library. He went first to London,
where he spent three weeks in constant visits with Joshua Bates, of
whom he subsequently wrote:

> To me he was a peculiar man. I knew him familiarly several years
> when we were both young; and if, after he established himself in
> Europe, I saw him rarely, still, whenever we met, as we did at
> seven or eight different periods on one or the other side of the
> Atlantic, I always found him, in what goes to make up the ele-
> ments of personal character, substantially the same. Indeed, during
> almost sixty years that I thus knew him, he was less changed than
> almost anybody I have ever been acquainted with . . . The rea-
> son, I suppose, is, that he was a true man, faithful always to his
> own convictions, and therefore little liable to fluctuations in his
> ways and character.

After reaching a complete and happy understanding with Bates
about the purposes of the library, Ticknor proceeded to the Continent, spending the fall, winter, and spring in Belgium, Germany,
Austria, Italy and France, where he made purchases totalling
£1,849/15/3. A month in the summer of 1857 he spent in London,
largely in completing arrangements with Bates and the agencies that
he had established on behalf of the library.

During Ticknor's absence abroad, Jewett and his assistants were
thoroughly occupied with the books that were pouring into 13 Boylston Place. Within a year and a half, 142 boxes, containing 21,374
volumes, costing $38,393, were received, unpacked, collated and
catalogued on cards. Lack of space made it necessary to repack after
cataloguing, and store in the basement of the new library, some forty
boxes. In addition to the catalogue cards, Jewett prepared a short-
title list on slips, corresponding in style to the catalogue that had
been printed earlier for the Mason Street rooms. These furnished
the exact entries for the accessions catalogue and were then classi-

fied by subject, so that when the new building in Boylston Street was occupied the arrangement of the books themselves would be purely mechanical.

While this feat of energy and skill was being accomplished by Jewett, the building was progressing. When Ticknor sailed for Europe Everett had replaced him on the Board of Commissioners for its construction. This in no way grieved Ticknor, for he had never wished to be involved in questions of construction, and as the work progressed he felt increasingly that the building was proving too expensive and less well adapted to its purposes than he could have wished. In any event, contracts for the interior finish were let in July 1856, and in May of the following year for shelving. Shortly thereafter the Commissioners began holding their meetings in already completed parts of the building, although final details dragged out over the remainder of 1857.

Meanwhile public use of the "narrow premises" in Mason Street was steadily increasing, with every effort made to keep the library supplied with "the current literature and fresh reading of the day." "Fresh" and "light reading" seem to have had different connotations in the Trustees' minds, for their 1857 report contains severely pompous strictures upon the second class.

> The best interests of the institution require that it should not be regarded as a depository of books of the latter description. They are so cheap that they can be otherwise obtained by almost every one who wishes to read them; they occupy space on the shelves better filled by better books; and they increase the resort of persons to the library whose wants might be easily supplied in other quarters, leaving the Librarian and his assistants to devote their attention to more earnest and thoughtful readers. The Trustees are persuaded that it was not the design of the judicious and public-spirited citizens who, as members of the City Council in years past, or at the present time, have liberally appropriated the public funds to the foundation and support of the library, to have it become the means of gratuitously supplying to a class of idle readers, the unprofitable, not to say pernicious trash, which is daily pouring from the press.

Here one detects the New England taste not only for self-improvement, but for the often involuntary improvement of others, intruding itself into a problem that became perennial for this and other libraries.

With a collection that now numbered 34,896 volumes and 16,053 pamphlets, *exclusive* of Joshua Bates's gifts, and with the approaching occupancy of the new building, there was natural concern about the future administration of the library. Under the ordinance of 18 October 1852, the Trustees were empowered to make rules and regulations for the care and use of the library and to appoint subordinate officers, but the Librarian's post remained in the political sphere. While the Trustees could recommend, it was the City Council that *appointed* the Librarian, and this annually.

Feeling that the library had advanced beyond a stage where its administration could safely be entrusted to the holder of an annual city appointment, the Trustees submitted a memorial to the City Council on 2 November 1857, setting forth their concept of the requirements. After discussing matters of routine, the memorial continued:

> But in addition to the work of this kind, there is much to be done, in a first class library, of a different and higher character. In order to meet the demands of the community and answer the ends for which it was established, it must within reasonable limits, promptly receive every important and useful new publication, in our own and foreign languages. To keep it supplied in this respect, it is necessary that some one, whose duty it is, should devote so much time to the various departments of science and literature, as to keep himself well acquainted with their progressive condition. To prepare judiciously and with discrimination, the requisite selected lists of books to be annually purchased at home and abroad would of itself, require a considerable part of the time of an accomplished bibliographer.
>
> An important part of the duty of those charged with the management of large public libraries is to attend to persons, both citizens and others, who resort to them for the purposes of scientific and literary research. Many persons will visit the Public Library in Boston for this purpose. It will contain very many valuable works of reference, and books too costly and rare to be put into circulation, but which will be consulted by those who visit the institution. It belongs to the management of a great public library to answer the inquiries and to facilitate the researches of persons of this class, and no small part of the time of some of its officers will be taken up in this way. An extensive knowledge of books, of ancient

and foreign languages, and of science and literature generally, is indispensable for the performance of this duty in a satisfactory manner.

In addition to these duties, to which specific reference has been made, the general management and administration of a first class library require an efficient and responsible head, possessing a degree of ability and qualifications, intellectual and literary, of a higher order than can be expected, on the part of young persons of either sex, however intelligent, who perform services of routine for a moderate compensation.

The memorial requested an amendment of the existing ordinance, so as to provide for a "responsible superintendent," endowed with the qualifications just enumerated, who would be "charged with the general administration of the Library under the Trustees." In opposing the annual election by the City Council, the memorial continued:

The Trustees conceive that this is too precarious a tenure for such an office. The place of Librarian in a great public library nearly resembles that of a professor in a seminary of learning. The Trustees are not aware that it has ever been deemed expedient, in any part of the country to subject the teachers or the librarians in our universities and colleges to the uncertainty of an annual election, by public bodies partaking largely of a political character. As the Trustees are directly responsible to the City for the condition and working of the institution, and as the duty of making the requisite regulations for its management and of seeing that they are carried into effect, devolves on them, they are of the opinion, for obvious reasons, that the appointment of the Librarian and of any other officer, who may be established in pursuance of the foregoing recommendation, should be devolved upon the Board.

The Trustees won at least a part of their point, for an amended ordinance, providing for a Superintendent of the library, was passed on 2 January 1858, even though annual appointment by the City Council, rather than permanent designation by the Trustees, applied both to this officer and the Librarian. The amended ordinance provided for the election by the City Council of a Superintendent, whenever the Trustees should recommend such action and make a suitable nomination, who was, unless removed, to hold office for one year or until his successor was elected. The Trustees might dispense with the office of Superintendent in any year by omitting to nominate a candidate, and the City Council might dispense with the Superintendent's services "whenever they concluded that the public interest does not require the services of such an officer." Whenever the office was vacant, the Superintendent's duties were to be performed by the Librarian. In spite of the ambiguous and unstable nature of the office, something had at least been gained, for Charles C. Jewett was immediately appointed Superintendent and remained in the service of the library until his death. Edward Capen continued to hold the title of Librarian, although that post was definitely subordinate to Jewett's and his duties were largely confined to the issue and circulation of books.

The 1858 Trustees' Report, in commenting upon the division of duties between these two officers, stated that "the operations of the Library are conducted with entire harmony and good feeling on the part of all persons employed in it." More conclusive evidence is furnished by the fact that Capen remained at his diminished post until 1874, when he resigned to accept the librarianship of the Haverhill Public Library, whose red brick building reflects on a reduced scale the design of the Boylston Street library. The same report contains the categorical statement that, after a single year of experience, the Trustees "cannot conceive of any state of things, in which the office of Superintendent, as now constituted, will not be absolutely necessary, in order to the efficient administration of the Library."

SOURCES

The history of the Boylston Street building is summarized in an appendix (pp. 117–172) to *Proceedings at the Dedication of the Building for the Public Library of the City of Boston, January 1, 1858* (Boston, 1858).

Robert C. Winthrop's somewhat boastful letter of 17 April 1855 is quoted by Allan Nevins, *Ordeal of the Union* (New York: Charles Scribner's Sons, 1947), I, 105. I owe this reference to the keen eye of Mr. Lee M. Friedman.

For Jewett's life, see Joseph A. Borome's biography, *Charles Coffin Jewett* (Chicago: American Library Association, 1951).

CHAPTER IV

Jewett in Boylston Street

A library has been defined to be "a collection of books"; but such a definition is as inadequate as to say that an army is a collection of men. To constitute an army the men must be organized for warlike operations. So, to form a library, books and titles must be rightly ordered for their appropriate use.

—CHARLES COFFIN JEWETT

ON the afternoon of New Year's Day 1858 the doors of the new library in Boylston Street opened to receive ladies invited to the dedication ceremonies. Gentlemen taking part in this happy occasion assembled rather at the City Hall in School Street, where a procession of municipal, legal, military and academic guests fell into columns of four. Escorted by the Boston Light Infantry, the male guests marched, to the music of the Boston Brigade Band, up School and Beacon Streets to the State House, down Park Street and through Tremont Street, arriving at the new library just as the clock of Park Street Church struck four.

The Commissioners who had carried their task to completion were on hand to receive the numerous guests, to the strains of Rossini's overture to Mahomet II, performed by Flagg's Cornet Band. They could well feel pride in this addition to the city's resources, for the combination of functional simplicity and great scale gave the building a quiet but monumental character. The red brick facade with huge round arched windows, dressed with Connecticut sandstone, surmounted by a heavy cornice, followed no recognizable historic model; it was, indeed, one of those designs that the late Walter H. Kilham in his study of Boston architecture classified as "plain American." The upper hall, where the guests assembled, had a clear area of thirty-eight by ninety-two feet, as the use of iron had permitted the magnification of the traditional library form to great size. It was no less than fifty-eight feet high, for along its lateral walls were three tiers of alcoves—thirty on each side—with clerestory windows above. Here, in quarters not unlike those still in use at the Peabody Institute Library in Baltimore, the majority of the institution's books were to be housed. But on 1 January 1858 the shelves were still empty, and a temporary platform, decorated with "several magnificent bouquets of natural flowers," supplied by John Galvin, the city forester, had been installed to make the dignitaries more visible to the sizeable audience.

Robert C. Winthrop, President of the Board of Commissioners on the erection of the library, delivered the keys to the Mayor with an account of his fellow Commissioners' stewardship. Mayor Alexander H. Rice received them, with suitably lengthy comment, eventually handing them on to Edward Everett, President of the Board of Trustees. Although disclaiming any intention of making a formal speech, Everett enlarged upon the happy occasion for forty-six minutes, so that it was close to seven o'clock before the guests were able to inspect the fine building which had, including the land, cost the city some $364,000.

The accidents of architecture inevitably shape the habits of insitutions. Throughout the life of the Boylston Street library the two floors—commonly designated as the "Upper Hall" and the "Lower Hall"—developed distinct and individual characters. From the central vestibule the main staircase led directly to the Upper Hall, where two hundred thousand volumes could be shelved, thus leading the reader bent on serious business to the second floor without reference to the more popular material housed in the Lower Hall. A door at the end of the central vestibule opened into the first floor Delivery Room—thirty-four feet wide and fifty feet long, with a twelve-foot ceiling—where a long counter for the issuing of books barred access to a thirty-four by seventy-eight foot hall extending across the back of the building, which had iron balconies designed for the circulating library and contained shelves for forty thousand volumes. From the Delivery Room opened the general Reading Room in the northwest corner, looking out on Boylston Street, with accommodation at tables for two hundred readers. A smaller special Reading Room in the northeast corner, seating one hundred, was provided for the use of ladies, although the high standard of decorum among users of the library made such segregation of the sexes unnecessary.

The extensive public use of the temporary Mason Street quarters, and the extraordinary number of books acquired while the library was under construction, made the occupation of this building, without unreasonably interrupting service, a thorny task. When one recalls that in 1850 Jewett had found only five libraries in the United States possessing fifty thousand or more volumes, the figures on the growth of the Boston Public Library quoted by the 1858 Examining Committee are all the more impressive.

YEAR	Number of Volumes	Number of Pamphlets	Increase of Books	Increase of Pamphlets
1853	9,688	961		
1854	16,221	3,950	6,533	2,989
1855	22,617	6,507	6,396	2,557
1856	38,080	12,638	15,463	5,879
1857	55,688	16,053	17,608	3,667
1858	70,851	17,938	15,163	1,885

It will thus be seen that, while the Boylston Street building was going up, Joshua Bates's generosity had created one of the major libraries of the country. Early in February 1858, when the last workmen were out of the building, Jewett began moving Bates's gifts from 13 Boylston Place. These, with the books stored in the Quincy schoolhouse in Tyler Street, and such as could be spared from the Mason Street library, were provisionally classified and placed on the shelves of the Upper Hall.

George Ticknor, whose faith in the value of a popular circulating library never wavered, made certain that the needs of that part of the institution should not suffer during the installation period. He insisted with firmness that the Lower Hall be opened as soon as possible, and that a separate index of its books be printed before the more imposing catalogue of the entire collection could be completed. The Mason Street rooms were finally closed in early August; on 17 September the Boylston Street reading rooms opened, and by

20 December 1858 the Index to the Lower Hall was printed and books were circulating once more for home use. Jewett, who, by the help of extra assistants, had accomplished this task in record time, thus described the character of the 15,000 volumes selected for the Lower Hall:

> These books constitute an admirable library for common use,— selected not in accordance with any preconceived theory, but solely because the experience of several years had shown that they were the books most wanted by the mass of the people. Viewed in connection with this fact our Library is of considerable interest in showing the literary tastes and demands of our citizens. It might not be supposed that, for a mere popular library, such works as De la Rive on Electricity, Mushet's and Overman's Papers on Iron and Steel, the various volumes of Balliere's Library of Standard Scientific Works, the writings of Jonathan Edwards, and of Leighton, the works of Jefferson and of Hamilton would require to be placed where they could be most easily reached. But such is the truth here, and it speaks well for the intellectual character of the city. It is indeed true that the greater part of the books in the lower hall are of a more popular character, consisting of attractive works in the departments of Biography, History, Voyages and Travels, Fiction and Poetry; but, generally, it is believed that the collection will be found eminently suited to promote the ultimate design of the Institution—the intellectual and moral advancement of the whole people. It would probably be difficult to select the same number of books, better adapted to the great end of sustaining and directing the mental activity awakened by the noble system of public instruction of which Boston is so justly proud.

Ticknor's biographer tells of the anxiety with which he watched operations on the opening day of the Lower Hall, and how

> . . . after witnessing the giving out of the books till eight in the evening, without seeing a moment's trouble or confusion, he went home feeling as if he had nothing more to do so far as this, in his view the most important, part of the institution was concerned.

His mind could well be at rest, for he had in Jewett a man who saw the mechanical techniques of library administration purely as a means to an end. The following observation from the Superintendent's Report for 1858 is well worth remembering.

A library has been defined to be "a collection of Books;" but such a definition is as inadequate as to say that an army is a collection of men. To constitute an army, the men must be organized for warlike operations. So, to form a library, books and titles must be rightly ordered for their appropriate use.

The northeast Reading Room, not having been required for the exclusive use of ladies, was fitted up for periodicals, 140 of which were available, in addition to two hundred volumes of encyclopedias, dictionaries, gazetteers, and other works of ready reference. Between the hours of nine in the morning and ten in the evening, half of its hundred seats were usually steadily occupied, but the most gratifying feature of the new Lower Hall was the constant circulation of its books for home use; 13,329 readers registered for the use of the library in the first fifteen months in Boylston Street, and an average of 588½ books left the building on each library day. This amounted to an annual circulation of 179,000 volumes, which was, as Jewett pointed out "for a library of 15,000 volumes, . . . equal to the loan of every book on an average nearly twelve times a year, or once a month." This speaks well for the skill of Ticknor's and Jewett's selections for the Lower Hall.

The new building opened with a staff of twenty-two, consisting of Jewett, the Superintendent, Edward Capen, the Librarian, a resident janitor, and eleven male and eight female assistants, who were chiefly at work on the books and in the preparation of the catalogue. It was hoped that when matters shook down the force could be reduced to fifteen, even with due regard to speed as well as economy of operation.

Although the Lower Hall was functioning by the close of 1858, it was 1861 before the Upper Hall collection was generally available for public use. The preparation of the printed catalogue for this major portion of the library would have been slow in any case, and the constant receipt of additional gifts made it a labor of Sisyphos. In August 1858, before the new building was even opened, the library of Nathaniel Bowditch was given by his sons Nathaniel I., J. Ingersoll, Henry I., and William I. Bowditch. As a poor boy in Salem in the seventeen eighties and nineties, Nathaniel Bowditch had pursued his studies in mathematics, navigation and astronomy through the help of books generously lent him by local clergymen and by the Salem Athenæum. Notwithstanding the practical experience of foreign voyages, he could hardly have published at twenty-nine his *New American Practical Navigator*—the "seaman's Bible"

BOYLSTON STREET UPPER HALL

of American ships—had uncommon scientific books not been within his reach during his teens. In his later and more comfortable years as actuary of the Massachusetts Hospital Life Insurance Company, Nathaniel Bowditch assembled a library of 2,500 volumes in his Boston house at 8 Otis Place. On his death in 1838, his children—with singular recollection of his need for books half a century before—made his library available for public use in that house. As the extension and widening of Devonshire Street twenty years later caused the demolition of the Otis Place house, Nathaniel Bowditch's sons offered his library, together with twenty-one volumes of his manuscripts, to the City, with the sole stipulation that the books not circulate but be kept together in one or more separate alcoves in the Public Library for reference use. Bowditch had been a Fellow of Harvard College, President of the American Academy of Arts and Sciences and a Trustee of the Boston Athenæum. With these connections, the offer to the Public Library (which did not exist in his lifetime) is a significant evidence of faith that, together with Ticknor's concept of books for popular reading, the new institution would encourage the growth of reference collections for more learned use. Its prompt acceptance, and the decision to keep it together in one department as the "Bowditch Library," established the less fortunate precedent of maintaining separate collections by provenance.

The scientific resources of the library were further augmented by the great series of Specifications of English Patents, presented by the Patent Commissioners of Her Majesty's Government, which were designed to contain in 500 volumes of imperial octavo text and 500 of folio plates, the specifications of all inventions for which letters patent had been issued in England from 1617 to the present.

The opening of the library in 1858 inspired not only gifts of books but of works of art for its decoration. An oil portrait of Benjamin Franklin, painted during his residence in Paris by Duplessis, was given by Edward Brooks, while a group of Boston gentlemen subscribed for the purchase of William W. Story's marble "Arcadian Shepherd Boy" as a suitable ornament for the Upper Hall. In the following year, 1859, another subscription secured for the library John Singleton Copley's large historical painting of Charles I demanding the impeached members of Parliament.

Of considerably greater extent and variety than the Bowditch Library was the legacy bequeathed in 1860 by the Reverend Theodore Parker, who had in the fifty years of an exceptionally active life assembled, with a view to writing a history of religions, a remarkable collection of ancient and modern works on theology, metaphysics, ethics, history, classical and modern literature and civil law. His widow generously relinquished her life-interest in the greater part of the collection and 11,061 volumes and 3,088 pamphlets were transferred to the library at once, a small residue coming to the library upon Mrs. Parker's death in 1881. The gift was particularly welcome, for the library was, as Thomas Wentworth Higginson observed, collected by Mr. Parker

> . . . with a view to actual use by himself, and prospectively by others, and this affected its very selection from the beginning. It was not a show library, or the library of a technical bibliomaniac; it was the collection of a specialist, but that of a specialist with a wide horizon. It was formed by a scholar upon the lines of his own particular studies, but projecting those lines far beyond what he could reasonably expect to accomplish in a lifetime. In the midst of a career so exacting and laborious that, in spite of a most vigorous organization, he died an old man at fifty, Mr. Parker was always making a collection of books that represented both his pursuits and his purposes.

In addition to these unanticipated gifts, the tried and established friends of the library continued unfailing support. Joshua Bates in 1859 gave five hundred books on the history of music, including many rare works of the fifteenth, sixteenth and seventeenth centuries, while in the spring of 1860 George Ticknor presented some two thousand volumes, chiefly of standard works in the ancient and modern languages, carefully selected by himself. In his letter of transmittal, written on 16 April 1860, Ticknor reviewed his own interest in the library:

> A part of the books that I have the honor to offer you are such, I think, as will be useful for the widest and most popular circulation. In this portion of the Library I have always felt and still feel the greatest interest. From the earliest suggestion of such an institution, it has been my prevalent desire that it should be made useful to the greatest possible number of our fellow-citizens, especially to such of them as may be less able than they would gladly be to procure pleasant and profitable reading for themselves and their families. This is known to all the Trustees with whom I have successively served, and our President remembers, that I never would have put my hand to the institution at all, except with

this understanding as to its main object and management. Nor has there been any real difference on this point among the different persons who have controlled its affairs during the eight years of its existence. The consequence is, that there has been spent for books of the most popular character, not merely an amount equal to all that, in successive years, has been saved from the grants of the City Government for the support of the Library, but other large sums derived from different sources, such as the income of the funds given by Mr. Bates and other generous friends of the Institution. In this way there has been collected in our Lower Hall, a library, which, considering the short time employed in gathering it, is, I think, both large and well fitted to its purposes, and one which is rapidly increasing, and growing more useful. The rest of our collection—the part of it, I mean, in our Upper Hall—has come to us almost entirely by gift, and chiefly from the rich donation of Mr. Bates, who, over and above the books purchased with the income of his fund of fifty thousand dollars, has sent us more than five and twenty thousand other volumes of great value.

The result is known. There has been an immense circulation,— one much larger than the most sanguine had anticipated. It was great from the beginning, and it has increased every year. In the ten months after December, 1858, when the Library was first opened in the new building, it rose to more than an hundred and forty-nine thousand volumes; and when the contents of the Upper Hall shall have been long enough accessible to the public to have their value felt, the number of books lent will, no doubt, be increased still further. Such a free circulation from a public library is, I suppose, without a parallel in any city not larger than Boston, and seems to be an appropriate reward for the munificence of its patrons and for the fostering care of the municipal government.

But, notwithstanding the precedence, which in my judgment should be given to this portion of the Library, there is another part of it which, it can hardly be doubted, deserves great attention,—I mean its books which do not circulate, but which are kept in the building, always at hand for reference and use . . .

After praising the utility of the British Patent Specifications and the Bowditch Library, Ticknor continued:

. . . Such collections, I need not say, are everywhere of the greatest importance to the progress of knowledge, but are of more value to persons who have not in their homes convenient arrangements for study, than to any others. We have, however, hardly any such collections in New England, and not one freely open for the use of all, like the Public Library.

I, therefore, fulfill now the intention I expressed to you so long ago, and send to the Superintendent a list of the books which, I hope, you will permit me to contribute to this part of the Institution. A few of them are already on our shelves, but it seems to be well that of these books, as of many others, a single copy should always be reserved in the Library, so that no person who may come there to consult and use it may be disappointed. Others of the books, I have the pleasure to offer you, may be infrequently asked for, but, when they are wanted, they will be found, I think, important, since copies of many of them cannot elsewhere be obtained, except after a troublesome search, if at all. I have wanted them much myself, and, because there was no public library in which I could obtain them, I have bought them,—often very reluctantly. I shall be happy if I am permitted to relieve others from this necessity.

Of the 2,418 volumes that accompanied this letter, four or five hundred were designated for general circulation. The remainder, which included such works as the Benedictine *Histoire littéraire de la France,* Du Cange's *Glossaria,* Schilter's *Thesaurus antiquitatum Teutonicarum,* Scherz's *Glossarium Germanicum,* and the *Classici Italiani* in 250 volumes, were considered as works of reference that should not normally leave the building. In addition to this large gift, George Ticknor also, during 1860, gave the library from ten to fifty copies each of such improving books as the life of Amos Lawrence, Bulfinch's life of Matthew Edwards, the boy inventor, Everett's life of Washington, Samuel Smiles's *Self Help,* and Florence Nightingale's book on nursing, wishing to try the experiment of multiplying available copies of books that were not only interesting but useful. This good idea worked less well than most of Ticknor's, for the Examining Committee of 1861, while turning its nose up at novels, had the honesty to admit that on 12 April 1861 49 out of 50 copies of Miss Nightingale, 16 out of 20 copies of Smiles, 10 out of 10 copies of Lawrence, and 17 out of 20 of Everett's Washington were on the shelf. "The demand had not increased since."

Notwithstanding the delays occasioned by these important additions, Jewett's staff pushed ahead with the preparation of copy for the Index of the Upper Hall. When this was finally printed, in the autumn of 1861, the entire resources of the library were available to readers. It also became possible for most of the 74,000 Upper Hall books to circulate. For this purpose borrowers were issued separate cards for Upper Hall use, which allowed the withdrawal of one volume at a time, without reference to the volume that might be permitted on a Lower Hall card. No great increase in circulation was anticipated, for it had always been the policy to place in the Lower Hall books that were likely to be in considerable demand, but the publication of the Index represented a notable step forward in making the total contents of the library available "to persons little in habits of study, as well as to those who devote themselves to the severest scientific investigations." While this index was in preparation, no less than four supplements to the 1858 Lower Hall index had been issued, for the volumes available in that division of the library had by 1861 increased from 15,000 to 19,161. With Theodore Parker's great bequest the aggregate for the whole institution had reached 97,386.

A year later, on the tenth anniversary of the establishment of the Trustees, the total had risen to 105,034. Capital funds for the purchase of books had been augmented by a $10,000 bequest from the Honorable Abbott Lawrence in 1860 and one of $20,000 from the Honorable Jonathan Phillips in 1861. The country was in the second year of the Civil War, and although many familiar faces were missing, there seemed no diminution of interest in the library, for the circulation of books for home use reached the new height of 180,302. In June 1861 some hundreds of duplicate books had been sent to Boston troops in the service of the United States, but those who remained at home also found use for the library services. The 1862 Examining Committee remarked:

> The library was most needed, it seems, at such a time. It has been frequented by those who were studying history and statistics with reference to our present crisis, and by those who were interested in the arts of war by sea and by land, in military engineering, and military surgery; and not only by those intent upon pursuits of

public import, but also by those who sought relief from the weight of anxieties and cares, pressing heavily upon every class of the community.

With the death of Joshua Bates at London on 24 September 1864, the Public Library lost its most valued friend and generous benefactor. Larger gifts than his followed in later decades, but none have had so decisive an effect, for it was the immediate response of Joshua Bates to the 1852 Trustees' Report that inspired the City of Boston to spend far greater sums of the public money to bring Ticknor's and Everett's dream into being. Before his intervention there were words; after it there was a library. Thus it was appropriate that the Upper Hall of the Boylston Street building should be renamed in his honor, and that the present Bates Hall in Copley Square should perpetuate the memory of this able, single-hearted and generous New Englander who passed most of his life overseas.

Four months later Edward Everett, President of the Trustees of the Public Library since their establishment, left the scene. His death on 15 January 1865 ended a life-long friendship with George Ticknor that, during the previous fifteen years, had led to almost daily meetings and the exchange of hundreds and hundreds of notes and letters concerning the library. Ticknor succeeded Everett as President, but with reluctance, for he was in his seventy-fourth year. In 1866 he passed the duties of the presidency on to William Whitwell Greenough—a close associate in the affairs of the library since his election in 1856—who continued in that office until 1888.

The disappearance of the founders underlines the passage of time. As the library became an established part of the community and ceased to be a novelty it alternately benefitted and suffered. The deposit in 1866 of the library bequeathed to the Old South Church in 1758 by its minister, the Reverend Thomas Prince, represented a tremendous gain. Although title to these books remained with the Deacons of the Old South Church, the physical custody of the remarkable collection made available to readers works of the highest rarity upon the early history of New England. On the debit side, as Jewett's report for 1866 points out, "instances of ungenerous if not of wanton and criminal abuse of confidence" multiplied in the misuse of books in the Lower Hall. Thieving fingers made away with periodicals and reference books; obscene words and drawings were scribbled, and someone even stole both a Bible and a Concordance! "One boy sold his father's card for four cents to another boy, who lent it to a third, who lost both book and card; but the three boys came to the Library, and united to pay for the book lost." To cope with these problems, periodicals were removed from tables and placed behind a desk under the care of an attendant who issued them upon written application. To keep more efficient track of books in circulation, Jewett abandoned the traditional method of recording loans in large ledgers and devised a system of charge slips which both increased the speed of service and furnished a rapid clue to the whereabouts of books not on the shelves.

Books in the library were arranged upon a "decimal system" originated by Dr. N. B. Shurtleff, by which the fixed shelves were so numbered that the figures in the place of hundreds denoted the alcove, those in the place of tens the ranges, and those in the place of units the shelves. Thus a book numbered 2236 would obviously be found, even by the dimmest intelligence, on the 6th shelf of the 3rd range of the 22nd alcove. To save the time of both readers and staff Jewett devised for the Delivery Room an "Indicator," which showed visually whether books belonging to the Lower Hall were in or out. This contraption consisted of a row of reversible pins for each shelf, with the number denoting the order of the book on the shelf on each end of the pin. The end containing the number in black on white ground was exposed when the book was known to be on the shelf. When it was taken out, the pin was flipped over, exposing the number in white on black ground, at the sight of which the intelligent inquirer would promptly go away without troubling anyone by asking foolish questions! The gadget was doubtless far from fool-proof, but its very existence shows something of Jewett's ideal of rapid and ingenious service.

The annually appointed Examining Committee, consisting of five citizens at large with a member of the Board of Trustees as Chairman, furnished a valuable check upon the policies and conduct of the library. No one of these had ever given as complete and searching an analysis as the 1867 Examining Committee, working under the chairmanship of Justin Winsor, a thirty-six-year-old literary man who had been elected a Trustee that very year. Winsor's group not only found good and bad features, but presented them with equal frankness. The building, after nine years of use, had not come up to expectations. Its main defects were

> A want of light in some of the alcoves of the Bates Hall, of ventilation in the lower story, and the absence of working-rooms. Moreover, a mistake had been made in the height of the alcoves, since moveable steps are required to reach the higher shelves,—a fault too late, probably, now to remedy.

Light and ventilation would not be improved without major rebuilding. Bates Hall, with its tiers of alcoves and galleries, *looked* very fine, but as the building was without working rooms for the staff, all collating, cataloguing and preparation of books for the shelves had to be done in the alcoves, where there was scarcely room for two people to pass beside the tables. Moreover, the binders who had been employed since 1863 in making repairs "are necessarily put to some inconvenience in timing the noisier parts of their trade to intervals when the hall is free from readers." The Reading Room was often overcrowded, and even the shelves were causing concern. Although the building, designed to accommodate 240,000 volumes, only contained 136,000 plus 35,000 pamphlets in 1867, subjects were already encroaching upon each other. "Accordingly, though the shelves of the Bates Hall will still accommodate a large accession of volumes, not many thousands more can be received without departing locally from the classifications so needful to make a library useful." Moreover the need of keeping the Parker Library together caused major disturbance, which would be increased by the acceptance of further gifts with like conditions. Consequently a series of independent rooms "to relieve the present hall of these minor consolidated collections, and not only to lodge, but to invite further accessions of a like character" seemed highly desirable.

In contrast to the defects of the building, the increase of books was highly satisfactory. With a total of 136,000, the Examining Committee felt that "there is reason to believe that the Boston Public Library is destined to become the largest on this continent," for it was then surpassed in size only by the Library of Congress. Furthermore, the record of gifts showed a sustained public interest in

the library. The catalogues were found adequate, with the comment
that "the *card* system for an *unprinted catalogue* with full titles is
more and more valued with experience." Records were in good order
and expenditures properly cared for. The pamphlet collection was,
however, getting out of hand, and additional help was needed to
keep it in useful order.

Closing for the annual examination of books during August, plus
52 Sundays and six holidays, reduced the number of open days to
approximately 278 per year. It was admitted that "the task of seeing
that every volume of a hundred and thirty-six thousand is in its
proper place is no small one, and the recess is not by any means a
season of relaxation to the attendants," but "it will be fortunate, if
in coming years, this work can be kept within the month."

The Committee felt that the library was conducted so as to be as
useful as possible to all classes.

> The institution was begun expressly on popular grounds. Mr.
> Everett, in his letter to the Mayor, in 1851, called it the comple-
> tion of our public school system, and that has been a favorite desig-
> nation of it ever since. In the preliminary report of 1852—the
> body of which was drawn by Mr. Ticknor—it was wisely recom-
> mended that a beginning should be made without any sharply de-
> fined plan, so that suggestions from experience could be made
> effectual; and it was not thought well to make it at once an impos-
> ing, learned or scientific collection, but rather to gather a library
> most fitted for the masses. Mr. Ticknor—whose contributions to
> the Library in time and experience cannot be overvalued—ex-
> pressly says, in a letter accompanying a valuable donation of books
> in 1860, that he would "never have put his hand to the institu-
> tion at all, but with the understanding that it should be made use-
> ful to the greatest possible number of citizens;" and he says that
> for eight years there had not been any *real* difference among the
> Trustees on that point, nor can we learn that there has been any
> since.

> Up to 1856 the system of purchases had looked to supplying
> the most popular wants. The collection, which had then grown to
> near 30,000 volumes, was deemed large enough to satisfy the
> most reasonable demands of a general kind; and it began to be felt
> that there were particular classes of our citizens, apart from the
> general body, whose wants deserved recognition. So about that time

we find that books in the foreign tongues began to be added, and
the higher departments of literature more fully developed. The
donations to the Trust Funds, now accruing, in being expended
for books of solid and permanent value, served to strengthen very
materially the upper classifications; while Mr. Bates' last munificent gift of books developed our weight in the same direction. The
time was now come when it was very properly agreed that there
was no department of learning, which some portion of the community was not interested in; and that every department should
be cared for to meet such requirements. So the two distinct collections have been developed—the Lower Hall to meet the ordinary demands of the people, and the Bates to serve the higher
requirements of the studious classes, or of investigators in special
matters—a scheme which your Committee cannot but think naturally evolved, and conducive to the satisfaction of every mental
grade, and answering the requirements of all the intellectual demands of the community.

The privilege of requesting books for purchase and the expeditious
service were favorably commented upon, while a series of arguments to justify the exclusion of readers from the shelves were set
forth.

The City Ordinance for the government of the library needed
improvement. A revision in 1865 had given the Trustees the right
to appoint the Superintendent and the Librarian, previously retained
by the City Council, but not the responsibility for fixing their
salaries.

In assigning duties to the various officers, they [the Trustees] are
not free to exercise fully their own judgment, until the apportion-
ment of the salaries goes with the assignment. They have this
liberty in all cases but with the Superintendent and Librarian, on
whom the most responsibility falls, and upon whose trustworthi-
ness they must depend before all others. It is eminently proper that
the City Council should fix the limit in the aggregate of all salaries,
but it seems to your Committee that it would be desirable to remove the restraint now existing, so that the Trustees may appor-
tion the recompense, as well as define the duties, of all under
them, within some aggregate limits.

In 1866 a further revision had doubled the representation from the
Common Council on the Board of Trustees and added one from the
citizens at large, making the new board to consist of nine rather than

seven members. The terms of tenure were altered so that five new members, or a majority, might come onto the board at a single election. This, to the Examining Committee, obviously opened the possibility of throwing the control of the library "into the hands of the inexperienced, or of those chosen, in obedience to some passion of the hour, on other grounds than their peculiar fitness." They urged that tenure be so altered that at least two successive elections should be required to change the predominant character of the board.

The most penetrating and original analyses of Winsor's Examining Committee concerned the circulation of books. To find an appropriate basis for comparison, the Committee resorted to statistics from the Manchester library, which since its opening in 1852 had been the pioneer in the British public library movement. At a new registration for borrower's privileges in Boston in 1866, some twelve or thirteen thousand cards had been issued and 183,714 books withdrawn from the Lower Hall, while at Manchester, with only 7,339 cards in use, very nearly the same number of books circulated. The Committee observed that the Manchester system of branch libraries "brings its books much nearer to a large number of households," and suggested:

> With a system of branch libraries with us, say one in Roxbury, one in South Boston, and one in East Boston, it seems probable that our popular circulation could be made far larger relatively, than it is even now to the most successful of such establishments at home and abroad. At Manchester, the system is well established and works successfully . . . The accumulation of duplicates at a central library is always less burdensome, when there are supplemental institutions among which to share them.

In Bates Hall the average daily delivery was 92 volumes, while the largest delivered in any one day was 206. Since the opening in 1862 the total number lent for home use had been 53,920, and the 13,-696 of the previous year set a record. In Manchester the Reference Library, although one-third the size of Bates Hall, showed three times the number of users. Nevertheless Manchester had twice the population of Boston and fewer rivals.

> . . . while within much the same area, and with a far smaller population, the Boston Public Library must share this class of more

or less cultivated frequenters, with the collections of Harvard College and the Boston Athenæum. Besides this, we in this community are uncommonly well supplied with lesser collections, accessible to persons making investigations, like the libraries of the Historical Society, the Genealogical Society, State Library, the Academy Library, the Social Law Library, the old Boston Library, the General Theological Library, etc., so that in the aggregate there are at least half a million volumes in our community, accessible to the public, or reached with ease by anyone desiring to use them.

The character of the reading in the two halls was contrasted. In the five years that Bates Hall had been in use, the *average* yearly use of books in the several classifications had been:

	Per cent
English History and Literature	17
Useful and Fine Arts	10
American History and Literature	9
Theology, Metaphysics, Ethics, Education	8
Periodicals	7
Mathematics and Physics	7
Medicine	6
French History and Literature	6
General History and Literature	4
Italian History and Literature	4
Natural History	4
Transactions of Learned Societies	4
German History and Literature	3
Greek and Latin	3
Other (including Oriental) History and Literature	3
Bibliography	2
Law and Political Economy	2
Miscellaneous	1

The preliminary report of 1852 had contended that, if the habit of reading could be engendered, it would go on improving in character. As the Trustees detected, or thought they detected, a "demand for higher and higher classes of literature," they became less willing to buy novels. "In 1859, it was reported, that only the best of the lighter class of literature was bought. The next year there was a marked falling off in circulation." Although attempts had been made to discover the genuine demand for fiction, it was only in 1866, when Jewett introduced the slip system of charging, that an accurate count became possible. Winsor's Examining Committee therefore offered the following analysis—the first accurate one to be made—of the 183,000 volumes circulating from the Lower Hall in 1866:

	Per cent
Fiction and Juveniles	68.2
Libraries, Collections, etc.	6.2
Science, Arts, Professions	6.6
Drama, Poetry, Rhetoric, Belles Lettres	4.7
Travels	4.8
History and Politics	2.9
Biography	3.9
Foreign Languages	2.7

As the class "Libraries, Collections, etc." included sets containing novels, the total of fiction circulating reached at least 70 per cent of the whole.

> This large proportion for a class of literature that ordinarily includes so much that is morbid or even pernicious, may alarm some of the good friends of the institution, but the subject is not to be dismissed without examination from many points; and your committee are of the opinion that although they might wish a different record, they must accept the condition as arising from the mental tendency of the masses of the community; and they hope to show that the result with us is no worse than elsewhere, and even sometimes creditable by comparison . . .

Fiction in the Manchester library as early as 1857 had accounted for five-eighths of the circulation, while three quarters of the current purchases of the New York Mercantile Library were novels.

> Your Committee, then, are not of the opinion that this large percentage of fiction with us, is anything that need surprise or alarm us. Good fiction is doubtless salutary, and the general character of juvenile literature is much improved over what it formerly was . . . We may say that the best novels are seldom read in a way to do the most good; but that is a circumstance of course beyond any library's control, and there is a good deal to say in favor of supplying the masses with reading of even an inferior order rather than

that they should not read at all . . . It needs must be that to most minds of a low intellectual culture, books must be of a character attractive in subject to that grade, or they will not be regarded at all. Once regarded, there is a fair chance of substituting for books attractive in subject, those attractive in manner, thus leading to a higher range of subjects.

A detailed analysis of authors in demand placed Cooper and Marryat far ahead of all competitors.

Winsor's report pictured as the result of fifteen years of honest experiment a library of great size, soundly administered although inconveniently housed, consisting—in the approximate proportion of four to one—of a learned collection scantly used because of resources available elsewhere in the region, and of a highly active popular circulating collection in which fiction predominated. The library had been designed for the people, and they were using it, but the improvement of popular taste was, it seemed, a slowish business.

SOURCES

For the Bowditch Library, see *Circular to the Patrons of the Bowditch Library with the documents on the occasion of its being presented to the Public Library of the City of Boston, August 28, 1858* (Boston, 1858).

CHAPTER V

The Winsor Decade

Mr. Winsor was the first librarian I ever saw
whose fundamental policy, never lost sight of for
a moment, was to get books used, even though they
should be used up.

—CHARLES W. ELIOT

THE year 1858 had opened happily and confidently with the
dedication of the Boylston Street library. Ten years later the
mood was sadly different, for on the afternoon of 8 January 1868
the indefatigable and invaluable Superintendent, Charles Coffin
Jewett, was attacked by apoplexy while working at his desk. Partially paralyzed, he was carried home to Braintree, where he died
soon after midnight. The Trustees might well enter in their minutes
that they "feel no common sorrow, and experience unwonted be-
wilderment," and resolve

that in the death of Charles Coffin Jewett this Library is deprived of a steadfast friend, and an officer of such ingenious mind
and such rare knowledge apposite to his duty, that we hardly know
where to find his equal,

for, although only in his fifty-second year, he had made a unique
place for himself in the rapidly expanding world of librarians. Since
coming to Boston in 1856, Jewett had quietly, rapidly and unerr-
ingly applied his considerable talents to converting Ticknor's and
Everett's plans into reality. Now when—with Everett dead and
Ticknor in retirement—Jewett was needed more than ever, he sud-
denly and without warning left the scene. Moreover, his principal
assistant, Professor William Everett Jillson, former Librarian of the
Patent Office, who had come permanently to Boston in 1865, was

far gone in consumption and spitting blood. Although soon chosen to succeed Jewett, Jillson was prevented by ill health from attempting the Superintendent's duties, and he too died within the year.

William F. Poole, who had aspired to the librarianship before the appointment of Edward Capen, now showed signs of wishing to succeed Jewett as Superintendent. At least on 15 February 1868 he resigned the post that he had held since 1856 as Librarian of the Boston Athenæum, without having any other pressing employment in view. It has been assumed that he took this unexpected step to indicate his candidacy for the Public Library vacancy, but, meeting with no more success than in 1852, he reached the culmination of his career in Cincinnati and Chicago, rather than Boston. After discovering that Jillson could not carry on, the Trustees of the Public Library, rather than consider Poole, took an imaginative step that proved to be as successful as it was both bold and unexpected. They appointed Justin Winsor Superintendent.

Winsor had been a Trustee for a year. He was a man of letters, without previous library experience, but in a few months he had taken better stock of the situation than most men would have in a decade. His report as Chairman of the 1867 Examining Committee showed his analytical and administrative powers. Indeed, as his successor, Mellen Chamberlain, recalled to the Massachusetts Historical Society thirty years later,

> This report attracted attention far and wide as a masterly, indeed as an unprecedented, presentation of all conceivable questions relating to the public library and its constituents.

Winsor happened to have chosen a literary career, but he was the kind of New Englander who would have made his mark at sea a generation or two earlier, for he had, as Judge Chamberlain pointed out, administrative and executive powers that would have made him equally able in managing a great railroad or a manufacturing corporation. When he took up his duties as Superintendent in July 1868, Winsor set about remedying with remarkable speed and precision the defects that he had noted in the Examining Committee report. Cotton Mather would undoubtedly have asserted that "the Lord raised up Justin Winsor to undertake this work." Even latter-day

Bostonians would agree that his appointment was in the nature of a remarkable providence.

One of Winsor's first moves was to discover what could be done elsewhere as a guide to what should be done in Boston. The 1868 library report bears on its inside cover this characteristic note:

> The Superintendent would respectfully invite correspondence with librarians and others interested upon points of library economy raised in this report; and in behalf of this library would particularly request, where it has not already been done, that sets of the printed reports, blanks, forms, etc., used in other libraries, may be forwarded to him.

Similarly Winsor's own report, after dealing with the inadequacies of the Boylston Street building, turns at once to the relative position of the Boston Public Library among comparable institutions in the country. It will be recalled that in 1850 Jewett listed but five libraries containing upwards of 50,000 books. In 1868 Winsor found ten, with his own in second place.

	Volumes	*Pamphlets*
Library of Congress	175,000	70,000
Boston Public Library	144,000	50,000
Astor Library, New York	138,000	
Harvard College Library	118,000	100,000
Boston Athenæum	100,000	70,000
New York Mercantile Library	98,000	
Philadelphia Library Company	85,000	
Library of Parliament, Ottawa	60,000	
Yale College Library	50,000	20,000
American Antiquarian Society	50,000	

Of all ten, Boston was the only library supported in the main by municipal grants, for in that group, Winsor found that only two other of the public libraries of this country had as yet assumed any considerable proportions, namely that of

| New Bedford | 21,000 volumes |
| Cincinnati | 20,000 volumes |

while the largest of the English public libraries, established by the Parliamentary acts that allowed an assessment of a penny in the pound valuation for their support, was Liverpool, with 84,000 volumes.

To obtain further information in this direction, Winsor circulated a questionnaire among several hundred libraries, American and foreign, explaining in his 1869 report:

> There is not a library in the country of a public nature but we are glad to be in correspondence with it, and to exchange the data of our experience and practice. The measure of our gift in this way may be, in the nature of the case, in many instances greater than the return; but we have not failed to profit by what has been given to us. The interchange of bibliothecal experience is almost alone wanting to carry the knowledge of library science to the limit of proficiency. The time may come, as Mr. Edwards remarks, when annuals of library progress may be as regularly published as the statistics of manufactures and trade. Till then, the exchange of documents and reports must supply the need. During the past year, I have done much to establish relations of good fellowship with the libraries of this continent; and our exchange list now numbers over four hundred different libraries, over one-quarter of which are foreign.

The results were tabulated in Appendices xxii–xxv to the report. In these forty pages, Winsor offered a more complete picture of libraries in the United States than had previously existed, together with notes on the practices of certain European institutions with which he had been in correspondence. In general, Winsor's reports exceeded Jewett's in usefulness, for he invariably included, in addition to the customary listing of donors, detailed statistics upon every conceivable subject concerning the library's books, their nature, growth, use and abuse. Comparative financial statements and detailed lists of staff members, with indication of their duties, soon appear. The Trustees rightly described Winsor's 1869 report as

> . . . a treatise upon the condition of our own and other libraries, forming an important contribution to a new department of literature, the science of management of popular libraries. It will render bibliographical and practical aid to a class of young men and women, now much desired in libraries, to whom special education needed for such positions had been heretofore entirely beyond reach.

The 1867 Examining Committee had been very frank about the inadequacies of the Boylston Street building. Ten years later Winsor wrote.

> Its faults are radical, and grew partly out of the inexperience of those, or rather a *majority* of the commission, superintending its erection, the records of that body showing a vote of four to three on all essential points concerned in arranging the plans, which induced an inability to comprehend the extent of work needful to be done in a rapidly growing Library, and partly from a sacrifice of fitness to a desire for ostentation.

The Examining Committee for 1870 minced no words when it said:

> It will be generally conceded, that whether we consider its external design or its internal plan, the building is equally a failure. With the former we have nothing to do, since no added beauty there would increase the conveniences of the officers of the Library or of the public who use it. But the sins of the interior cry aloud continually and in vain for a remedy. The crypt-like Delivery Room, the narrow and ill-lighted Reading Room, the dark staircase with its wretched landings, where one stands groping for the handle of the door which should not be needed, the pretentious Hall above, fit enough for a music hall or an exchange, but as little like a library-room as it could well be made, the dark alcoves piled up three stories high, and shrouding the books in an almost impenetrable gloom; finally, the inexcusable absence of ventilation throughout the building; these are the daily and hourly misfortunes of all who have occasion to pass much of their time within these walls. To remedy the faults of the present building is impossible.

As it was sometimes necessary on short winter afternoons to suspend delivery of books in Bates Hall because the staff could not read the book numbers in the Stygian alcoves, Winsor first provided the runners with "dark lanterns." Subsequently he installed gas jets and later broke windows through the exterior walls. Similarly he moved the noisy binders from Bates Hall alcoves to the basement, and by 1869 had three of them working busily there in a "permanent and suitable apartment . . . with every necessary appliance in all departments of the trade." After such obvious improvements had been made, Bates Hall, at least to the casual visitor, had an air of dignity and decorum. An article on the library in the 2 December 1871 issue of *Appleton's Journal* thus describes the vast room:

It is fifty-two feet high, clear. It contains three stories of alcoves on the sides. Twenty-two massive pillars, with bases of marble, enclose the space used by the public, and in the rear of them are the shelves. Between the bases of the pillars are heavy desks, turned outward, and supplied with conveniences for writing. Large oval tables, six feet long, are distributed in the apartment, and the chairs are cushioned.

The colors of the wall are neutral, and the tints are subdued. The ceiling is richly ornamented, and, to an American, its elevation is startling. The floor is tiled, and every step and tone resounds as if the place were a cavern. The effect is impressive. The stairway emerges into the centre of the hall, and the space over one's head is clear and unbroken by galleries.

Twenty or thirty people are usually to be found here, some writing, most of them reading hard, and a few gazing about them. All are quiet. Few sounds break the silence, except, now and then, the tap of the cancelling stamp at the desk, a footfall in the corridors, or the faint rustle of book-leaves.

The noise of the street sinks to a muffled hum, and one catches, through the windows, a sight of the verdure of the beautiful Common. There is no more civilizing place in the country.

Civilizing amenities hardly extended to the Lower Hall Delivery Room, where the lion's part of the library's business was transacted.

It is in this somewhat limited apartment that a visitor gets his first hint of the magnitude of the operations of the library. At all hours of the day groups of people throng it and quietly pursue their objects. At one desk they return the volumes which are read, and apply for others; while at another desk the distinct but monotonous voice of the attendant calls, at intervals, the names of those for whom books are ready, or those whose applications have been fruitless.

At six in the evening, when the schools have emptied, and all workers of both sexes are free to go to their homes, this room becomes one of the sights of the city. It fills to repletion. Children throng its floor, and are wonderfully sharp to the little tricks of competition for early attention. It is amusing to see with what rapidity an old stager of twelve years, with a cropped head and a quick eye, will put his errand through. He will monopolize a wide section of desk-room with extended elbows, pounce in a single flourish upon the exact catalogue out of the many, get his number out of the multitude of other numbers, pencil it and his name with precise care upon his paper and deliver it up to the clerk, all the while an unaccustomed visitor will be engaged in the first part of the transaction, namely, deciding what book he would like to have. This well done, the boy must await developments; and, American-like, he improves the interval. He goes to the adjacent reading-room, and, securing an illustrated paper, sits himself down within sound of the attendant's voice, to wait and read until his book or disappointment turns up.

The assembled crowd is often motley. But, the more motley, the more various and dissimilar its ingredients, the better the proof of the wide-spread influence of the library. Rich and poor assemble together and alike in this narrow dispensary, and a great many of them too.

So many, in fact, that Dr. George Derby, Secretary of the State Board of Health, considered the Delivery Room air on crowded winter afternoons to be more foul and unwholesome than that of any other room in Massachusetts. As early as 1869, the Trustees were marvelling "how many are willing to submit to the inconvenience of such a crowded, ill-ventilated apartment."

As *these* were the readers for whom the library had been founded, Justin Winsor took steps to discover who they were, as an essential preliminary to finding out what they wanted and devising better means of getting it to them. His 1869 report contains an analysis in tabular form (Appendix XIX) of the occupations of over eleven thousand readers who had registered the previous year. Forty-six per cent were women, while "what may be called the educated classes form 10 per cent of the whole number, including women, and not including any of the 37 per cent of the whole number, male and female, who gave no occupation." The picture, in summary form, appeared to be:

	Males	*Females*	*Totals*	*Per cent*
Trades, Manufactures, etc.	1,001	584	1,585	15
Dealers, Shopkeepers, etc.	234	6	240	2
Mercantile callings	2,006	116	2,122	19
Professional classes	746	396	1,142	11
Official classes, etc.	165	3	168	1
Laboring classes	242	3	245	2
Miscellaneous classes	1,038	434	1,472	13
No occupation given	585	3,708	4,293	37
	6,017	5,250	11,267	

Had Joshua Bates been alive, the primacy of the mercantile classes would have confirmed and strengthened his faith, for 926 clerks, 417 salesmen, 320 merchants and 237 bookkeepers appeared among the library's readers. The professional classes, even when represented by 394 teachers, 132 physicians, 107 lawyers and 82 clergymen, were not so creditably represented as the trades. It is less surprising to note 161 printers than 154 carpenters, 31 piano makers, 25 organ builders, and 25 blacksmiths. In Winsor's statistics only a solitary representative appeared in each of the occupations of artificial leg maker, butcher, embalmer, tallow chandler, liquor dealer, pawnbroker, minstrel, alderman, ballet girl, sheriff and billiard hall keeper, although 60 porters and 49 laborers were registered. Moreover, among the crowd jostling each other in the foul-smelling Delivery Room might be found as many as 9 bartenders, 4 Sisters of Charity, 4 oyster openers (one male and three female) 3 street waterers, 2 wood choppers and 6 washerwomen. Eleven readers described themselves as gentlemen.

After this analysis of his parishioners, Winsor was in no way surprised that novels accounted for three quarters of the circulation of books from the Lower Hall. It did not disturb him, for in 1869 he had observed:

> When Whately affirmed that the mind, like the stomach, did not thrive on concentrated food, but needed bulk of matter as well as nutriment, it was a proposition very closely touching this question. Most novels show some good purpose or give some fractional information, which would be disregarded if concentrated into moral pith or educational precept. A hand-book of "Good Manners" or "Etiquette" will not make many gentlemen, and many novels have a far more effective influence to that end. "I often see," says Mr. Emerson, and no doubt truly, "traits of the Scotch and French novel in the courtesy and brilliance of young midshipmen, collegians, and clerks."

Similarly in 1871 Winsor wrote:

> I have in the past discussed the question of the large amount of fiction read in popular libraries. It is an inevitable experience, and the dreams of those hopeful for a change are in vain. The multitude not only crave fiction,—something imaginative as a counterpoise to the realities, often stern, of life,—but, in consequence of

there being comparatively few trained imaginations, the style of fiction that is craved is oftenest of a low order. We may perhaps find a moral in the old fable of the thirsty starling, who got at the water in the urn by dropping pebbles into it one by one. The reading books which we may grow to despise, like the service of those valueless fragments, may imperceptibly raise the fountain of intelligence to a higher level, and this no doubt sometimes happens; but the general results in libraries will not vary, since new readers begin at the level from which the old readers advanced, and thus keep up the relative debasement.

Notwithstanding the cool realization that missionaries are never going to run out of heathen to convert, Winsor prepared a list of historical novels, poems and plays, which he hoped, entirely correctly, "might become the stepping-stones to the less imaginative works upon the corresponding periods of the world's history." This *Chronological Index to Historical Fiction,* which appeared in 1871, was followed in 1873 by *A Catalogue of Books belonging to the Lower Hall of the Central Department in the Classes of History, Biography and Travel . . . with Notes for Readers under subject-references,* where Winsor embarked upon a wholly new theory of notes for the guidance of readers. Of this experiment he wrote retrospectively in his 1877 report:

In 1873 the Library made an innovation in the bibliographical matter which was made an adjunct of its popular Catalogues. The new departure was a natural one, and followed as a matter of course in the development of the influence which it was the aim of the fathers of the Library to bestow upon the public. Mr. Everett, its first president, enunciated a sentiment that has never been lost sight of, when he claimed that its mission was to supplement the schools; and a happy embodiment of the idea has found shape of late in the phrase of "The People's College." With the growth of any collection the ease of consultation naturally gives way to an indecision in the face of accumulated titles on every subject, and without some guide to a choice of books discouragement is likely to ensue from any haphazard selection out of many, for any particular purpose. A consideration of these difficulties ripened the plan. As preliminary the thought occurred of alluring the pastime reader, of whom all Libraries, in any degree popular, have a large following, by easy steps, to become a reader of better purpose. I am too much a believer in the general straightforwardness of ingrafted impulses ever violently to counteract them. I believe men can be led rather than pushed. The implanting in mankind of the story-telling faculty, and the enjoyment of it in others, was not an idle creation; and the imagination has done too much for amelioration of mankind not to deserve our acceptance of it, as a handmaid of virtue and a promoter of intellectual advancement. This assistance was accordingly invoked in a list of historical fiction, which was prepared in chronological grouping under countries, as calculated to instigate a study by comparison, and lead the mind to history and biography by the inciting of the critical faculties. I have reason to believe the idea was not a futile one, from the interest manifested in the movement, and the avidity with which more than one edition of it was taken up. This was but a trial. The next step was the more serious one of endeavoring to direct the ductile perceptions of the less learned among readers. The effort was not to propound positively any course of reading, for there is danger always in dogmatism, however right its foundation may be. The notes which were appended to the subject-references in the History, Biography, and Travel Catalogue of the Lower Hall, in 1873, served to render the ordinary reader more able to choose to his liking when an undistinguishable mass of equivalent titles perplexed him.

These pioneering efforts in bibliography for the masses inspired both praise and emulation here and abroad. Although attempting by such means to raise the standard of choice, Winsor, nevertheless, was admitting with complete frankness that "the great effort is to get people to read at all." When social workers found Public Library books in tenements with broken windows, leaky roofs and no fires, Winsor reasoned,

> There can be no question if there is any mental amelioration or intellectual pastime to be enjoyed from a popular library by the lowest classes, that, if you confine your selection of fiction to Scott and Miss Edgeworth alone, as some good people would have you do, you debar the vast majority of such from becoming readers at all. If we exclude the positively vicious books, we have gone as far as we can without thwarting the desires of the great masses of readers, which are legitimate because arising from their conditions and wants.

In the 1867 Examining Committee report, he had raised, for the first time in Boston, the idea of extending the usefulness of the library by means of branches, patterned on the British model. The revised City Ordinance of 1869 had empowered the Trustees of the Public Library "from time to time to establish Branch Libraries of popular and useful books and periodicals in sections of the city distant from the main collection"; a plan that Winsor immediately hailed as "one which promises more effectually than any other to induce more people to read our books and to read more of them." East Boston was chosen as the part of the city least accessible to Boylston Street. Thus far 1 in 8 of the population of Boston proper used the library; in Roxbury the proportion was 1 out of 14, in South Boston 1 out of 16, while in East Boston only 1 in 26 took any advantage of the institution. Therefore in 1870 the Trustees requested an appropriation for establishing an East Boston Branch Library. Rooms on the second floor of the old Lyman schoolhouse were made available by the City; books selected from Lower Hall duplicates and specially purchased were supplemented by the collection of the Sumner Library Association, founded by the late General William H. Sumner, and by 28 November 1870 the new Reading Room was open. Circulation began on 27 January 1871, and, the printing of the catalogue having been completed by early March, a formal dedication took place on 22 March, with an address by William W. Greenough, President of the Board of Trustees.

A second branch, in hired quarters in the new Savings Bank Building in Broadway, South Boston, was dedicated with similar ceremonies on 16 May 1872. Just as the Sumner Library Association had turned over its books for the use of the East Boston Branch, the Mattapan Library Association—having fallen on evil days— generously made its collection of 1,470 volumes available for the new South Boston Branch. With books bought for the purpose, 4,350 volumes were on the shelves in South Boston and ready for use on 1 May. Both the new branches duplicated many of the Lower Hall holdings, but cards issued in either of them were also valid for use in Boylston Street either in the Lower Hall or in Bates Hall.

In Roxbury the task of establishing a branch library was made easier by a private benefaction organized under the will of Caleb Fellowes, a seafaring man out of Gloucester who had prospered in trade at Calcutta. Although he had only lived in Roxbury for a part of his life, Fellowes's will—upon his death in Philadelphia on 8 November 1852—was found to provide for the establishment of an Athenæum "within half a mile of the Rev. Mr. Putnam's meeting house in Roxbury," the building "to be as nearly as practicable like that of the Philadelphia Athenæum, and to be used, as that institution is, for literary and instructive purposes." As the will provided for reinvestment of income until an adequate capital sum had accumulated, no immediate steps were taken. In December 1871, the Trustees of the Fellowes Athenæum in Roxbury—incorporated in 1866—approached the Boston City Council with the proposal that they erect a building that would be rented by the City for a Roxbury Branch Library and operated jointly. As this plan would give the city a good building and several thousand dollars a year for books over and above the ordinary appropriation for a branch library, agreement was soon reached and construction begun during 1872 at a site on Bartlett Street, Roxbury, near Shawmut Avenue.

Justin Winsor seized the opportunity to work out with the architects, N. J. Bradlee and W. J. Winslow, his ideas of a practical and convenient library. His chief objection to Bates Hall was that it was

> . . . unfortunately planned to produce the largest instead of the smallest average distance of books from the point of delivery,— a defect which requires some sacrifice of supposed architectural claims to avoid, and which, in consequence of the inability of architects and building committees to recognize the paramount demands of administrative uses over the meretricious attractions of vistas of books and displayed alcoves, has disfigured some of the more important and recently erected library buildings in this State and at the West.

The exact opposite was tried in the plan for the Fellowes Athenæum, where an ample ground floor Delivery Room of 36 by 37 feet, easily accessible from the street, opened directly into a library stack, capable of eventual shelving for 50,000 volumes, where no book would be above the reach of a normal arm. A Reading Room, 37 by 45 feet, occupied the second floor. In 1871 Winsor had suggested establishing a separate "Juvenile Library" in Boylston Street, with a view to "restoring the almost abandoned rights of adults" in the Lower Hall. Although such a plan was not included in the Fellowes

Athenæum, its Delivery Room was bisected by a barrier that confined adults and youths to separate areas.

Most unhappily, after construction had begun, the Metropolitan Horse Railroad Company bought land completely surrounding the site of the Fellowes Athenæum. The prospect of a library hemmed in by stables and perfumed with horse manure proved so intolerable that in August 1872 the Trustees of the Fellowes Athenæum incontinently sold out to the Horse Railroad Company, and began their building a second time in more salubrious surroundings on Millmont Street. Although six months' time was lost by this contretemps, the Roxbury Branch was in full working order by the time of its dedication on 9 July 1873.

By the annexation to Boston in 1874 of Charlestown and Brighton, existing libraries in those two communities became branches of the Boston Public Library system. The Charlestown Library, owning 15,788 volumes at the time of the merger, had, since its opening in 1862, been housed in two rooms on the second story of the City Hall. With the consolidation of city offices, the entire second floor became available, and, as Winsor observed in his 1875 report, the rooms of the Charlestown Branch, "ornamented as they are with the large paintings which were a legacy from the old city government of that district, now present one of the most conveniently planned and cheery-looking of our dependencies."

The Holton Public Library in Brighton, organized in 1864 through a bequest of James Holton, took over the collection of the Brighton Library Association, which had, upon its foundation in 1858, absorbed the Brighton Social Library of 1828. At the 1874 annexation of the city, the Holton Library, of 11,037 volumes, was housed in crowded quarters, while an imposing building was under construction on Rockland Street. After some alterations in plan to make it more suitable for use in its new function, this building was completed and opened for use as a Brighton Branch of the Boston Public Library in August 1874, although the formal dedication was deferred until 29 October 1874, when Mr. Greenough delivered one of the addresses inevitably associated with such occasions. Thus the fourth and fifth branches were acquired, almost ready-made, by process of municipal accretion.

The sixth, in Dorchester, was foreshadowed in 1874 appropriations, accommodated in the new city building at Field's Corner, and opened in January 1875. The presence of a local resident, Mr. William T. Adams—better known under his pen name of Oliver Optic—among the speakers at the 18 January 1875 dedication must have amused any of the audience who recalled President Greenough's pious hope, uttered three years before at similar exercises in South Boston, that "boys and girls may come to desire something more profitable than Mayne Read and Oliver Optic." Mr. Adams gracefully expressed his pleasure that our public libraries were aware of the dangers of supplying "the young with books of doubtful tendency," and, after reviewing his literary career from the Sunday-school onward, alleged that he had never "written a story which could excite the love, admiration and sympathy of the reader for an evil person, a bad character."

> I am willing to admit that I have sometimes been more "sensational" than I now wish I had been, but I have never made a hero whose moral character, or whose lack of high aims and purposes could mislead the young reader.

The next enlargement of the library system was by offshoots from the branches in the form of delivery stations. Such an experiment was tried in 1876 at Dorchester Lower Mills, where a friendly storekeeper offered space in which a library attendant might, during the late afternoon, issue library cards and take orders for and deliver books that were shipped daily from the Dorchester Branch. A similar experiment in Jamaica Plain, tied in with the Roxbury Branch, proved so successful that by 1877 Winsor considered that the region would soon require a branch of its own. In addition, two or three hundred books were shipped each month to a sub-delivery station established at Deer Island for the benefit of the isolated city institutions in the harbor, while similar service was given to thirteen of the Fire Department engine-houses and to the fire-boat. In the spring of 1877 comparable arrangements were being planned for the Police Department and the Charlestown Navy Yard.

The Trustees, in their 1874 report, had stated that "a book never accomplishes the object of its production unless in the hands of

some one who wants it." With Justin Winsor's downright passion
for *pushing* books into readers' hands, the library's circulation increased fantastically during the decade of his administration, as one
can see by the figures offered in his 1877 report.

DEPARTMENTS	1868	1869	1870 9 mos.	1871	1872
Central Library					
Bates Hall	33,874	42,905	47,597	65,205	50,251
Lower Hall	141,853	175,772	163,366	231,110	254,246
East Boston					
Branch				26,130	75,846
Totals	175,727	218,677	210,963	322,445	380,343

DEPARTMENTS	1873	1874	1875	1876	1877
Central Library					
Bates Hall	59,264	72,313	80,737	114,329	141,618
Lower Hall	238,057	253,097	272,834	348,842	405,732
East Boston					
Branch	68,212	81,091	85,548	90,987	102,627
South Boston					
Branch	102,322	108,566	112,525	115,530	135,179
Roxbury					
Branch		67,342	89,539	101,297	146,829
Charlestown					
Branch	-	33,391	79,375	85,815	106,816
Brighton					
Branch		9,642	21,842	24,805	29,792
Dorchester					
Branch			16,017	66,016	71,979
Totals	467,855	625,442	758,417	947,621	1,140,572

The most casual glance at these figures will show the instantane-
ous success of the branches. It will also disprove fears felt that Boston was hazarding the chances of making the Central Library an important one by dissipating its resources among lesser projects, for
against a circulation of 175,727 books in 1868, the number of books
issued from Boylston Street alone had in 1877 increased more than
three-fold to 547,350, although six branches were in active operation. Notwithstanding the good that the branches had accomplished

in many directions, they had clearly done nothing to relieve the perennial problem of congestion in the Lower Hall Delivery Room.

Winsor's ingenuity was constantly taxed to make the Boylston Street library habitable under the greatly increased use and growth. No one liked the building, except possibly Robert C. Winthrop or some other survivor of the commission that had built it; certainly no one who attempted to work in it had a good word to say on its behalf. In 1869 the Trustees stated publicly their unwillingness to recommend any further expenditures for building on that site because of the want of light and air. Change was considered so inevitable that in 1870 they stated that "when the Library is removed, it should go to a site where it may remain for the future without disturbance of light and air." A scheme of moving Bates Hall to another location, and making the entire building available for popular use was considered and rejected by 1871. As books were coming in at an alarming rate, and as any move would require large expenditure and the passage of several years, Winsor was constantly devising means to make do in Boylston Street. In 1870 he rigged rooms in the southeast basement to shelve newspapers and duplicates. The following year he installed in parts of Bates Hall deep drawers that permitted three or four banks of books to be shelved, one behind the other, while in 1872 more extensive changes were made. Although observing of the building that "its defects are radical and not to be remedied," Winsor reported that "work has been done, and is now in progress, which will much improve it for administrative uses." A subdivision of Bates Hall alcoves, completed in the autumn of 1872, produced space for an additional hundred thousand volumes, while the rebuilding of the gallery level of the Lower Hall furnished two large and six small rooms for staff use. Additional adjacent land was purchased in 1872, and as Winsor reported in that year, "these changes, which strongly indicate the abiding of the Central Library in its present site, must also lead to others at a not very distant future," the great Boston fire of 9 November set everyone to worrying about the future of the institution in so crowded an area. A standpipe to provide water was installed in the southeastern tower at the back of the building in 1874; hoses were stowed on each floor, and iron shutters added. In the same year a wing was run out from the southwest angle of the rear of the building that, on its completion in the spring of 1875, furnished decent accommodation for the Patent Collection, the Catalogue Department, certain special libraries, and increased working room for the rapidly growing staff. The construction of still another wing would have been requested in 1876, had it not been for the nationwide financial depression, which limited any improvements to the addition of a somewhat dubious wooden extension covered with sheet iron, of 45 by 16 feet, to the rear of Bates Hall. This contrivance, although frowned upon by the Examining Committee, at least gave extra room for students below, and space for the order department above. In spite of these expedients, the Lower Hall was still entirely unsuited to the increased volume of business. Seats in the Reading Room were insufficient; the Delivery Room was overcrowded; ventilation was atrocious, and the water-closets inadequate for the staff, to say nothing of readers. On this point the 1876 Examining Committee spoke with feeling:

> Every Library of the first class in Europe affords similar provision for the wants of its frequenters. A greater obligation than exists in the Old World lies upon the authorities of our city to maintain such accommodations; for, in European cities, public structures, conveniently situated, and where recently built, unobtrusive and neat in appearance, abound for the use of all classes. Here, in New England, so strong are the fetters of a past provincialism, that the reader at the Library, if obliged to leave the building, hardly knows where to turn for relief.

The inadequacies of the building were emphasized not only by increased use, but by the phenomenal growth of the library's holdings. When Winsor became Superintendent in 1868, the Boylston Street building contained 144,000 volumes. In May 1877 the count was 242,885, divided between 35,478 in the Lower Hall and 208,-411 in Bates Hall. With 69,125 books in the branches, the total holdings of the library system amounted to 312,010. Although the emphasis had been upon popular reading, the scholarly collections had not been forgotten during this decade. In 1869 Winsor had explained that the library's purchase of new books depended partly upon specific orders and partly upon the discretionary selection of foreign agents in London, Paris and Leipzig, who shipped books once or twice a month, and a Florentine agent who forwarded an annual consignment. "Of American publications, our agents have orders to send for our inspection everything published, and half our additions in *new* books bear American imprints." In bibliography, literary history and bibliothecal science Winsor aimed to buy nearly everything of any value; in American history he aimed to be thorough.

> It seems desirable that every library which can spare from its resources the requisite means should select some subject, strength in which will give them character and a value beyond their immediate dependencies. The free library of Birmingham very opportunely seized the occasion of the recent Shakespeare Tercentenary to found a special Shakespearian library as a part of their general collection . . . Our own collection of Shakespeares and works illustrative of him is very good; but we have not thought of giving it anything like completeness. An effort has been made during the year to gather what was possible of the different translations of Hamlet, and as an indicative part of the subjects, it may be worth our while to keep up the search.

In the same year, the Examining Committee had urged the doubling of the trust funds for books, which stood at $96,000, so that in times of political and financial crisis the library might avail itself of "opportunities, which now and then occur, of purchasing special collections of books which money itself is impotent, in ordinary times, to obtain." This recommendation had its inspiration, no doubt, in the negotiations currently under way with Mrs. Thomas P. Barton of New York for the purchase of her late husband's library, which included among the works of English and foreign dramatists a remarkable series of Shakespeare folios and quartos. Although valued at $60,000, the Barton Library was offered for $45,000, with the stipulation that the books should be shelved together as a collection, and should not be allowed to circulate. Negotiations broke down in January 1870 for want of funds, but Mrs. Barton's desire to have her husband's books permanently preserved in Bates Hall was so strong that she subsequently made concessions in price, which made their purchase possible in May 1873 for $34,000. This was the first occasion upon which a sizable appropriation of public funds had been spent upon rare, rather than currently useful, books, for the majority of such additions had been received by gift.

George Ticknor's generosity in enlarging the scholarly holdings of the library has been previously noted. In addition to the books that he had given in 1860, he had in October 1862 presented a collection that his friend, William H. Prescott, had assembled with a view—never carried out—to writing a life of Molière. Although with advancing years he had withdrawn from the Board of Trustees, George Ticknor's interest in the library that he had helped to found never flagged. Upon his death, on 26 January 1871, it was learned that his magnificent collection of Spanish and Portuguese literature had been bequeathed to the Public Library, with a fund of four thousand dollars for future purchases in the field. Altogether his gifts totalled 8,201 volumes and 1,265 pamphlets. Thus Ticknor's memory has been kept green, not only by the marble portrait bust by Martin Millmore, given by several gentlemen of Boston in 1868, but through the much loved books that he had used to such admirable purpose in the preparation of his *History of Spanish Literature.*

Another major gift that had opened broad horizons was the collection of some thousands of engravings, assembled by Cardinal Tosti, that was purchased in Rome in 1869 for the library by Thomas G. Appleton, one of the original Trustees. In 1872 Gardner Brewer— the donor to Boston Common of the bronze fountain by Liénard, the grace of whose water-splashed figures of Neptune, Amphitrite, Acis, and Galatea is too seldom appreciated by the shoppers emerging from the Park Street Subway—presented the library with a Greuze portrait of Franklin, which formed an admirable counterpart to the Duplessis likeness earlier received from Edward Brooks. The 1865 Examining Committee, under the chairmanship of Henry I. Bowditch, had taken a dimly austere view of such acquisitions, considering it

. . . as wholly inappropriate to the Reading Room of any Library that is habitually used by students for consultation and the reading of books, that any works of pictorial or plastic art should be placed therein. Beautiful in themselves, they excite—nay, seem to demand,—conversation and criticism. Conversation, save what is absolutely necessary in the obtaining of books, is, of course, wholly inadmissible.

One of the same committee had spent nearly an hour in Bates Hall, "and all the while a gentle 'tete-à-tete' was being carried on by a young couple, who found the luxurious chairs a pleasant spot in which to pass an agreeable hour." This was quite in the tradition of the Boston Athenæum, in whose secluded upper rooms various nineteenth century Bostonians did their courting and became engaged, but it greatly distressed the 1865 Examining Committee. Fortunately that committee's views upon the unsuitability of works of art in libraries were not generally shared, and the Public Library —again like the Athenæum—developed a pleasant receptivity to such offers as that of the gold medal commemorating the evacuation of Boston on 17 March 1776, presented to General Washington by Congress, and given to the library on the hundredth anniversary by fifty citizens of Boston. Such gifts, in Winsor's day, were appreciated as amenities, even if they did, now and then, "excite conversation."

To keep ahead of the extraordinary expansion of books and readers during the 1867–1877 decade, quick thinking and sound improvisation were required. With everything happening at once, there were no established precedents to fall back upon. It was assumed in the sixties, for example, that libraries had to close once a year for examination of the shelves. This meant not only that all books had to be recalled from borrowers at one time, but that readers were entirely debarred from the library during the fortnight or month required for the location, cleaning and checking of every book. It was a lot of work for the staff, and a nuisance to the readers, yet how otherwise could one tell what had been lost or stolen during the year? When the Boylston Street library was first opened, only eleven days had been required for the task, but the building was then new and the shelves barely filled. Winsor's 1867 Examining Committee, in considering the question "Is the Library open as much as possible?", observed that with 136,000 volumes, one would be fortunate to keep the work within a month. The 1868 committee questioned the whole practice, suggesting that the same result might be accomplished without closing by dividing the library into twelve sections, one of which would be examined each month by a person who made that his sole occupation.

> The principal objection to this plan is the expense, which would be greater than it now is, as it would be necessary to have one or two persons in each Hall, in addition to the present force. Yet if the public can be better served in this way, their convenience should be considered rather than the cost, if it be moderate.

Winsor, although not without misgivings, agreed that the expense would be the chief disadvantage. It was successfully attempted, for the first time in any great library, during 1869, and worked without a hitch. Winsor's method was to establish a separate Shelf Department, manned by a Custodian with three assistants. These new workers went from shelf to shelf each morning, comparing the books *in situ* with the shelf-list and noting missing volumes. The numbers of the latter were then checked against borrowers' charge slips and bindery schedules. Any not accounted for in that way were set down as missing, although all but 19 books in Bates Hall and 70 in the Lower Hall were subsequently found to have been misplaced in alcoves that were examined later. The system worked so well that in 1870 it was permanently adopted.

The establishment of a Shelf Department suggested to Winsor the wisdom of more specific assignment of duties than had previously been made. In Jewett's day, Edward Capen—although continuing to bear the designation of Librarian, as he had since 1852— was actually the functionary responsible for the Lower Hall. The unfortunate Professor William E. Jillson, during summer vacations from Brown University and Columbia College, Washington, where he taught modern languages, had assisted Jewett in preparing the Bates Hall Catalogue, but it was only in October 1865 that he joined the library staff on a full-time basis. Although dignified only with the vague designation General Assistant, he was described as the second officer of the institution. It was such vagueness that doubtless led the 1865 Examining Committee to urge a classification of the duties and responsibilities of all employees. In a roster of the library staff, published for the first time as Appendix xx to Winsor's

1869 report, Jillson's successor, William A. Wheeler, appears both as Assistant Superintendent and Chief of the Catalogue Department. A total staff of 43 consisted of the Superintendent, an Accountant, a Catalogue Department of 10, a Shelf Department of 4, a Bates Hall Circulating Department of 6, a Lower Hall Circulating Department of 16, a Janitorial Department of 2, and a Binding Department of 3. None were lavishly paid, for the total salary expenditure was under twenty-five thousand dollars. In November 1869 James L. Whitney joined the Catalogue Department as Wheeler's Deputy, and by 1872 had become in addition Winsor's second mate, with the title of Principal Assistant. Wheeler's early death from typhoid pneumonia on 28 October 1874, in his forty-first year, deprived Winsor of a valued "coadjutor and friend," for Wheeler's work in preparing the Prince and Ticknor catalogues, but more particularly his efforts upon the printed public card catalogue of the entire library—begun in 1872—had been of a high order. Upon Whitney's promotion to Wheeler's dual posts, he was succeeded by the Reverend James M. Hubbard, while Frederic B. Perkins—formerly an editor of the *New York Tribune* and of *Old and New*—assumed the duties of third mate, with the title of Office Secretary and sub-executive officer.

A separate Ordering and Receiving Department is first mentioned in the 1873 report, while by May 1875 there were 116 employees, 47 in the branches and 67 in the Central Library. In May 1877 the number had risen to 55 in the branches and 84 in the Boylston building. The staff was truly of the Superintendent's choice and training, for although William E. Ford, the Chief Janitor, had settled in the basement of the Boylston Street library on its opening in 1858, less than ten of the 139 antedated Winsor's stretch at the helm. The President of the Trustees, William W. Greenough, had, it was true, walked with the patriarchs and founders, for he had been elected to the board in 1856, but the next in point of service, Weston Lewis, had only become a Trustee with Winsor in 1867.

The library had grown enormously. Thanks to Winsor's genius for organization and administration it was efficiently run, for he always kept his eye on the shape of the forest. In this vein he once remarked to Samuel Swett Green of the Worcester library that, while he appreciated very highly the services of his accomplished assistants Wheeler, Perkins, and Whitney

> . . . he considered it a failing in them all that he could not induce any one of them to slur work; that is, he wished perspective to be used in doing work and thought that with limited time and resources it is best to omit certain details of work or postpone them for the sake of having energy to employ in effecting the higher objects for which an institution exists.

Winsor's treatment of the problem of catalogues strikingly illustrates this view. Jewett's two printed volumes of Bates Hall catalogues, issued in 1861 and 1866, were received "as a contribution to the facilities for acquiring knowledge through the use of large libraries, such as has not been afforded elsewhere," but, admirable as they were, the rapid growth of the library rendered them more obsolete every week. In October 1867 Jewett issued, in similar format, a *Bulletin* of new books; designed for quarterly appearance, to give readers prompt notice of what they would not otherwise discover without fishing through an interleaved copy of the printed catalogue. Winsor carried on the *Bulletin,* not only enlarging it, but making it a vehicle of communication with readers by including notes, comments, and essays. He attempted to produce a third volume of the Bates Hall catalogue, but finally in 1871 threw up the sponge and turned instead to a public *card* catalogue. By organizing the flow of work, and using mechanical means of duplicating entries, twenty rather than five or six thousand volumes a year passed through the Catalogue Department.

Winsor looked beyond parish boundaries where the convenience of the reader and the welfare of the library were concerned. In an era when pride of possession lent glamour to bulky accessions, and many institutions shared the small boy's view of "You stay on your side of the fence," it is refreshing to read in his 1876 report:

> The work upon the newspaper catalogue has been kept up to date, and, as subsidiary helps, a record has been made of files which are preserved in the Libraries of the Athenæum and of the Historical Society, partly to guide the inquiries of persons seeking beyond what we have, and partly to prevent increasing our collection by the purchase of bulky accessions, when other accessible libraries can supply what is wanted.

Ink was first allowed to be used in Bates Hall in 1869. The hour for opening that hall was in the same year pushed back from ten o'clock to nine, to conform with the rest of the library, while its closing—formerly vaguely approximating sunset—was fixed at six o'clock in winter and seven in summer. When in 1873 the Lower Hall Delivery Room closing hour was pushed forward from eight to nine o'clock, the quitting time for attendants, which had formerly varied from six to eight, was set uniformly at seven o'clock and a special force organized for evening service.

Sunday opening had long been a bone of contention that inspired antagonism and pamphleteering. The issue had been publicly debated in 1859, 1864 and 1867, the latter year producing a particular ludicrous effort entitled *Protest or Remonstrance of M. Field Fowler against opening the doors of the Public Library, Boston, on the Lord's Day.* Although stoutly refuted by Charles M. Ellis in his *Argument for Opening the Reading Room of the Public Library of the City of Boston on Sunday Afternoons,* Mr. Fowler remained unconvinced, and as late as 1872, enraged by the suggestion that horsecars would take the pious to church, treated Boston readers to a further statement of his views in an *Essay on the Sunday Library and the Horse Car Questions.* Also in 1872 the Reverend Henry Ward Beecher's New York pamphlet with the rhetorical title *Should the Public Libraries be opened on Sunday?* resoundingly answered, "Yes." The experiment of opening the Periodical Reading Room on Sundays from two to nine o'clock was first tried on 9 February 1873. Attendance was nothing startling, but Winsor noted with pleasure "that a large proportion of the Sunday visitors are not such as are seen in the rooms on week-days." So far as he was concerned libraries should be open when people will come to them— "all night, if they will come all night, in the evening certainly, and on Sunday by all means."

One of Winsor's first acts was to move the bindery out of Bates Hall alcoves into basement quarters where noise was of no account. Another was to arrange that all foreign books be received bound rather than in wrappers. Although work for the Lower Hall and the binding of periodicals and newspapers was divided between two outside firms, the basement bindery attended to Bates Hall books, mounted maps, made portfolios and pamphlet cases, and generally proved a convenience and an economy. It also helped staff morale, for Winsor would send there as an apprentice an occasional page boy who had outgrown his job but lacked the education that would fit him for other library duties.

Winsor's imagination flashed from one point of the compass to another with incredible speed. At one moment he is investigating buckram as a binding material that will resist gas-lighted and heated rooms.

> The article has never been introduced into this country, but I have brought it to the attention of importers of Scotch linens, who will introduce it at once.

At another he has the simple inspiration of making readers fill out their own charge slips, thus enabling the library "to deliver nine or ten thousand volumes a day with much less confusion and more expedition than fifteen hundred volumes were delivered ten years ago." Hard on the heels of Alexander Graham Bell, he was, in 1877, speculating on the likelihood of

> . . . greater favor being accorded to the Branch system by devices for increasing the promptitude of the business by means of telegraphic wires for the transmission of messages, and not unlikely with telephonic attachments.

But with all this went hard-headed Duxbury economy. The library was beyond question costing money. The budget for 1858 was $19,890; in 1867 it was $52,658 and in 1877 $117,800. Yet, as Winsor pointed out:

> If the annual expenditure be divided by the amount of circulation, it will show that the measure of the Library's usefulness, as indicated by such reckoning of the cost of issue per volume, has been reduced from twenty-five cents in 1867 to less than ten cents in 1877.

It is small wonder that Winsor's busy days were interrupted by requests for advice from other institutions, here, there and everywhere. The first issue of *The American Library Journal* (30 September 1876) bears at the mast-head the quotation:

We have no schools of bibliographical and bibliothecal training whose graduates can guide the formation of, and assume management within, the fast increasing libraries of our country; and the demand may perhaps never warrant their establishment; but every library with a fair experience can afford inestimable instruction to another in its novitiate; and there have been no duties of my office to which I have given more hearty attention than those that have led to the granting of what we could from our experience to the representatives of other libraries, whether coming with inquiries fitting a collection as large as Cincinnati is to establish, or merely seeking such matters as concern the establishment of a village library.

JUSTIN WINSOR

The article that opens the issue, "A Word to Starters of Libraries" —one of the happiest examples of Winsor's combination of wisdom and humor—begins:

Every well-established librarian occasionally or even frequently receives letters of which the following is a fair sample:

PUNKEYVILLE, July 10, 1876

"Dear Sir: The Honorable Hezekiah Jones, of our town, has donated [by the way, *given* has dropped out of the dictionary with such people] $_____ to found a library in this his native place, and we wish the library to reflect honor on him and credit on Punkeyville. Accordingly we would be obliged for any information you can give to enable us to establish this trust on a correct basis.

"Very respectfully,
"For the Committee,
"JOHN BROWN

"P.S.—I hope you will send us your catalogues, your charter, and your rules."

Mr. Brown is very likely an estimable person, whom the benefactor has designated as suitable for the head of the trust. Perhaps he is a clergyman, and if you should ask him to tell you the way in which to run a church and take care of a parish, he would remind you that, if it were not for writing the next Sunday's sermon, he might find time to enlighten you. Perhaps he is a physician, beloved of the people, and trusted above all by the Honorable Mr. Jones; but if you asked him something about the theory and practice of medicine, he would refer you to the journals of his profession or recommend a course of study in the schools . . .

It was in no way surprising that when the American Library Association was organized at Philadelphia in October 1876, Justin Winsor should be elected its President. Nor was he any less appreciated at home, for in the 1877 Trustees' report—in reviewing the first quarter century of the Boston Public Library—President Greenough wrote:

> Of the obligations of the Library to his [Jewett's] successor, the present Superintendent, the Trustees cannot speak too strongly. The Library has increased since his appointment, with the addition of the six branches, to the position of the largest collection on the continent, now numbering 312,000 volumes, and having in nine years increased its circulation more than five-fold,—having distributed and placed in the hands of readers during the past year 1,140,000 volumes. The requirements of the office have been most completely filled, but at the expense of the most unremitting labor at the Library and at home, and beyond human strength to sustain for a series of years. The scholastic and administrative demands of this great institution, with its six branches, have not only been fully met, but the methods of public contact and usefulness have been simplified, as well as extended and improved. The catalogue, under his direction, has received a new value,—having become not only a key to the books, but a manual for readers and scholars. It is proper to say that the class lists printed for the Boston Public Library have given it a reputation and a following both in America and in Europe, most flattering to a city, now more extensively known throughout the world by this than by any others of its institutions.

Here for once was the right man in the right place at the right time. The Boston Public Library had crowded on sail, but, with Winsor at the helm, there seemed no doubt of a safe voyage, and strong likelihood of maintaining the markedly advanced position that had come from an early start and favoring winds.

SOURCES

The fullest treatment of Winsor is in Joseph A. Borome's 1950 Columbia University Ph.D. dissertation, *The Life and Letters of*

Justin Winsor, which is available on microfilm as Publication 1834 of University Microfilms, Ann Arbor, Michigan. See also the remarks on the death of Justin Winsor at the November 1897 meeting of the Massachusetts Historical Society by Charles W. Eliot and others, and Horace E. Scudder's memoir of him in *Proceedings of the Massachusetts Historical Society,* second series, XII (1897–1899), 30–44, 457–482. Winsor's article "The Boston Public Library" in *Scribner's Monthly* for December 1871, pp. 150–156, is illustrated with views of the interior of the Boylston Street library. The crowded Lower Hall is well described in Albert G. Webster's article, "The Boston Public Library," *Appleton's Journal of Literature, Science and Art,* VI (1871), 629–631.

CHAPTER VI

In the Doldrums

It is unfortunate that, just as we are congratulating ourselves on the great strides of our public library system as a factor in social and political growth, there comes this blow in the face from Boston.
—AMERICAN LIBRARY JOURNAL, 1877

TWENTY–FIVE years had produced wonders. In that short time the Boston Public Library had been transformed from a reasoned hope of George Ticknor and Edward Everett to the first library of the United States. Moreover, it was the first not only in size and use, but in imagination and leadership. It is not hard to attribute this success to first-rate and original minds, exploring unhampered, with generous support, fresh and uncharted territory. Robert Cowtan, who had recently published his *Memories of the British Museum,* wrote Justin Winsor on 26 January 1872, acknowledging receipt of the latest Boston cataloguing experiments, with the comment:

All the reforms that have taken place in our library have been effected by slow and hardly fought battles against old customs and precedents, and it wants a Panizzi now and then to gather up all the improvements that crop up and so present them to the powers that be that they *must* be adopted. You have no old usages to combat with and can therefore adopt the best plans at once, and they appear to have worked so admirably that I beg to offer you my humble but most hearty congratulations.

Notwithstanding the generosity of Joshua Bates and other private benefactors, the people of Boston, acting through their City Govern-

ment, footed the bill, for in 1877 the library trust funds of $105,-
335.13 produced an income of only $6,300, while the total annual
expenditures reach $124,396.86. The City Council had been ex-
traordinarily generous, which was not surprising when the mayors
had included such genuine friends of the library as Josiah Quincy,
Jr., John P. Bigelow, Dr. N. B. Shurtleff and Henry L. Pierce, who
had in 1873 made a personal gift of $5,000 to the book funds. Al-
though the library was booming in the seventies, one could not say
as much of city finances in general. As the panic of 1873 had been
disastrous not only to speculators but to more sober owners of Boston real estate, there was, in the years immediately following, a
demand not only for reduction in real estate assessments but in
municipal expenses. Frederick O. Prince, though without previous
political experience, was elected mayor in December 1876 on a
retrenchment platform, and during the winter the City Council
began injudicious tinkering with the minutiæ of the library budget
which led to disaster.

Although the 1858 ordinance had left the election and salary of
the Superintendent in the hands of the City Council, the choice of
all other library employees and the fixing of their pay had been the
responsibility of the Trustees. An attempt to defeat Jewett's re-
election as Superintendent because somebody disliked his politics
had led, in 1865, to a revision of the ordinance that gave the Trustees the right to appoint the Superintendent, although the determination of his salary remained with the City Council. So matters
proceeded until the winter of 1876–1877, when the Council sud-
denly adopted an order regulating the salaries of more than thirty
officers of the library. No one questioned the right of the City
Council to reduce the *total appropriation* for the library; that was
a matter of municipal policy and finance. But both the Trustees
and the 1877 Examining Committee very much questioned the be-
havior of the City Council in meddling, without adequate knowledge, in the detailed use of the appropriations, particularly when
their intervention was so capricious and ignorant that, under guise
of general reduction, salaries, in two instances, instead of being
lowered, were actually *raised*. Such political intervention upset
commitments made in good faith by the Trustees, and set at nought

an orderly system of "fixing the salaries at even grade when the duties were first assumed, and raising them as length of service and qualification justified." Moreover the City Council rewarded Justin Winsor's years of unremitting and fruitful effort by docking *his* pay as well.

This incident is the one sour note in the 1877 report, which otherwise records the inexorable progress of the library during its first quarter century. The Examining Committee, while making it abundantly clear that they did so without Winsor's knowledge, or without a hint from him, spoke their mind forcibly upon this injustice.

The committee cannot praise too highly the administration of the Library in all its details. The credit of this redounds to the honor of the city and its citizens, but is really due to the distinguished ability and untiring zeal of the Librarian. Mr. Winsor has won for himself, for the Library, and for the city of Boston, the foremost place in the management of free public Libraries. His principles and methods are watched in all parts of the civilized world, and accepted as models for imitation. His position as a skilful, energetic, and successful library administrator, if not actually the first in the world, is certainly second to none. The aggregate value of the property under his charge is more than a million dollars; the force employed numbers nearly a hundred and forty individuals. The influence which his measures exert upon the education and future welfare of the citizens is beyond computation. The character and attainments requisite in the incumbent of such a post are in no wise inferior to those sought for in the President of Harvard University or of any great institution of learning. President Eliot receives what is equivalent, it is believed, to $6,000 a year. The Mayor, Solicitor, Auditor, and Treasurer of this city receive $5,000 annually; the City Engineer, $4,500; the City Clerk and the City Collector, $4,000. In marked contrast to these salaries stands that of the Superintendent of the Public Library, this year reduced from $3,600 to $3,000, which does not exceed that of a well-paid assistant or chief clerk. This salary does not correspond to the duties and responsibilities of the position, to the remarkable ability and high professional standing of the present incumbent, or to the salaries assigned to other officers of similar grade by the City of Boston. The committee is unanimously of opinion that this salary is discreditably small, and should be made equal to those given to the heads of the other higher departments of the public service.

Although undated, this report was apparently completed at the beginning of May 1877.

In the middle of the same month, John Langdon Sibley, the veteran Librarian of Harvard University, notified President Eliot that he wished, after thirty-six years' service, to retire. Mr. Eliot promptly offered the post to Justin Winsor, giving him until 25 June to reach a decision. The prospect was attractive, for the Harvard post carried the rank of professor, with a $4,000 salary and the long academic summer vacation. Moreover it was free from the strife of political maneuvering. This was especially tempting, for, as Horace E. Scudder said of Winsor,

> . . . with his generous nature he was keenly sensitive to any act of meanness; he has come once or twice into collision with members of the city government when he was administering the library, and he had a profound distrust of municipal politics as he saw it in operation.

Nevertheless Winsor was loath to consider President Eliot's offer. He was heart and soul in his work. He had, through two-fifths of its life and more than one-fifth of his own, guided the Boston Public Library to a position of unique eminence, and he sincerely believed that it had a great future. President Greenough, seeing that the wolf was at the door, thought it well that the city authorities should have an opportunity either to repent or to "be allowed to place themselves deliberately in the wrong." The Trustees of the Public Library therefore hit upon a petition to the City Council for authority to make a five year contract with Winsor, effective retroactively to 1 May 1877—the date of the salary cut—at a salary not exceeding $4,500. Because of this Greenough asked Eliot to grant Winsor an extension of time for his decision, so that he might learn the result of the petition before making an irrevocable choice, and the Harvard Corporation allowed him until 7 July.

On 2 July, when the Trustees' petition was considered by the Board of Aldermen, Charles Burnham, Chairman of the Joint Library Committee, praised Winsor and his accomplishments and asked that the order be passed, pointing out that Winsor only desired permanency of tenure. Alderman Hugh O'Brien, speaking as if rubbish collection were under discussion, protested that the order would create a bad precedent and that other department heads and superintendents would soon be in looking for a raise. Winsor had been educated on the job, and it was time to give another man a chance. Alderman O'Brien was so inexpert a prophet as to allege that there were "hundreds of citizens who could fill that place after a few weeks' experience with just as much ability as Mr. Winsor." Moreover, the library was costing more than its founders ever dreamed of; enough had already been spent on it. He was, of course, proud of it, but all such institutions had to be kept "down to an economical mark." Although Alderman Francis Thompson vigorously combatted these views, and Alderman John T. Clark testified to the need of having an experienced Superintendent of Winsor's ability, Alderman Richard Robinson took the opposite view. Robinson spoke upon principle rather than knowledge of the circumstances when he said:

> I never was in the Public Library but once. I have a library of my own, and do not need the Public Library. But what particular qualifications are required in cataloguing books I am not able to see. I have always been of the opinion that when a person became so valuable to the city or a corporation that they could not get along without him, the sooner that man left the corporation the better for it.

Nevertheless, the order increasing Winsor's salary to $4,500, but without the five-year provision, was passed by a vote of 10 in favor to O'Brien and Robinson in opposition. On 5 July this action was unanimously approved by the Common Council, and Winsor wrote President Eliot declining the Harvard post. In notifying William W. Greenough on the seventh of his decision to remain with the Public Library, Winsor wrote:

> I feel content with the assurances which are given to me that not only the salary of my office is fixed with the solemnity if not with the legal surroundings of the faith of the City; but that the friends of the library will make strenuous efforts to secure, next winter, from the State Legislature, such provisions by enactment as will give the library a stability which it can never have with the instabilities of a municipal council.

Thus it seemed that, through Greenough's prompt action, the Public Library was to have Winsor at the helm during its second quarter

century. Alas for such hopes, it was soon learned that, by an amendment of which the official record made no report, Winsor's salary
was to be increased from the passage of the order, rather than from
1 May 1877. This bit of pettiness so disturbed Winsor that, on the
tenth, he wrote Greenough:

> The variation is small, but it has destroyed my confidence. You
> tell me that in your opinion it was an accident; but as you are
> aware our experience is that we can only judge of the purpose of
> that body by the acts it does.
>
> I am therefore under the necessity of severing my connection with
> the library.

On 11 July Winsor wrote President Eliot accepting the Harvard
post.

When it was learned that Justin Winsor would take up his duties
in Cambridge on 1 September, there was public consternation. Boston newspapers invited the dissident aldermen to produce the names
of the numerous candidates who were so well qualified to fill the
post made vacant by the resignation. *The American Library Journal,*
in its 31 July 1877 editorial, thus summed up general opinion:

> It is unfortunate that, just as we are congratulating ourselves
> on the great strides of our public library system as a factor in so-
> cial and political growth . . . there comes this blow in the face
> from Boston . . . The Public Library, we had said to ourselves,
> was the one thing in Boston which Boston would not permit to be
> touched, and Boston was the one city in which institutions were
> intrenched behind intelligence. Yet in the City Council of Boston
> itself we hear the very same voice which is making itself heard in
> other parts of the country through the rapine and bloodshed of the
> railroad strikes—the voice which insists that intelligence is worth
> no more than ignorance, and that every man must be ranked on
> an equality with the lowest—and this voice is attacking that best
> gift of the people to itself, the public library. This is of dreadful
> significance, but it presents a fresh motive to the friends of public
> libraries, in the fact that they furnish the most effective weapons
> against the demagogic ignorance that glorifies ignorance and chal-
> lenges civilization. Light is always the one cure for darkness, and
> every book that the public library circulates helps to make Alder-

man O'Brien and railroad rioters impossible. The measure proposed for the safety of public libraries during the present maladministration of our cities is their incorporation, by the state legislature, out of the reach of city demagogism.

It is an ill wind that blows nobody any good, and the consolation to the friends of library development in the present case is, first, that Mr. Winsor, outside of the Library and out of the reach of the city government, will be better able to make a stronger fight against encroachments upon it.

The prediction was correct, for as Winsor himself wrote half a dozen years later in his sketch "Libraries in Boston" in *The Memorial History of Boston* that he edited:

The friends of the library rallied in its defense; and even the city council, on a sober second thought, did not oppose an application to the State Legislature for an act of incorporation for the library, which was in due time secured. This practically limited the interference of the city government to defining the gross limits of expenditures, so far as they were met from the city treasury.

Although this good was blown by an ill wind, one cannot explain away the genuine tragedy of Winsor's departure. When he crossed the Charles River to Cambridge in September 1877, the Boston Public Library wandered into a wilderness from which it did not emerge for eighteen years. However highly one may regard the desirable developments of more modern times, there is no blinking the fact that the library has never again regained the position of unquestioned national pre-eminence that it held in Winsor's day. For this we chiefly have Aldermen O'Brien and Robinson to thank. It is only charitable to assume that they did not realize what they were doing on that second day of July 1877 when they made their fine speeches.

When Henry L. Pierce, a friend of long standing, returned to the mayor's office in 1878, he proposed, in his inaugural address, legislative action for ensuring the sound permanent administration of the library. Consequently the Trustees were made a corporation by Chapter 114 of the 1878 Acts of the Massachusetts Legislature, approved on 4 April.

AN ACT TO INCORPORATE THE TRUSTEES OF THE PUBLIC LIBRARY OF THE CITY OF BOSTON

Be it enacted by the Senate and House of Representatives in General Court assembled, and by the authority of the same, as follows:

SECTION I. The trustees of the public library of the city of Boston for the time being are hereby made a corporation by the name of the Trustees of the Public Library of the City of Boston; and said trustees and their successors in office shall continue a body corporate for the purposes hereinafter set forth, with all the the powers and privileges and subject to all the duties, restrictions and liabilities in the general laws relating to such corporations.

SECTION 2. Such corporation shall have authority to take and hold real and personal estate to an amount not exceeding one million dollars, which may be given, granted, bequeathed or devised to it, and accepted by the trustees for the benefit of the public library of the city of Boston or any branch library, or any purpose connected therewith. Money received by it shall be invested by the treasurer of the city of Boston under the direction of the finance committee of said city; and all securities belonging to said corporation shall be placed in the custody of said treasurer; *provided, always,* that both the principal and income thereof shall be appropriated according to the terms of the donation, devise or bequest, under the direction of said corporation.

SECTION 3. The trustees of the public library shall be seven in number. In the month of April in the year eighteen hundred and seventy-eight and annually thereafter in the month of January, the city council shall elect, by concurrent vote of the two branches, one member of the board of aldermen, and one member of the common council, to be members of said board of trustees, to hold office during the remainder of the municipal year in which they are elected, and until others are elected in their places. And in the month of April in the year eighteen hundred and seventy-eight, the mayor shall appoint, subject to the confirmation of the city council, five citizens of Boston, not members of the city council, to be members of the board of trustees of the public library, one of whom shall hold office for five years, one for four years, one for three years, and one for two years, and one for one year; and upon such election and such appointment and confirmation, the terms of office of the trustees of the public library then holding office shall cease and determine. And annually thereafter, in the month of April of each year, the mayor shall appoint, subject to the confirmation of the city council, one citizen at large as a trustee of the public library, to serve for a term of five years from the first Monday in May in the year in which he shall be appointed. The trustees shall at all times be subject to removal from office for cause by a vote of two-thirds of each branch of the city council present and voting thereon. Whenever any vacancy shall occur in said board of trustees by death, resignation or otherwise, said vacancy shall be filled by the election or appointment, in the manner aforesaid, of another trustee, who shall hold office for the residue of the unexpired term. No member of said board of trustees shall receive any pecuniary compensation for his services.

SECTION 4. The members of said board shall meet for organization on the first Monday of each May, and choose one of their number as president. They shall have power to make such rules and regulations relating to said public library and its branches, and its officers and servants, and to fix and enforce penalties for the violation of such rules and regulations, as they may deem expedient: *Provided,* that the same shall not be inconsistent with the provisions of this act, and shall be subject at all times to such limitations, restrictions and amendments as the city council may direct.

SECTION 5. The said trustees shall have the general care and control of the central public library now located in Boylston street in said city and of all branches thereof, which have been or which may hereafter be established, together with the buildings and rooms containing the same, and the fixtures and furniture connected therewith, and also of the expenditures of the moneys appropriated therefor.

SECTION 6. The said board of trustees may appoint a superintendent or librarian with such assistants and subordinate officers as they may think necessary or expedient, and may remove the same, and fix their compensation: provided, that the amount thus paid shall not exceed the sum appropriated by the city council for that item of expense, and the income of any moneys which may lawfully be appropriated for the same purpose from funds or property held by the said trustees under the provisions of this act.

SECTION 7. The city council shall have the power to pass such ordinances not inconsistent herewith to other laws of the Commonwealth as to the duties and authority of said board as they may from time to time deem expedient.

SECTION 8. This act shall take effect upon its passage.

By an amendment to the City Charter in 1885, making members of the City Council ineligible for membership upon executive boards, the number of Trustees of the Public Library was reduced from seven to five citizens at large. This arrangement continues to the present, as do the main points of the 1878 Act. Subsequent amendments of detail have been of minor significance.

Although the incorporation of the Trustees stabilized the administration of the library in relation to the City Government, it in no way eased the problem of replacing the irreplaceable Winsor. In the weeks between his resignation and departure for Cambridge, a South End Branch—based upon 18,000 volumes given by the Mercantile Library Association—was opened, and arrangements were completed for enlarging the delivery station at Jamaica Plain into a full-fledged branch library. Dr. Samuel A. Green, one of the Trustees of the Public Library from 1868 to 1878 and the high-handed and extremely cantankerous Librarian of the Massachusetts Historical Society from 1868 until his death in 1918, was placed in a temporary position as "Trustee in charge" that continued for more than a year. *The American Library Journal,* in commenting on Winsor's resignation, had observed:

> In the mean time the Library will doubtless "run itself" without difficulty, for it is the part of a great organizer to gather about him such men as will make him unnecessary for any given time, or until a crisis comes or fresh progress is to be set on foot. It is to be trusted that this, which is the best testimony to Mr. Winsor's success, will not be accepted from the demagogues as evidence that like ability is no longer needed at the head of the Library.

One can gather enough about the formidable Dr. Green from scholars now living, who met him at their peril in later years at the Massachusetts Historical Society, to make one aware that he was hardly the ideal successor. Obviously the library ran along, for it was not only well organized, but Winsor had persuaded his valued assistants Whitney and Hubbard to restrain their natural inclinations to resign also. Even the newspapers were worried about "fresh progress to be set on foot" and aware that, once momentum is lost, a fresh start is painful. The *Sunday Herald* of 30 December 1877 dealt truthfully but subtly with the problem by publishing a fable entitled "How a steamer went to sea without any captain."

There was once a fine steamer named the *Joshua Bates,* after one of the famous firm of Baring Bros. & Co., in London, well manned and equipped, with a full cargo and many passengers. The captain was a good seaman, who knew every rope in the ship and every wind that blew. People said he was born to sail a ship. So the owners of another ship offered him higher pay to come to them and sail their old craft, and, as his owners would not agree to keep him for several voyages more, he prudently left their service for the other parties, who always kept their men till they died. Naturally the chief mate should have taken the ship for the voyage, but he and the second mate were set to keeping the log by the owners' agent, and so they remained below perpetually writing the log. Whether the ship went ahead or astern, they kept on writing their log. But some one must sail the ship. And it chanced that some of the part owners were on board, and they hit on the idea of sailing her themselves. One was an apothecary, one was a lamplighter in the city, and the other had never done anything at all, and none of them had ever been to sea before. But no matter, they thought they could run the vessel as well as any other man, till they could find a new captain; so they sailed the ship. And I must not omit to say that one took charge of the bow, and another of the stern, while the one who had never done anything at all continued to do nothing. He sat and looked at the others, but counted for one, just the same as if he did something. One of the assistant engineers thought he had had enough of the sea, and concluded to retire. Did they look for another? Oh! no; they said, "we have more waiters in the saloon than we need for our passengers. Let us take the head waiter and let him run the engine, and he will do it for the same pay, or we can let him go, which he will not want to do!" So they put the head waiter in to run one of the engines. The committee did not think it worth while to buy much coal, and but a small stock of provisions, though they were bound on a long voyage and there were many passengers. Neither did they think it necessary to get new sails or replace ropes that were old. The officer of the deck, too, who, you know, watches the compasses and makes himself generally useful, besides talking to the passengers and telling them which way the wind blew, and how she headed, and when she would probably get in, and all that; him the committee considered entirely useless, and put ashore at the lower light. By and by the ship sailed. I wonder when she landed and what condition she was in. If she ever *should* arrive, it will be well for the rest of the owners to look after that committee.

This was preceded by some sharp observations concerning the Trustees' experiments "in the direction of incommoding its patrons, diminishing the circulation, and impairing the usefulness and acceptability of the library" that had involved the removal of Henry Ware, Keeper of Bates Hall, and Arthur A. Brooks, Assistant Keeper of the Lower Hall. The *Sunday Herald* suggested to the Trustees "that they let well enough alone until they are in position to offer the vacant superintendency to a man qualified to carry on the institution, and leave the change and new experiments to him."

The advice was not promptly heeded, for no appointment was made until the fall of 1878, and the action taken then had a certain unexpected and accidental quality. The Honorable Mellen Chamberlain, a New Hampshireman of the Dartmouth class of 1844, who had settled in Chelsea and had sat for a dozen years on the bench of the Boston Municipal Court, happened by, while "endeavoring to promote the election of a friend," and was chosen himself. Judge Chamberlain was a man in his fifties, of scholarly tastes and collecting habits. Elected to the Massachusetts Historical Society in 1873, he was a faithful member, who regularly, until his death in 1900, contributed papers on phases of colonial history. These historical and literary tastes he carried into the search for autographs and manuscripts, assembling a sizeable collection that he gave to the Boston Public Library in 1893. He was not only a man of wide interests, but of a "clubable" disposition, that made him, in later years, an agreeable companion at the St. Botolph Club. His qualifications bore at least a superficial resemblance to those of Justin Winsor, who had been appointed in 1868 with no previous professional training in running a library. There is, however, as skilful military strategists know, a danger in planning an operation upon the experience of the last war. The trench warfare of 1914–1918 led to the construction of the Maginot Line, which proved entirely calamitous in a mechanized war of movement. Apparent similarities, derived from too rigid a devotion to the precedents of history, may get both military commanders and boards of trustees into trouble. Judge Chamberlain was a sincere and conscientious administrator, who introduced night watchmen, devised schemes for dusting the books, and generally took his duties seriously, but he had none of Justin Winsor's clipper ship flair for crowding on sail and steering a direct but sound course at record speed. The best sailors do not confine themselves always to keeping before the wind.

Judge Chamberlain took over his new duties on 1 October 1878, but as Librarian rather than Superintendent. The latter title may have been devised in 1858 at least partly to introduce Jewett to the scene without unreasonable damage to the sensibilities of Edward Capen, the first Librarian. As Capen had emigrated to Haverhill in 1874, both posts were vacant, but there is a reasonable inference that Chamberlain was not designated Superintendent because the "owners' agents," having had a taste of steering the ship themselves proposed, for better or worse, to continue.

In his 1879 report, beside questions of housekeeping, the new Librarian raised the question: "How can the Public Library be made to participate more efficiently than at present in the work of public education?" The answer to this rather wordy discussion appeared the following year in Chamberlain's account of a request received from the principal of the Wells School for fifty copies of Mrs. Whitney's *A Summer in Leslie Goldthwaite's Life* and of George M. Towle's *Pizarro; his Adventures and Conquests* to be retained for an indefinite period. Although there were only two or three copies of each in the library and no funds from which more could be properly purchased, a friend came to the rescue and provided fifty dollars for the books, with gratifying results. The effort, however well meant, hardly had the Winsor touch.

Although Judge Chamberlain had not known Winsor during his Boston service, they became good friends in subsequent years, a process possibly made easier by Winsor's election to the Massachusetts Historical Society in June 1877. Chamberlain's genuine admiration for his predecessor's accomplishment is clearly expressed in the tribute that he paid, after Winsor's death, at the November 1897 meeting of the Massachusetts Historical Society.

No sooner had I taken my chair than with special pains I endeavored to understand the nature and extent of Mr. Winsor's library views, plans and labors during his ten years' incumbency. This endeavor included not merely a cursory examination of the annual reports of the trustees, the examining committee, and the librarian, but a study of them with a thoroughness which I had brought to few things save those relating to my profession. I was not only amazed, but quite dismayed at the prospect of attempting to fill an office which I had not sought, but to which I had been elected while endeavoring to promote the election of a friend . . .

When I came to the Public Library, I found it in perfect order and running itself, so to speak, without the need of a directing head. This was due to the efficiency of Mr. Winsor's administration. He had trained his assistants to self-discipline and correct habits. Others in various fields of administration have done the same; but with a tendency, as is too often seen, to relapse when the strong personality has been withdrawn. But what seems to me most remarkable is, that during my twelve years of administration I discovered no such tendency; for Mr. Winsor had not only formed correct habits in his associates, but he had also formed their *permanent character,* as may be seen in those who now survive him, twenty years after his retirement from the Library.

While those of the old staff who remained doubtless deserved Judge Chamberlain's praise, not all of Winsor's associates cared enough for the changed conditions to outstay him long. His second and third mates, James M. Hubbard and Frederic B. Perkins, took their departures within two years of Winsor, and went into vociferous public opposition to the library's current policies. Perkins, who went first to the Cooperation Committee of the new American Library Association before becoming Librarian of the San Francisco Public Library, ventilated his views upon the inadequacies of the situation in three letters to Mayor Prince. These documents, dated 1 February, 15 March and 29 April 1880, were highly critical of the library's standard of cataloguing, but even more vehement in their opposition to the practices of the Trustees. Perkins explained that he addressed himself to the Mayor rather than to the Trustees "because it is precisely the composition and methods of the Board, which need reforming; and therefore to address it directly is the least likely method to reform it." The core of his complaint concerned "the administrative disorganization which has been silently introduced into the Library."

As you know, as every other good business man knows, every large institution, government, bank, mill, insurance company, church, college, must necessarily be conducted, if successful, by one central head. The Continental Congress tried to govern the United States by a set of committees. Every historical student knows the miserable mess they made of it, and how out of their imbecility arose our own wisely framed government with a single executive. I appeal to your own administrative experience as Mayor of Boston as a proof, so close before our eyes, of the indispensable necessity of this mode of business organization.

The Public Library has at present no executive head. It is—not governed, but fumbled,—by a set of committees. While Mr. Winsor was superintendent, he was (in the words of the by-laws) "the proper executive officer of the Trustees and their committees." This was as it should be. After Mr. Winsor left, this clause was struck out of the by-laws, and now there is no "proper executive officer." Judge Chamberlain is only a head clerk, without the official dignity or authority to which his high personal character and his official station entitle him. Whether he is a good librarian or not, he has not had an opportunity to show. As for the service of the Library, it goes on, to a considerable extent, because the great administrative abilities of Mr. Winsor "set up" the machine so strongly that it runs, so to speak, of itself. But every man of insight and close observing power who has watched the Library will feel the truth of this following statement of mine to wit: —since Mr. Winsor left the Public Library, it has lost its leadership among the libraries of America; what Judge Chamberlain could do to maintain that leadership he has not had a chance to show; and while the Library is mismanaged in this radically vicious and helpless way, it will certainly nòt gain, and in all probability will continue to lose, in efficiency and reputation. This executive clause in the by-laws of the Trustees should be at once replaced.

Perkins's barbs obviously hurt, for the 1881 library report contains a singularly pompous and legalistic defense of the Trustees' administrative policies that is as damning as any confession of guilt. The Trustees alleged that "the principles which have given this institution its great success were laid down by the original Board of Trustees, and have not been varied from in principle since," and that "while the principles at the outset were right, they were not derived from a corps of librarians and the heads of the different administrative departments of a great library." They invoke a "faith once for all delivered to the saints" in the paragraph:

The Trustees of the Library have no power to lay aside their responsibility. By the by-laws of the institution they have given to the Librarian, the chief executive officer, all the authority which may reasonably and properly be given to such an administrator of its affairs. The institution is to be managed for the greatest good of the largest number of people, and so it has come down to the present from former Boards of Trustees. The original ordinance requires it.

This explanation of motives—only partially summarized here—was signed by President Greenough, the Reverend James Freeman Clarke (a Trustee since 1879), Professor Henry W. Haynes (a Trustee elected in 1880), Alderman Hugh O'Brien and Councilman Charles E. Pratt, who had been designated by the City Council since 1879 and 1880, respectively. George B. Chase was in Europe, and Samuel A. B. Abbott, a lawyer of the Harvard class of 1866, who had become a Trustee in 1879, expressed his dissent by the uncommunicative statement: "I cannot sign the foregoing report."

To express his conviction that "God's in his heaven; All's right with the world," Judge Chamberlain prefaced his report by a statement that "though he has no vote in the proceedings of the Trustees, and, therefore, no responsibility for the result of their deliberations, yet, when these take form in legislative acts, he is brought into immediate relation to those acts in their execution, and with that his responsibility begins, and is limited only by the requirements of successful administration." In 1871 any discussion would have been about the means of getting books read; in 1881 we have instead this dancing of a legal minuet over powers and responsibilities. The completeness of the change of atmosphere naturally leads to speculation about its cause. Two explanations are possible. Either Mr. Greenough had, late in life, been seized with a sense of his own omniscience, or his recently elected colleagues had brought the infection of that disease to the board with them. It is hard at this distance to tell which, but the strictures upon the library's policy of book selection made by the 1884 Examining Committee suggest the former. That group, which included Thomas Sergeant Perry, Robert Grant and Brooke Herford, made the following comment:

The ultimate decision as to what books shall be purchased rests nominally with the Book Committee of the Trustees; in fact, the

selection from the books recommended is made by the President of
the Board. As long as the President is willing to devote so much
time as at present to this work there can be no doubt that it is
practically as well done as it could be in any other way; but it
seems to this committee that this is too important a work to be
allowed to remain dependent upon the power and health of any
single honorary officer.

In assuming this responsibility, Greenough no doubt felt that he was
merely carrying on the tradition of Ticknor, whom he had succeeded
in the presidency in 1866, and who gave great attention to the catalogues of publishers and booksellers. Ticknor had been, however,
not only a remarkable scholar but a modest one, as will be seen by
the following letter that he had written to Jewett.

PARK STREET, Oct. 3. '60

My dear Sir,
 If you will send to my house about ½ past 2 o'clock today, I
will have ready a mass of books and pamphlets, which, in arrang-
ing my Library, I find I cannot conveniently have room for. Some
of them have more or less value; some are, no doubt worthless.
But I do not wish to give anything to the public which ought not
to be kept, in the reasonable hope that it may be useful. Be good
enough, therefore, to look the whole over and throw out whatever
you do not think worth a place in the Library; offering *only* the
remainder to the Trustees at their next meeting.
 You *may* find among the city documents, the reports of societies, &c, separate tracts that will help to complete our sets; and
among the accounts of foreign galleries there are catalogues by
Welcker, Matthaei, Waagen &c that are worth preserving. Otherwise both these lots should, I think, be thrown away, in the most
ruthless manner. If I had time, I would sift them a little myself
but I am excessively occupied and have none too much strength for
my work. Besides I cannot exactly tell what you may want out of
what I account nothing worth. But, in no event, keep trash. We
have too much of that already in our dark room; and it is time
we should remember that there is a great deal of matter in print
that never ought to have been printed at all and that will only
serve to cumber any shelves it may be put on.

Yours sincerely,
GEO: TICKNOR

C. C. JEWETT, Esq., Public Library

Please let Mr. Ford come. He will need a stout man to help him,
and four or five boxes.

Three years after Mr. Greenough's retirement from the presidency in 1888, the 1891 report referred to him as having "been in effect the manager of the present Library for twenty-two years." Regardless of individual responsibilities, the Public Library was during the eighties quite thoroughly in the doldrums, thanks to committee management.

As no choice of books, however conscientiously made, will suit all tastes, the Public Library received its fair share of criticism on this score. One approach is represented by an anecdote from the *Boston Traveller,* reprinted in the *American Library Journal* for 31 October 1877.

> "Say, mister," said a small boy to one of the assistants at the public library, "I can't find the books I want to git into these here catalogs. I wish yer'd find 'im for me." "What work do you wish to draw," paternally inquired the official. "Well, hev yer got *Mulligan the Masher, or the Gory Galoot of the Galtees?*" The man shook his head. "Well, I'd like *Red-Headed Ralph, the Ranger of the Roaring Rialto.*" "We don't keep any of that kind of trash, my boy." "Wot sort of a libery is this, anyway?" retorted the gamin; "wy, it's just like everythin' else in this country—run for the rich, an' the poor workingman gits no show at all."

The 1878 Examining Committee faced squarely those critics who implied that the library was overstocked with Mulligan-type fiction, by affirming that "the character of the books supplied" was desirable. They admitted that some poor specimens had crept in; "not directly and positively beneficial, concerning which the best you can say is, that they form a taste, that they whet and sharpen an appetite for reading." Concerning these, the Committee spoke, as Justin Winsor might have:

> Banish them from the Library, as some advise, and you banish their readers also. Keep them in the Library and you keep their readers also; who, with constantly improving taste, will finally select books of unquestionable excellence and profit.

They advised leaving the whole problem to the Superintendent and the Trustees. The latter body, although reminding parents of their obligation to look after their children's welfare, gradually attempted to reduce the purchase of "sensational and vapid productions."

Although the 1880 circulation fell in consequence, the restriction was not severe enough to suit James M. Hubbard, who, late in that year, began a press campaign against the library's policies regarding both popular and scholarly books. His departure from the library indicated his views clearly enough, but in the *Sunday Herald* for 21 November 1880 he aimed a charge of buckshot at many targets. Stating that the Boston Public Library had been founded to ensure the education of the people, he inquired whether the Trustees—whose committee methods he abhorred—were still carrying out this object. In answering his own question, he found that

> Great labor is spent in searching sales catalogues, but it is exclusively in the interests of scholars, and a very large proportion of the money available for books is spent for works not intended for general use. Last spring a trustee—on his own responsibility, I have good reason to believe—took $2,400, nearly a tenth of the annual appropriation, to a sale to spend for books not one of which could be of general use. Seven years ago, $34,000 was paid for a collection [the Barton Library] still inaccessible to the public, and not fit for circulation, many of the books on account of their value, many on account of their character.

Hubbard seems to have had a weak stomach, for, after slurring the "character" of the Elizabethans in the Barton Library, he took a fling at the popular fiction, alleging that "many distinctly bad books, openly attacking morality and religion, and giving 'lively descriptions of the demi-monde,' are put into the hands even of children." This kind of tirade was unsympathetic to Winsor, who was no doubt referring to Hubbard's extravagancies when, in his opening presidential address at the February 1881 meeting of the American Library Association in Washington, he remarked:

> I would not be blinded to the fact that mischief, and enough of it, may lurk in books. It will do its work in spite of us; but, if we would keep it at its minimum, we do not wisely make this mischief prominent. Our emphasis should be upon the wholesome, and upon that which healthfully stimulates . . . I must decidedly differ from those who, for the common good, take to the method of magnifying an evil the better to eradicate it. I believe that under cultivation the weeds succumb.

Hubbard was not easily squelched, for in October 1881 he published a pamphlet, *The Public Library and the School Children, An Appeal to the Parents, Clergymen, and Teachers of Boston,* and continued his campaign with further appeals in 1881 and 1882. His earlier diatribes evoked from the Trustees, in their 1881 report, a reasoned and dignified statement of the Library's attitude to questions of censorship inspired by external pressure.

> While they carefully exclude from circulation, especially among the young, all books of an immoral influence, they do not consider themselves in the position of parents, or guardians to the community, bound to select for it only such books as suit their own tastes. The argument of Milton, in his Areopagitica, against a censorship of books largely applies to the present question. He opposes the prohibition of books which might possibly be injurious, on the ground that it was not the intention of the Almighty to place us in a world from which all temptation is excluded. Any standard of taste that would deprive the Public Library of such books as *Jane Eyre, Adam Bede,* and *The Scarlet Letter,* would not satisfy the just demands of the community.

The problem continued to be argued in some quarters. Although a majority of the 1882 Examining Committee strongly supported the library's policy, and commended Judge Chamberlain's efforts "to improve the moral character of the books circulated," a minority—consisting of the Reverend Leighton Parks and Colonel Homer B. Sprague—urged the hiring of a special staff to weed out books of "a positively immoral character," those "tending to lower the moral tone of the reader," and any "tending to encourage a spirit of irreverence concerning religion and virtue." The majority of the committee replied, in a postscript, that

> . . . it is not asked of the Trustees and officials of the Library that they shall turn Puritan in their literary tastes when public sentiment fails to justify such action. They are the servants of the public, not the censors of their morals and manners.

Hubbard's criticism of the Barton Library purchase may well have inspired Judge Chamberlain to ask H. H. Furness to give his opinion on the value of the library's Shakespeare collection. A letter from that eminent scholar, printed in the 1882 report, placed the Boston

Public Library's Shakespeare holdings as the finest in the United States at the time, and inferior only to the collections of the British Museum, the Bodleian, and Trinity College, Cambridge. In a similar attempt at appraisal, the 1883 Examining Committee induced Thomas Wentworth Higginson to describe the Parker Library, and Thomas Sergeant Perry to evaluate the French literary holdings, while William F. Apthorp made specific suggestions concerning the musical department.

A greatly increased use of books in Bates Hall so inspired additions to the library's scholarly possessions that in 1890 the City Council appropriated $20,000 for the purchase of books at the sale of the late Samuel L. M. Barlow's library. From the dispersal of this collection, which offered a unique opportunity to secure works on early American history, the library obtained, among other things, the Latin version of the first letter of Columbus, and a manuscript "True Copie of the Court Booke of the Governor and Society of the Massachusetts Bay in New England," containing some local records not duplicated elsewhere. This excursion into the upper levels of the auction market obviously rested heavily on some consciences, for the Trustees in 1892 were tentatively explaining that, if the State would only take the "Court Booke" off their hands for the $6,500 it had cost them at the Barlow sale, they would have money enough to carry out the improvement of the musical department recommended in 1883 by Mr. Apthorp. Such purchases though flattering to self-esteem, were edging the library away from Ticknor's concept, and by 1893 the Examining Committee was concerned over the widening gulf. After rehearsing the principles of book selection included by Ticknor in the 1852 report, the committee noted with some dismay that in twelve lists of recent accessions, selected at random, and containing about 2,200 titles, 950 were in foreign languages, mostly German and French, but including Norwegian, Sanskrit, Russian, Welsh, Arabic and Volapuk.

> About one quarter of the English books are starred, and therefore not intended for circulation, and many of those so marked are of little common interest, being reports or memorials, or treatises on technical subjects. The small remainder, probably not more than a hundred, of works of a general literary character, is almost hid-

den among the many strange and curious titles . . . Your committee would suggest that more discrimination be exercised in the choice of popular books. There are now none too many, but they might be better chosen.

The committee further found that the special bibliographies included in recent quarterly *Bulletins,* although of value to a small group of students, did little towards furthering Ticknor's ideal "that the means of general information should be so diffused that the largest possible number of persons should be induced to read and understand questions which are constantly presenting themselves."

Appendices to the Librarian's reports continued, in the pattern set by Justin Winsor, to give very full details upon the growth and use of the library. Anyone with a speculative fondness for statistics will find these documents of absorbing interest in their reflection of popular taste. In general they show a steady growth of books and a relative diminution of their use. Circulation (which included books used *in* the library in addition to those withdrawn) fell off after an 1878 peak of 1,183,991. In fact, such a figure was not again reached until 1890, although the total volumes owned in that year amounted to 536,027 against a count of 345,734 in 1878. Against a permanent decline in Lower Hall circulation—generally attributable to the restriction of the *Mulligan the Masher* type of fiction—the use of Bates Hall increased several times over. Something of the pattern may be seen in the following figures, chosen to show the extent and use of the library at five-year intervals.

YEAR	Volumes in Library	Total Circulation	Bates Hall Home Use	Bates Hall Hall Use	Circulation Lower Hall
1877	312,010	1,140,572	66,832	74,786	405,732
1882	404,221	1,040,553	63,782	103,540	250,792
1887	492,956	934,593	61,183	138,870	183,988
1892	576,237	1,715,860	77,401	231,541	191,391

The branch library system moved slowly in the eighties. The South End Branch, originally established at the corner of Tremont and Newton Streets, in the basement of the Mercantile Library Association, which had given its books for the purpose, caused considerable misgiving. Finally when in 1881 the branch moved to better quarters elsewhere, the Association, deprived of its library, entered upon a steadily less successful career as a social club that came to a dusty and inglorious end in 1952. A North End Branch, opened in the Hancock school-house in 1883, was the target of severe criticism in 1890. The Examining Committee of that year, claiming that branches were inadequately supervised and that a revival of the old post of "Inspector of Circulation" was needed, stated:

> Were such an officer to visit the North End Library during the hours in which it is open, he would at once report that it is unfit for human occupancy . . . In all their visits to this Library the Committee have never met both attendants on duty at the same time, as one or the other has been absent on account of sickness incurred by living several hours a day in a fetid atmosphere, only improved by opening windows upon a back alley, concerning which the Committee have asked the Trustees to complain to the Board of Health. The people of the North End have to some extent learned to stay away from a room with noxious odors without and a gas-consumed atmosphere within.

This iniquity was soon removed by shifting the branch to a second-story room at 166 Hanover Street that was both better ventilated and less accessible to mischievous boys.

In 1893, with nine branches and sixteen delivery stations in operation, the principal unsatisfied need was for a West End Branch. When the West Church, whose pulpit had been ornamented by Jonathan Mayhew and Charles Lowell, went the way of many city churches in 1892, Andrew C. Wheelwright—with outstanding public spirit—bought its dignified meeting house at the corner of Cambridge and Lynde Streets. Mr. Wheelwright held this fine building, designed by Asher Benjamin in 1806, until the City took it off his hands in 1894 for conversion to library use. Thus the combined imaginativeness of a generous citizen and the Public Library Trustees succeeded in saving, for a changing quarter of the city, one of its outstanding beauties, and converting this landmark of the past to new and vital uses for the future. The conversion is all the more creditable when one considers how little thought had been previously given to the preservation of historical monuments in Boston. The Hancock house was wantonly destroyed as recently as 1863, and the first real instance of civic consciousness in such matters was the campaign of 1876 that succeeded in saving the Old South Meeting House in Washington Street.

WEST END BRANCH

The matter which most concerned everyone interested in the Public Library in the years following Winsor's departure was the inadequacy of the Boylston Street building. From 1878 onward the desire was to escape at the first opportunity, but opinions as to ways and means were diverse. The complicated story of the planning that eventually led to the construction of the present library in Copley Square will, for the sake of clarity, be reserved for the following chapter. It will suffice here to summarize the administrative changes that occurred prior to the occupation of the new library in 1895. William W. Greenough, having served the library without stint of time since his election to the board in 1856, resigned the presidency in April 1888. His successor, Professor Henry W. Haynes, who, through service in 1858–1859 had also known the founders, and who had been a Trustee since 1880, resigned as President after occupying the chair for the six days of 7 to 12 May 1888. Samuel Appleton Browne Abbott, a Trustee since 1879, was then elected, and exhibited greater staying powers as a presiding officer. Like Greenough, Abbott carried out his duties with extraordinary fidelity and, often a controversial figure, left his mark both upon the library and upon the city.

Judge Chamberlain offered his resignation as Librarian because of ill health on 1 July 1890, to take effect on 1 October. When it was accepted, on 8 July, President Abbott was "authorized to act with all the powers and duties of the Chief Executive officer of the Trustees." Nothing was done about filling the vacancy, for the Trustees were not only intensely preoccupied with the details of the new building, but happily confident of their ability to meet all administrative requirements without professional assistance. The failure to appoint a Librarian only confirmed the dim view of the library held by outside observers during the previous thirteen years, for it appeared that Abbott, in addition to undisputed and indefatigable control of building the new library in Copley Square, now proposed to add the detailed current management of the library to his other responsibilities. Boston newspapers had grumbled so much about "Trustee-Librarian Abbott" that the hope expressed by the 1891 Examining Committee "that the trustees will soon feel it possible to appoint a librarian to fill the vacancy which has now existed for more than a year," accompanied by the polite explanation that "such an appointment would relieve the trustees and officers of their present unusual responsibility," was like a red flag to a bull. The Trustees' comment left no one in any doubt.

> In regard to the suggestion that the appointment of a librarian will relieve the trustees of unusual responsibilty, they would say, that whether or not a librarian is in charge of the building their responsibility remains the same. They are given by law the con-

trol and management of the Library and all its branches, and their responsibility cannot be shifted to any other shoulders.

The wonderful success of the Library has been due to the fact that the present trustees and their predecessors in the trust have felt the full weight of this responsibility, and have at all times refused to delegate any part of it to subordinates.

It might be noted parenthetically that the weight of this responsibility must indeed have been considerable to conscientious men, when one reflects that, at their semi-weekly meetings, the Trustees carefully deliberated over such matters as the change in one female assistant's dinner hour on Mondays, the disposition of two books from a branch library whose borrower had been stricken with scarlet fever, and the relative merits of various brands of plumbing fixtures. As perfectionists, they reasonably resented criticism of faults that were not their own, as when, in 1888, they made it clear that

> The darkness of the halls of the Library is not attributable to the Board of Trustees. The building was constructed by a commission composed of four citizens-at-large and three members of the city government of the day.

Again in 1890 a criticism by the Examining Committee had evoked the somewhat querulous comment:

> The Trustees are not surprised that the "poor quality of gas is a subject of complaint at Jamaica Plain." In this respect the branch suffers in common with the Central Library and other branches. It is feared that it is an evil that cannot be remedied by the Trustees.

A few years earlier it might have been, for Mr. Greenough had been Treasurer of the Boston Gas Light Company from 1852 to 1887.

After congratulating themselves so modestly upon the "wonderful success of the Library" the Trustees assured the 1891 Examining Committee that they had considered the subject of the appointment of a librarian with great care.

> The qualifications for a librarian are peculiar, and it is difficult to find any person possessing them. When the trustees are satisfied

that this position can be filled for the best interests of the Library, a librarian or superintendent will be appointed.

The name of Theodore Frelinghuysen Dwight had been considered as early as March 1891, but no action had been taken. Dwight, who was born in 1846, had, following a brief passage through a San Francisco banking house in the early seventies, turned to publishing before becoming secretary and librarian to the historian George Bancroft. After thirteen years in Washington, as Librarian of the Department of State, he had resigned to take charge of the extraordinary archives of the Adams family at Quincy. Henry Adams, writing to Elizabeth Cameron in 1888, had described Dwight as

> . . . a sort of literary factotum, [who] will soon be in general charge of the establishment, from the kitchen to the barn. I don't know how he can manage a farm, but I do know that neither my brothers nor I can do any better, so you may see him milking a cow, and reading an old MS. at the same time. We none of us know our whole genius till we've been tried.

The name of this versatile genius was brought up once again on 23 February 1892, when it was voted that the salary of a Librarian, when one shall be appointed, was to be $5,000. On 1 March 1892 the Trustees first amended their by-laws so as to provide that no person shall hold *two* of the offices, President, Clerk and Librarian, and then proceeded to elect Mr. Dwight Librarian. The amendment, in juxtaposition to the election, seems all the more discourteous when one recalls that Jewett, Winsor and Chamberlain had all served as Secretary or Clerk of the Trustees, and thus had—although without the power of voting—full knowledge of the board's deliberations both on matters of major policy and trivial detail. The decision to exclude Dwight, and to appoint his future second-in-command, Louis F. Gray, as Clerk of the Corporation, could hardly have eased administrative frictions any more than the by-law providing that the positions and duties of all persons employed in the library were to be determined by "the Corporation *or* the Librarian."

Dwight became Librarian on 13 April 1892, but on 19 December 1893 announced his intention to withdraw from the office as of 30 April 1894. He was then granted leave of absence, as he requested, for the remainder of his term. The official explanation given to the press was "poor health and inability to stand the cares and responsibilities of the office." Nearly a year elapsed before his successor, Herbert Putnam, arrived in February 1895, bringing with him a fresh breeze that rapidly sped the Public Library out of the doldrums.

SOURCES

The early volumes of the *American Library Journal,* which began publication on 30 September 1876 with Melvil Dewey as managing editor, contain numerous references to Justin Winsor's departure for Cambridge and its effect upon the Boston Public Library. See, in particular, the editorial of 31 July 1877, I (1876–77), 395–396; the article "The Change of Boston" of the following week (pp. 401–402). The *Boston Sunday Herald's* bitter little fable "How a steamer went to sea without any captain" was reprinted in II (1877–78), 225.

From this period onwards I have found many useful newspaper references in the collection of scrapbooks preserved in the Trustees' Room of the library.

Frederick B. Perkins's letters to Mayor Prince were privately printed. I have used the Boston Athenæum copies (:XL5.B656p) that he sent to Charles A. Cutter.

George Ticknor's letter of 3 October 1860 to Jewett is in the Boston Public Library miscellaneous volume T.R. 15.10.

CHAPTER VII

Building the New Library

These chosen precincts, set apart
For learned toil and holy shrines,
Yield willing homes to every art
That trains or strengthens or refines.
—OLIVER WENDELL HOLMES

THE Boylston Street library represented generous faith on the part of the City Government. It was a noble experiment, but, built in years when nobody knew what a popular public library might become, it simply did not meet the needs of its users. When ten years old it was considered unsatisfactory; at twenty it was intolerable. Much thought and a good deal of money had been spent upon its improvement during Winsor's decade, but by 1878 everyone had had enough. The Examining Committee of that year, recognizing that it could never be made absolutely fireproof, quiet, and decently ventilated, urged the Trustees to ask the State Legislature to give the city a square of Back Bay lands on which a wholly new library might be built.

Only those with a taste for eighteenth century maps remember today that Boston was once a peninsula, connected with Roxbury by a neck so narrow that a single gate—near the present intersection of Washington and Dover Streets—would bar all access from the mainland. It is one of the few places where hills have literally, as well as figuratively, been cut down to fill in the valleys, for from 1814, when tidal dams carrying toll roads were first pushed through the Back Bay, water was steadily being replaced by land. Haphazard filling was regulated in 1850, when the City took steps that led to the orderly development of the South End. The handsome prospect of Columbus and Harrison Avenues and the extended Tremont and

Washington Streets, with regularly intersecting streets, parks and squares, suggested the wisdom of filling the remaining portion of the Back Bay. This was undertaken by the Commonwealth in 1857, and when, by means of endless dump-carts of gravel, the metamorphosis of the Back Bay from water to land had been completed, the mill dam became an extension of Beacon Street; Commonwealth Avenue, Marlborough and Newbury Streets were laid out; and Boylston Street was prolonged into the new territory. Although the majority of lots were sold by the Commonwealth, certain areas were freely given to the City and to institutions. The Massachusetts Institute of Technology, incorporated in 1861, had been granted a large part of the Berkeley-Clarendon block of Boylston and Newbury Streets, while the Boston Society of Natural History had, in 1864, put up on the rest of it the building now transformed into Bonwit-Teller's store. The Museum of Fine Arts, incorporated in 1870 as an outgrowth of the Boston Athenæum, had in 1876 moved into a new building in Copley Square. This land—the site of the present Sheraton-Plaza—had been granted in 1870 by the City, which had received it from the Boston Water Power Company, the promoters of the tidal mill dams. Almost as the Back Bay came into being, the residents of the equally attractive South End abandoned their properties and scrambled into the newer development. Following the movement of fashion, the parishioners of Trinity Church, burned out of Summer Street by the great fire of 1872, chose Copley Square for a new home, while the Old South Church was in 1876 displaying unseemly haste to be profitably rid of its historic meeting house in Washington Street so as to pay for its new building at Boylston and Dartmouth Streets. Here was a whole new Boston rapidly rising, like Venus from the sea, in which the new public and learned institutions were happily settling, through the generosity of the Commonwealth and the City. The Public Library had proved its usefulness. Why should not it too share in this municipal expansion?

Mayor Frederick O. Prince, in his inaugural address of 1879, agreed that an addition to the Boylston Street Library would be merely temporary relief, and vaguely suggested moving the Lower Hall and Reading Room "to some convenient place, until the time shall arrive when it will be proper to erect a new building." Professor Haynes, commending to the 1879 Examining Committee the policy "which almost thrusts a book into the hands of every inhabitant, and insists upon his reading it," found that the reference library was inadequately used because of overcrowding. The committee, impressed by his findings, urged that land be acquired for a new building of quadrangular form, part of which should be built immediately "to accommodate the books used for reference and consultation." It should contain ample space for students, and be capable of future enlargement. This would leave the entire Boylston Street building for the adequate housing of the Lower Hall collection.

> The committee would urge this matter at the present time, because the land, which could now be obtained at a moderate price, will soon be built upon, and could not be bought without a much greater outlay of money. We are convinced that such a building must be built not long hence, and it can be done much cheaper now than in the future.

These opinions led to the passage, on 22 April 1880, of Chapter 222, Acts 1880, by which the Massachusetts Legislature granted the City of Boston a parcel of land on the southerly corner of Dartmouth and Boylston Streets, on condition that construction of a library building begin within three years. The plot had a frontage of 264 feet on Boylston Street and 125 on Dartmouth Street, extending to a back alley, dignified by the title of "public passageway," that had been laid out to provide service entrances to houses that would front on Boylston and St. James (now Blagden) Streets. The Harvard Medical School was then raising money for the new building that it completed in 1883 on the adjacent Boylston and Exeter Street corner lot, while Samuel N. Brown's house already occupied the corner of Dartmouth and St. James Streets. As the lot granted by the Commonwealth appeared unduly restricted, the City Council authorized the purchase of a sufficient number of lots fronting on St. James Street, to make the proposed site nearly square, provided Harvard University would agree to closing the back alley that bisected it. Harvard was cooperative, but, as the owners of the Brown house were not, the Legislature empowered the City, by Chapter 143, Acts 1882, to take the land if necessary.

With a site thus in hand, only the problem of planning a suitable building remained, but that proved so protracted an undertaking that on 21 April 1883 the Legislature, by Chapter 141, Acts 1883, generously extended for another three years the time limit by which construction must begin. The 1880 Examining Committee, recognizing that the chief defect of the Boylston Street library was the sacrifice of all other considerations to the monumental appearance of Bates Hall, urged that

> The new building should contain numerous moderate-sized rooms and wide corridors, both well lighted and not too high-studded, in some of which there should be conveniences for students who, under special circumstances, should be allowed access to them. The waiting and reading rooms should be separated from the room for general delivery. In one of the reading-rooms there should be a reference library, in which, under proper conditions, every one should be permitted to take down and consult books at pleasure. The present building could then be used in the place of the Lower Hall, and the South End Branch for the storing and delivery of popular books, and for a reading-room of periodical literature. It should be borne in mind, in making plans for the new building, that fitness must not give place to show.

The Trustees, reporting in June 1881 that they had requested the City Council to permit them to consult the City Architect, George A. Clough, outlined their theories of a functional library.

> No elegant edifice is to be designed in which the books are to be deposited in conformity to the architectural or ornamental structure of the building; but it should be erected over the books, the arrangement and classification of which for convenience of use must determine the form and details of its great hall, in which they must necessarily be stored, and thus outline the walls of the building. The other conditions of the Library can easily be fashioned to conform to this first necessity . . . The Boylston-street structure is one of the ornaments of the city, externally and internally, but is a singular instance of inconvenient and costly construction. It was, however, built upon such information and knowledge as were accessible at the time, . . . but the theories upon which it was based have not withstood the proof of service . . . No similar edifice can meet the present and coming wants of the institution, and it is to be hoped that none such will be attempted.

Clough was a competent architect, whose most notable work for the City was the recently completed English-High and Latin School on Warren Avenue and Montgomery Street, justly admired as the largest structure in the world then used for a free public school. It was indeed so generously planned that the City Council, seeing pupils rattling about in its fifty-six rooms, instructed the Trustees of the Public Library to consider the fitness of the building for their purposes.

In compliance with this order of 9 March 1882, the Trustees studied the problem with Henry Van Brunt—co-architect with William R. Ware of Memorial Hall at Harvard College—and concluded on 2 May, by a vote of six to one, that it was unsuitable. As the dissenting Trustee, William H. Whitmore—the scholarly Chairman of the Boston Record Commissioners—served notice of his intention to submit a minority report, it became clear "that in order to show more distinctly what was not wanted, it would be necessary to draw plans which would show approximately what was wanted." The Trustees therefore called upon Van Brunt to submit plans for an adaptation of the school, and invited Clough to make drawings for "the first approximation towards an arrangement of a building" for the Copley Square site, clearly intending to demonstrate conclusively thereby the advantages of starting afresh rather than cobbling over an existing structure. The results were embodied in a report, signed by President Greenough on 1 August 1882, which restated the Trustees' conviction that the English-High and Latin School simply would not make a satisfactory library.

Van Brunt's plans called for using the western half of the school for library purposes, constructing a book stack 123 feet long and 30½ feet wide in the courtyard, and adding a wing fronting on Dartmouth Street for reading rooms and a new Bates Hall. This, he estimated, would provide accommodation for a million volumes at a cost not exceeding $250,000. Van Brunt further submitted a sketch for a building on the Copley Square lot, in which two six-story book stacks, each capable of receiving 476,280 volumes, were placed in the courtyard of a rectangular library with Bates Hall on the front, administrative offices on the back and small rooms for special collections along the sides, the whole linked together by internal corridors and bridges connecting with the book stacks. No cost was estimated. Clough's design for the Copley Square site involved a rectangular plan in which a stack, with capacity of 1,100,-000 volumes, divided the interior in two courts and extended along the back. This building, which would cost about $450,000, occupied only part of the lot, leaving space for an addition that would house another 400,000 volumes. All these designs foreswore the great alcoved hall and copied the stack principle of a metal framework, carrying tier upon tier of compact shelving, that had been evolved by Van Brunt and Justin Winsor in the 1877 addition to Gore Hall at Harvard College.

William H. Whitmore disagreed so completely with his colleagues that he independently persuaded Clough to draw plans for the conversion of the English-High and Latin School, and presented these to the City Council with a minority report. Whitmore contended that the entire school could be occupied as a library as it stood, with only the expense of fire-proofing, not exceeding $100,000, while a new schoolhouse could be built for $218,000. In Copley Square $200,000 would be required for taking the additional privately owned land on St. James Street, plus $450,000 for the building. Thus $332,000 could be saved by settling in the schoolhouse without further argument. The majority of the Trustees were in favor of the new Harvard stack principle; Whitmore saw no sense in it.

> To use a plain simile, it is like a wire bottle-rack as compared with ordinary wooden shelves and bins. The gain is solely in space, but the objections to the plan are several. In the first place the books become merchandise. They are *stacked,* and must be removed to other rooms for use. The extra space thus required for those consultation-rooms must be put as an offset to the gain in the close stack.

He much preferred the idea of housing the books in the numerous schoolrooms, where, as in the Athenæum, they could be seen and used.

> In the "stack system" no one but the officials can be allowed to see and handle the books; everything is sacrificed to economy of space. But the student or the booklover regrets the necessity which deprives him of the pleasure of seeing his treasures about him. The

wisest student cannot carry all his facts in his head, and the sight of a book on a shelf adjacent to the one he is consulting may remind him of other authorities, or new fields of thought. Having, as I have shown, on two floors of the school building, four times the space required to shelve all our Bates Hall books, we can afford to combine the two systems represented in this vicinity by the College library and the Athenæum library. In the one, the applicant examines a catalogue, orders a book, and it is brought; in the other he is free to range around the shelves, to stand entranced on a ladder, like Dominie Sampson, or to sit down at a table surrounded by as many books for reference as he may desire.

Thus separate rooms might be assigned to every department of literature, with ample space not only for reading and writing but for shelving the next half century's probable accessions. Even if a stack *were* required, one could be built according to Clough's plans and still not have the remodelling of the school cost over $250,000. Whitmore's final thrust was the question, "What can the City afford?"

There must be a limit, both to the advantages of collecting books, and of the expense attendant thereon. Last year, out of $121,000 spent on the Library, $25,500 were spent for books, and $2,000 for binding. The remainder was used in making them available . . . It should be remembered that the Bates Hall Department, or Reference Library, is an enterprise quite apart from the public library usually established by a city or a town. It is mainly for the use of scholars and authors, and, however useful, is of value chiefly to those classes. The ideas of our present Trustees soar to a rivalry with the national libraries at London, Paris, Rome or Washington. Elsewhere it taxes the revenues of a nation to maintain such a library; can our City incur the expense, or should it attempt so to do?

Whitmore saw the alternatives of using the schoolhouse "as was," or being prepared in 1883 to take the first steps toward spending $650,000 in Copley Square. There was no doubt in his mind that the former was preferable.

The majority and minority reports did not reach the City Council until 3 October 1882, and although the matter dragged through the winter, a decision against using the schoolhouse was reached by spring. On 14 April 1883 Mayor Palmer approved orders authorizing special appropriations of $180,000 for the purchase of the additional St. James Street lots and of $450,000 for the erection of a new library on Copley Square according to plans approved by the Trustees. At this juncture it was still anticipated that the Boylston Street building would be retained and remodelled for the Lower Hall popular circulation library; only the Bates Hall books were destined for Copley Square. Although Clough had already drawn preliminary plans, it did not occur to anyone to proceed without an open competition for designs, in which anyone who could draw was welcome to try for a prize. The advertised requirements called for a three-story brick building with brown-stone trimmings, with seven-story iron book stack capable of containing at least 700,000 volumes. The first floor must contain separate rooms for the patent library, public documents, and periodicals; the second a large hall on the front of at least 7,500 square feet, a public catalogue room and offices, while on the third floor space was required for the ordering, receiving and catalogue departments, an art room and a photographic room. Somewhere, although the floor was not specified, seven rooms had to be provided for special libraries and two for special students. Prizes of four, three, two and one thousand dollars each were offered for the best designs submitted before 1 June 1884. As these printed specifications were not finally distributed until January 1884, the time allowed was subsequently extended to 1 August of that year. While the twenty sets of plans submitted were being studied individually by each Trustee, the Corporation Counsel concluded that the library board had no authority to make awards. This embarrassment remained an open question until 1 January 1885 when a new administration—headed by Hugh O'Brien, entering on the first of his four terms as Mayor—cut the knot by authorizing the Library Trustees together with the City Architect (who was by then Arthur H. Vinal) to award the prizes.

Mr. Vinal's judgment coincided with the Trustees' as to the four best plans of the twenty. He also agreed with them "that no one of the plans is suitable to build on." Thus, in the typical manner of public architectural competitions, in which the absurdity of the requirements deterred really competent firms from entering, $10,000 had been spent to no other result than wasting a year's time. In

March 1885 Vinal was directed to prepare plans that would not only meet with the Trustees' approval but that could be carried out at a cost within the $450,000 loan authorized by the City. Time was pressing, for even with the generous extension allowed in 1883, it was still necessary to begin construction by April 1886 in order to hold title to the land granted by the Commonwealth. As further studies were made, it became apparent that, to stay within the sum appropriated, it would be possible only to provide for about twenty-five years' growth of the Bates Hall Library. Vinal was uncommonly slow in producing plans, and far from being either communicative or cooperative. Nobody seemed greatly pleased with his design, which Ralph Adams Cram—then a devout young worshipper at the feet of H. H. Richardson—described half a century later as "an example of what Richardson's own style could become at the hands of a sincere but incompetent disciple—it was a chaos of gables, oriels, arcades and towers, all worked out in brownstone." But construction had to begin not later than 21 April 1886, and at 4:18 p.m. on that very day the first pile was driven!

The Trustees requested Vinal on 20 July 1886 to contract for the foundations of the building, and by 17 December $73,600.20 had already been spent. But, as Cram recalled it, "by the time the designs were revealed, the real work of Richardson had had some effect on the enlightened sector of public opinion and there was a growl of rage and indignation." Professor T. M. Clarke of the Massachusetts Institute of Technology growled so specifically to President Greenough that the Trustees spent much of December 1886 and January 1887 reexamining Vinal's piling and foundation plans. Work had been suspended and the foundations covered for protection against the winter, when matters took an unexpected and dramatic turn. The Legislature intervened, by the passage on 10 March of Chapter 60, Acts 1887, amending the act of incorporation of the Trustees of the Public Library so as to give them "full power and control of the design, construction, erection and maintenance of the central public library building, to be erected in the city of Boston." They were further empowered to select and employ architects of their choice, and supervise construction, with the sole proviso that work shall not be begun "until full general plans for the building shall

have been prepared." Thus the problem of the new building, removed from city politics and city architects, was, for better or worse,
made the sole responsibility of the library board. The act accom-
plishing this was said by Samuel A. B. Abbott to have been "started
by the architects in order to put the matter into the charge of the
trustees, so that the work and management could be better carried
on than it had been." Newspaper comments during the preceding
months had emphasized the inpropriety of leaving the new library
in the hands of the City Architect, as if it were a fire station or a
tool house for storing equipment. Arthur Rotch, testifying at the
legislative hearings on behalf of the Boston Art Club—which had
occupied its new house at Dartmouth and Newbury Streets in 1882
—made it clear that all members of the club, representing every
branch of business and professional life, felt, quite as strongly as
his fellow architects, "the keenest anxiety that this opportunity of
making a building worthy of our far-famed Public Library should
not be lost from the want of full and efficient powers on the part of
the trustees of the Library, who alone are competent by study and
experience to carry out this great work." Few "growls of rage and
indignation" have led to as rapid and desirable results, for within
the month McKim, Mead and White, the coming architectural firm
of New York, had replaced Arthur H. Vinal. However this came
about, one can only be grateful that the Legislature intervened and
prevented a repetition of the ineptitudes of the Boylston Street
library.

Charles Follen McKim, although a Pennsylvanian practicing in
New York, was no stranger to Boston. He entered Harvard College
with the class of 1870, but, after a year chiefly memorable for his
performance in right field of the 1867 varsity baseball team, took
off for Paris to study architecture. Returning to New York in June
1870, he worked for a time in Gambrill and Richardson's office,
engaged in part on the drawings for Trinity Church, Boston, which
H. H. Richardson had been commissioned to design in July 1872.
On leaving later that year to hang out his own shingle, he turned
over this work to Stanford White, who subsequently in 1879 joined
him and William Rutherford Mead in establishing the firm of
McKim, Mead and White. The Newport Casino, designed by them

in 1881, had led to commissions for both country and town houses, of which the most striking was the group built for Henry Villard on the east side of Madison Avenue, between 50th and 51st Streets. McKim's second wife had been a Bostonian—Julia Amory Appleton—who died early in January 1887 while he was at work on his designs for the Algonquin Club in Commonwealth Avenue. He was therefore entirely at home in Boston, where he had numerous friends.

When the Trustees found themselves rid of Mr. Vinal and free to choose, they first considered Edward C. Cabot, who forty years earlier had built the present Boston Athenæum at 10½ Beacon Street. But before going further with him, Samuel A. B. Abbott, who greatly admired the Villard houses, hurried off to New York to consult McKim. They talked for four hours on Saturday, 19 March 1887, and met again on Sunday to such purpose that Abbott asked McKim to meet his fellow Trustees, President Greenough and Professor Haynes, at the Brevoort the next day. McKim described this in his memorandum book as a "very successful interview." So successful, in fact, that the Trustees, at home again in Boston on the 26th, voted to direct the President to make a contract with McKim, Mead and White, and to ask Mr. Cabot to defer any further action on library plans. Greenough and McKim signed the contract on the 30th, and on the same day a quorum of the Trustees approved it. William H. Whitmore remained unreconciled to the prospect of building in Copley Square. Having missed the 26 and 30 March meetings, he protested by letter on the 31st against three members of the board having visited New York without having asked him and the Reverend James Freeman Clarke to join them, stating clearly but uncivilly: "I feel myself entirely released from any responsibility in regard to the construction of the building." He did not feel free, however, to refrain from impeding and harassing his colleagues whenever possible.

The architectural problems facing McKim, Mead and White were complex. There was no precedent in the United States for a library of this size and character. Moreover, the site chosen was bordered by a singular variety of recent buildings, inspired by various aspects of the middle ages. The Romanesque masses of Richardson's Trinity

Church dominated Copley Square from its commanding position at the east. To the north, an unobtrusive block of brick and brownstone houses, broken by the low façade of the Second Church—an academic exercise in the revival of English Gothic—fronted on Boylston Street, while at the far corner, beyond Dartmouth Street, the north Italian Gothic campanile of Cummings and Sear's New Old South Church supplied a vertical accent that could not be ignored. Across the way Sturgis and Brigham had housed the new Museum of Fine Arts in one of those unhappy red brick and yellow terra cotta approximations of Gothic that make one wish that John Ruskin had never gone to Italy, while at the corner of Dartmouth Street and Huntington Avenue S. S. Pierce and Company sold their excellent groceries in a building that at once parodied Richardson's style and sought to recreate the picturesque roof lines of old Nuremberg. Truly it was no easy matter to fill the vacant lot to the west with a structure that would have architectural quality of its own and still not swear at its motley and aggressive neighbors, while simultaneously creating for the first time in America "an ideal library" within the confines of another man's foundations!

Temperamentally Charles Follen McKim was a man of the Renaissance both in his exuberance and in his love for combining the arts of architecture, painting and sculpture. Remembering the European squares where buildings of many centuries and styles merge harmoniously, he early determined to bring Copley Square out of the middle ages, while benefitting by the superb mountainous Trinity Church and the graceful tower of the New Old South. His biographer, Charles Moore, thus described the early stages of McKim's reasoning.

As the problem presented itself to McKim's logical mind, there was first the straight line of Dartmouth Street, passing directly in front of the site and prolonged on either side—an important thoroughfare. The new building must recognize the street. It must also oppose itself to the irregular, vertical masses of Trinity. Therefore it must emphasize the horizontal lines, and thus by contrast itself enhance and be enhanced by its picturesque neighbor. Moreover, in the community of dark and colored stone and brick, in which romantic characteristics prevailed, the Library must be white in color, severely simple in outline and classical in style. So, although comparatively small, it would hold its own among its motley neighbors.

Although that decision was reached, a good year was required to produce a reasonable set of plans, for as McKim recalled the process,

> It took us about six months to lose our vanity in connection with the subject, and it took us six months more, having found out that we couldn't make a scheme which we felt would go down the pages of time and be enduring, to propose to the trustees what else could be done.

It was, first of all, found necessary to abandon any idea of confinement to Vinal's existing foundations. In seeking suitable precedent for inspiration, McKim considered and rejected first the Louvre pavilion, then the Farnese Palace and finally Félix Duban's façade of the École des Beaux-Arts. Eventually Henri Labrouste's Bibliothèque Ste.-Geneviève appeared to provide a workable springboard, for as McKim recalled:

> We finally, however, settled upon a model for a library building, which we founded on the St. Genevieve Library, in Paris, which we recognized and believed to be the best type and the best scheme in its outward expression, and also in its arrangement.

But although the Paris library, completed about forty years earlier, furnished a suggestion in masses and in locating a great hall with arched windows on the front of the second floor, McKim's design and details were very much his own.

On 30 March 1888, a year to the day after signing the contract, the Trustees approved McKim, Mead and White's plans, and voted to go ahead with as much of the construction as appropriations already made by the City would permit. In mid-April plans and a plaster scale model were placed in the Old State House for public inspection and comment, and a series of heliotype reproductions of drawings was issued as a supplement to the Trustees' thirty-seventh annual report. The plans proposed a rectangular granite building, the rear half of which was devoted to book stacks, surrounding an arcaded courtyard. A vaulted entrance hall gave upon a stairway of noble proportions which led to a new barrel-vaulted Bates Hall, 218 feet long, 42 feet wide and 50 feet high, which occupied the entire front of the second floor, and whose great arched windows determined the character of the façade. This noble apart-

BATES HALL

ment bore no resemblance to its book-lined and alcoved predecessor in Boylston Street, for in McKim's preliminary sketch it was entirely free not only of bookcases but of chairs and tables. It suggested rather the hall of a great Roman bath with decorative elements of the Italian Renaissance superimposed. Its semi-circular ends, separated by low screens from the body of the hall, were designated for use as writing and catalogue rooms. Adjacent to the catalogue area, and accessible from the staircase, was a Delivery Room overlooking

St. James Street; at the opposite Boylston Street end of the building was a large room for scientific periodicals and three rooms for special students. The area on the ground floor under Bates Hall and these rooms was, to the left of the entrance, assigned to the ordering and catalogue departments; to the right, space was provided for housing bound newspapers, maps and duplicates. Although the building appeared from the exterior to be only two stories high, a third floor, lighted from the courtyard, was provided for the accommodation of the special libraries. The main outlines of the building were established in these drawings; it was only in matters of internal arrangement in the side and rear sections that important changes were made. Certain improvements of detail were achieved on the façades and in the courtyard arcades before construction, but McKim's strenuous year of planning had produced substantially the building that exists today. It is worth observing, as a straw in the wind, that although the plans called for an extremely elegant oval Trustees' Room, they showed no visible accommodation for the Librarian, who seemingly did not enter into anyone's calculations.

The public exhibition of the plans was on the whole well received. While there were captious critics who likened the building to the old Beacon Hill Reservoir or a Roman market place superimposed upon Fort Independence, a contributor to the *Transcript* characterized the drawings as "a revelation" and observed:

> The magnificence of the conception of the plan of the building carries one quite off one's feet. Laying out that great hall entirely across the front of the building was a stroke worthy of the great masters of architecture. Mr. Richardson would have loved that.

Another correspondent expressed his feeling of "profound relief" that "there was no yielding to a current fashion for novelty or strangeness," and commented on "the Roman repose" and the simplicity and dignity of the design. *The Boston Herald* felt that "so far as the external appearance of the new building is concerned, it would be hard to raise adverse criticisms," while the *Boston Daily Advertiser* observed that "when we consider the remarkable diversity of buildings already in Copley Square . . . we begin to realize what a saving grace the simple Roman strength of this new library will be to that locality." Indeed, after fifty years' reflection, Ralph Adams Cram—who loved Richardson's church—wrote:

> No greater contrast could be imagined than that between Trinity Church and the new Library across the way. On the one hand, an almost brutal, certainly primitive, boldness, arrogance, power; on the other, a serene Classicism, reserved, scholarly, delicately conceived in all its parts, beautiful in that sense in which things have always been beautiful in periods of high human culture.

With his plans for the library, McKim submitted a sketch for the improvement of Copley Square, so simple and so completely right as to be a work of genius. It required nothing more than to eliminate the triangular plots of mangy grass that quite unnecessarily marked the passage of Huntington Avenue, to pave the square and to place a simple Roman fountain in the center. It is a thousand pities that this scheme was never carried out, although it is still not too late to do so.

Anyone could see that this monumental structure could not be built within the original $450,000 appropriation, of which—after the payment for competition prizes, Vinal's abortive foundations, and more recent expenses—about $358,000 remained. As the City Council wished to have some estimate, McKim was called upon to produce one within a week. The time was totally inadequate, particularly as his plans were not completed in detail, but in response to pressure he cobbled up the best figures he could and on 23 April 1888 reluctantly offered the sum of $1,165,955. This led to a vote of the City Council on 7 May, authorizing the Trustees to go ahead within that greatly increased limit. About this time, William W. Greenough, who was nearing his seventieth birthday, felt unable to cope with the increased obligations of construction and resigned from the board, and in June the Reverend James Freeman Clarke died. In their places former Mayor Frederick O. Prince and Phineas Pierce were appointed Trustees, while after a week's incumbency by Professor Haynes, Samuel A. B. Abbott, who had been the moving spirit in employing McKim, Mead and White, was elected to the presidency.

Proposals for the construction were advertised in July, and, after harassing tactics by William H. Whitmore, who continued tooth and nail opposition to everything, the bid of Woodbury and Leighton was accepted on 23 July 1888. Wednesday, 28 November 1888, was fixed for the laying of the cornerstone. This ceremony, performed by Mayor Hugh O'Brien, was graced by the celebrated Dr. Oliver Wendell Holmes, who, by direct wire from the Muses, transmitted the following poem:

> Proudly beneath her glittering dome,
>   Our three-hilled city greets the morn;
> Here freedom found her virgin home,—
>   The Bethlehem where her babe was born.
>
> The lordly roofs of traffic rise
>   Amid the smoke of household fires;
> High o'er them in the peaceful skies,
>   Faith points to heaven her clustering spires.
>
> Can freedom breathe if ignorance reign?
>   Shall Commerce thrive where anarchs rule?
> Will Faith her half-fledged brood retain,
>   If darkening counsels cloud the school?
>
> Let in the light! from every age
>   Some gleams of garnered wisdom pour,
> And, fixed on thought's electric page,
>   Wait all their radiance to restore.
>
> Let in the light! on diamond mines
>   Their gems invite the hand that delves,—
> So learning's treasured jewels shine,
>   Ranged on the alcove's ordered shelves.
>
> From history's scroll the splendor streams,
>   From science leaps the living ray,
> Flashed from the poet's flowing dreams
>   The opal fires of fancy play.
>
> Let in the light! these windowed walls
>   Shall brook no shadowing colonnades,
> But day shall flood the silent halls
>   Till o'er yon hills the sunset fades.
>
> Behind the ever-open gate
>   No pikes shall fence a crumbling throne,
> No lackeys cringe, no courtiers wait,—
>   This palace is the people's own!

Heirs of our narrow-girdled past,
  How fair the prospect we survey,
Where howled unheard the wintry blast
  And rolled unchecked the storm-swept bay!

These chosen precincts, set apart
  For learned toil and holy shrines,
Yield willing homes to every art
  That trains or strengthens or refines.

Here shall their sceptred mistress reign,
  Who heeds her meanest subjects' call,
Sovereign of all their vast domain—
  The queen—the handmaid of them all.

The arts were indeed provided with willing homes, for, as the concept of a "palace for the people" gradually replaced in the Trustees' minds the earlier theory of a functional library "erected over the books," architectural painting and sculpture entered into McKim's plans. The day after his first talk with Abbott in March 1887 he and his partner, Stanford White, had spent Sunday afternoon walking with Augustus Saint-Gaudens. Their thoughts had early turned to decorative adjuncts to the proposed great building, and McKim's plans soon involved bronze sculptured groups, flanking the entrance, by Saint-Gaudens, and a pair of monumental Siena marble lions on the main staircase by his brother, Louis. Although Stanford White was rather inclined to procure European painters for the decoration of the public rooms, Augustus Saint-Gaudens insisted that there were "strong men of American fiber who should be employed." Thus, although Puvis de Chavannes—described with an engaging stammer in Herbert Small's ten cent *Handbook of the New Public Library in Boston* as "almost, if not quite, the most distinguished of living French painters"—was persuaded to decorate the main staircase, John Singer Sargent and Edwin A. Abbey were also brought into the scene. McKim, White and Saint-Gaudens clearly saw, in the words of Charles Moore, "the possibilities opening before them for the creation of the greatest combined work of the architect, painter and sculptor ever achieved in America up to that time." Abbott, whose taste and enthusiasm often outran his tact and discretion, readily fell in with their plans; the role of patron suited him, and, as he was giving his time without compensation he could readily persuade himself that it was all in the public interest. When veterans of the 2nd and 20th Massachusetts Infantry Associations proposed erecting memorials to the valor of their Civil War comrades in the library, it was clear that Louis Saint-Gaudens's staircase lions were just the thing. That solved one problem, but, although formal contracts were postponed and sources of funds remained vague, Sargent was informally commissioned to decorate the third floor gallery and Abbey the Delivery Room. McKim brought Augustus Saint-Gaudens and the two painters to Boston in May 1890, and a dinner with the Trustees clinched the matter. In various summers Abbott went abroad, usually with McKim, studying details of European libraries, seeking sources of marble, or looking into possibilities of decoration. In the hope that Whistler might be persuaded to decorate the Boylston Street end of Bates Hall, an agreeable dinner *à quatre* was arranged at Foyot's in Paris by Sargent, for himself, McKim, Abbott and Whistler. It was a charming evening. Whistler responded, drew sketches on the tablecloth, and his companions marvelled. But the tablecloth went into the wash, nothing tangible came of the meeting, and Bates Hall is free from peacocks.

While all these exciting plans were being made, construction progressed and expenses mounted. Early in 1889 the Trustees were rid of William H. Whitmore's opposite-minded and dampening company. On 10 January he sent a letter to the Mayor stating that "he was entirely opposed to the erection of the new library building, mainly on account of its cost," and, as he felt that the board should be united, offered his resignation. It was accepted, and William R. Richards was appointed in his place. This was just as well, for, although Whitmore was an accomplished scholar and a highly intelligent man, his economical views and Abbott's expansiveness could never have been reconciled. As the decision for a monumental palace had been made, it was as well to carry it out wholeheartedly.

To provide the funds necessary to complete the building according to McKim's estimate, the Legislature, by Chapter 68, Acts 1889, empowered the City of Boston to issue bonds for one million dollars, outside the legal limit of indebtedness. This act, passed on 1 March 1889, provided that, before the maturity of this loan, the Trustees should sell the old Boylston Street Library and the land on which it stood, turning in the proceeds toward the redemption of the bonds. The optimism of McKim's estimate of the preceding year was soon apparent, for the Trustees in their thirty-eighth report made it clear

STAIRCASE

that the amount of loan was less than they had requested, and that it would not be enough to enable them to complete the building. In fact, by the end of 1890 it was estimated that the total cost, including shelving but no other furniture, would be $2,218,865. To show that they were not the only body guilty of underestimating costs the Trustees appended a list of contract prices and actual costs of fourteen public buildings constructed since 1885. The parallels were striking, but nobody else had achieved quite as resounding a miscalculation as the Trustees of the Public Library. Once again the City Council responded, and the Legislature, by Chapter 324, Acts 1891, permitted the issue of another million dollars worth of bonds outside the authorized city debt limit.

With the pains and expense that were lavished upon the new building, it was disheartening to find it unsympathetically viewed by the library profession. During Judge Chamberlain's term of office the Public Library had not maintained the position of unquestioned leadership it had held in Jewett's day and in Winsor's. There had been frequent criticism, both deserved and unfounded, but matters came to a head in September 1890 when the American Library Association met in Boston. During that meeting William F. Poole, then based in Chicago, spoke his mind plainly about the new building. He claimed first of all that Bates Hall, "with throngs of visitors coming to pass comments on the beautiful architecture and frescoes," would be as unsuitable for quiet study and reading as the street outside in Copley Square. He then disagreed with the theory of isolating books in a great stack, and after citing other grievances said, "Here you will have, indeed, a beautiful façade, but not a library building." In attempting to explain how this all came about, Poole continued:

> Mr. Greenough acknowledges that he consulted no librarians, for, he says, they are inexperienced persons with bees in their bonnets. "I had the advice of architects," he adds, "and did as well as I could." The result is you have a library building, in the construction of which librarians, who are generally supposed to know something about such matters, have not had a thing to say.

In an effort to draw attention away from these Cassandra-like remarks, the chairman called upon Judge Chamberlain, obviously hoping for refutation. Instead the former librarian merely confirmed Poole's allegations by saying: "I acknowledge our building is merely the library building of the architect. No librarian, so far as I know, has been consulted." In a later interview with the *Advertiser* he admitted, "I had no knowledge of the plans until they were substantially determined upon."

Abbott reacted so vehemently and discourteously to Poole's criticism in the *Boston Herald* of 20 September 1890 that there was some ground for Poole's rejoinder:

> Mr. Abbott has much to learn before he sets up business as a library expert, but there is still hope for him. I commend him to a rigid course of training under the instruction of the accomplished persons employed in the Boston Public Library, and recommend that he put his feet in a cold bath and apply a bandage of ice water to his head whenever he assumes a controversial attitude on those matters; and finally, that he give his overworked expression, that the statement of his opponent "is unqualifiedly and absolutely false," a vacation.

Much of the ink spilled during the building of the Public Library makes one wish that Bliss Perry had not waited until his ninetieth year to send a very brief letter to the Mail Bag of the *Boston Herald,* "Very few men and no women write well when they are angry." He might so well have sent it sixty years earlier and shamed various angry men out of committing their recriminations to print.

Prior to the granting of the second million dollar loan, the City Council held hearings at which Abbott and McKim testified concerning the cost of the building. On the basis of these statements, the City Government Committee on the Library Department submitted on 13 April 1891 a report (Document 54—1891) which concluded with the statement that if the building could be completed for the estimated sum of $985,000

> . . . the city will have a building of rare beauty—"a palace for the people,"—built at a cost not more extravagant than that of many other public buildings.

That should have ended the matter, and the building might have been rapidly completed had not political tangles, inspired by irresponsible journalism, complicated the scene. In November 1891 the *Boston News* began beating a drum and inventing scandals that did not exist. Day after day, with that peculiarly mealy-mouthed hypocrisy by which journalists of a certain type invoke the public good as a cloak for tricks aimed at increased circulation, the *News* attacked the library. First it was claimed that the admirable Milford granite used in the library façade was so rotten that stones had to be stuck together with shellac. To demonstrate the wickedness of the "Public Library Octopus," a reporter stole three inch-square cubes of waste granite, sent them to the Watertown Arsenal to be tested for crushing strength, and published an Army report of findings that proved nothing. After exhausting the granite theme, the *News* looked for new outrages to denounce. They celebrated New Year's Day 1892 by publishing "on excellent authority" that the Trustees "have omitted to make any provision in the new building for the extensive collection of books now situated in the lower hall of the library building on Boylston Street." The *Boston Daily Globe,* in its role of "the people's paper," took up the cry on the 4th by pointing out the indignities to which the Lower Hall readers—"the people who are not overblessed with this world's goods"—will be submitted if they

> . . . have to go into the enormous Bates Hall along with everyone else, and rub elbows with the Beacon st. swell, the teacher and all the varying classes of people who are now accommodated in Bates Hall, upstairs, and are away from the plain people, who are glad to avail themselves of the "lower hall."

The *Globe* painted a tear-jerking picture of the poor teamster whose hour of leisure would be ruined by having "to brush against fine ladies and rub elbows with men who are spick and span in their fashionable clothes." Even the *Boston Evening Transcript* joined in the fray by printing, on 9 January, an article by Arthur W. Brayley describing some of the odd personalities that Joshua Bates did not have in mind when reflecting upon the educational value of a library.

> Probably the most original of the habitues of the reading room is a German by birth, his English being very bad. Every evening at 6:30 he enters the Lower Hall, walks over to the registration desk and looks at the clock. He then crosses the room where hangs the thermometer, at which he takes a good look. Turning, he makes a line for the thermometer in the reading-room and reads the condition of the temperature. If he is satisfied, all is well; if not, he expresses his disapproval very decidedly. He then calls for the *Pilot* and takes his favorite seat in the front of the room. At about eight o'clock he is asleep. He has not missed an evening since 1880. Another celebrity may be noticed among the readers

with a large handkerchief or nightcap on his head. The "trio" is composed of an Irishman, Englishman and Scotchman, who have for over ten years spent the time between Deer Island and the library. One of these walks by the aid of two canes and is generally the first to make his appearance at the room. He calls for the London *Tablet* and occupies a comfortable corner. First one and then the other member of the set comes in, who in turn call for the Dublin and London papers and are soon seated together, where they read and discourse hour after hour, the only intermission being when called by nature to nourish their physical being, when they sally forth on an expedition of "grabbing." This will continue for two or three weeks, when they begin to show signs of inebriation, which indication grows stronger each day, until first one and then the other disappears "down Duck," only to make their reappearance after their expired term of office, wearing clothes on which the creases made by long confinement in the wardrobe of the island institution are still fresh.

All this hullaballoo sprang from some advance intimation that the 1891 Examining Committee had some doubts about the wisdom of merging the more popular part of the library with Bates Hall. Their report, when later published, contained only a mild suggestion that the old scheme of division be continued in the new building, but the false scent started brought a pack of journalists rushing in full cry. They in turn created such a clamor that Mayor Matthews, on 4 January 1892, sent a letter to the Trustees expressing his surprise at hearing for the first time on the previous day that the Trustees "had made no provision in the new building for the delivery of books, and that it was their intention to retain the Public Library on Boylston Street in addition to the new one when completed." He asked what truth there might be in the statement, and requested various facts and figures.

A more ill-founded rumor could hardly have wasted a chief magistrate's time, for McKim's first plans in 1888 had provided a spacious room for the delivery of books, and Chapter 68, Acts 1889, in appropriating the first million dollars for the completion of the new building had specifically required that the Boylston Street library be sold. The Trustees promptly denied the rumor, and in their 1891 report, adopted on 29 January 1892, amplified their excellent reasons for proposing to merge the two parts of the library. In commenting upon the Examining Committee's recommendation, they wrote:

> What is now called the "lower hall" in the old library, was established soon after the Library was founded, as a room connected with the main hall of the Library where books of a popular character would be more easily accessible to the public. For many years there was no division of the catalogue of the two rooms, and probably there would never have been a division had they not been located upon different floors. The separation was the result of an effort to relieve persons desiring books in the lower hall from the inconvenience of mounting stairs to consult the catalogue which was then in the Bates hall.

> In the new building no such inconvenience will exist; all books in the Library,—which will contain a copy of every one now in the lower hall,—will easily be accessible to the public. Those who now use the lower hall will find ample accommodation in the new Bates hall, which is designed as a general reading-room for the whole people, and not for any special class. In other parts of the building there will be provided for students desiring to prosecute any particular line of research, almost three times as much space as is contained in the new Bates hall. While it is possible in the new building to provide, without alteration of the present plan, a room with ample accommodations for the collection in the lower hall, with separate and convenient access from the street, the trustees do not propose, at present, to set apart separate accommodations for that collection. If experience show that they are in error, and that the public desire a separation of classes, future trustees will be able to provide that separation without changing the present arrangement of the building. The present trustees, however, are of the opinion that the new building is built for the accommodation of all the citizens of Boston, without reference to so-called "class" or condition; and they are further of the opinion that the new Bates hall will not be too good for the users of the present lower hall, and that they would be false to their trust if they made any regulation which might result in an apparent separation of the poorer users of the Library from the richer.

There was, indeed, no logic in perpetuating a division that had sprung from pure architectural convenience in another building, and which was, moreover, creating an implication that certain groups of readers were second-class citizens. One respects the Trustees for insisting that, in a public library maintained by the City for the free use of all inhabitants, there was no ground for dividing reading rooms and multiplying entrances in the manner of a British pub.

These clear statements only scotched the rumors, for on 2 February Mayor Matthews served notice of his intention to investigate the whole subject of the expense and convenience of the new building before authorizing the expenditure of any part of the latest loan. He undertook, with the Corporation Counsel and the City Architect (then E. M. Wheelwright), to sit as a Commission of Inquiry. By this time the façades, interior masonry walls and fireproofed floors were completed; the tile roof was in place; Bates Hall was progressing, and Louis Saint-Gaudens's noble lions were already installed on the stairway. Construction had already been delayed while negotiations for the second million dollar loan were in progress during the spring of 1891; it was to be even further retarded by Mayor Matthews's unwillingness to have that loan used. The Trustees in April furnished a full report of all expenditures and contracts, including the verbal agreements for decorations with Abbey and Sargent, and waited patiently for many months before receiving permission to proceed with the completion of the building.

During this interval there occurred one of the small comedies that punctuated the construction of the library. McKim had sought to relieve the severity of the granite façades by introducing decorative carvings and inscriptions, replete with historical and literary allusions. In the spandrels of the window arches were round medallions, carved by Domingo Mora, derived from the marks or trade devices of the earliest printers and booksellers, while below the great arched windows memorial tablets were carved with the names of literary men, artists, scientists, statesmen and soldiers, which served not only as decorative relief but constituted a kind of roll of honor. The names were intermingled, without regard for century or subject, in a kind of pleasant hodge-podge that suggested the diversity of riches to be found within. Then, on 27 May 1892 the *Boston Evening Record* began screaming that there was more to these names than met the eye, for at the left of the Dartmouth Street façade this combination occurred:

MOSES	MOZART	WREN
CICERO	EUCLID	HERRICK
KALIDASA	ÆSCHYLUS	IRVING
ISOCRATES	DANTE	TITIAN
MILTON		ERASMUS

The *Record's* shocking "discovery" amounted simply to the fact that the architects, like certain scribes in medieval scriptoria, had amused themselves by working an acrostic of their names into an inscription primarily conveying an unrelated meaning. The Trustees took the matter as the harmless joke that it was, but the *Record* magnified it out of all proportion:

> The Public Library will have that architect's adv. wiped off, or The Record will find out why.

A correspondent to the *Transcript* proposed that

PRAXITELES	SOLON
EURIPIDES	OVID
ARISTOPHANES	ARISTIDES
RHADAMANTHUS	PLINY
SOPHOCLES	

be carved on two of the vacant tablets; other wags suggested acrostics of the Trustees' names, and comment became so heated that the offending inscription was unfortunately erased.

Early in July 1892 the Trustees reminded Mayor Matthews that his investigation had already delayed the completion of the building by five months, and tactfully suggested that enough time had been wasted. In reply, the Mayor proposed eliminating certain ornamental work, bronze doors and statuary, to effect a saving of two hundred thousand dollars. This notion was extremely unwelcome, but as the chief necessity was to get on with the building, the Trustees compromised sufficiently to make advertising for bids for final contracts possible in September. Eventually, through a memorial signed by Richard M. Hunt and other distinguished artists from other cities, and through the interest of such citizens as Major Henry L. Higginson and Professor Charles S. Sargent, Mayor Matthews came to see the desirability of decorative elements and ceased his opposition. Thus on 28 October 1892 President Abbott was authorized to contract with Augustus Saint-Gaudens for two groups of statuary to be placed on pedestals flanking the main entrance, at a cost of $50,000, "and to reduce the verbal contracts for decorative painting entered into about November 7th, 1890 with Messrs. John S. Sargent and Edwin A. Abbey to writing." In May 1893 a contract was authorized with Puvis de Chavannes for the decoration of the main staircase, thus bringing to fruition negotiations begun by McKim and Abbott during their European travels in 1891. Private generosity supplemented public funds to allow two young Boston painters to have a share in the decoration of the library. In 1891 Dr. Harold Williams had proposed a subscription among friends for work by John Elliott—son-in-law of Julia Ward Howe—and two years later he was assigned a ceiling in the Patent (later to become the Teachers' Section of the Children's) Room, while Arthur Astor Carey made possible the decoration of a "Venetian Lobby" on the second floor by Joseph Lindon Smith. Dr. Charles G. Weld gave a bronze statue of Sir Harry Vane by Frederic Macmonnies, now in an entrance vestibule niche. In July 1894 Abbott was empowered to exute a contract with James A. McNeill Whistler to decorate the wall at the northeasterly end of Bates Hall for the sum of $15,000, and in September a $25,000 contract was authorized with Daniel Chester French for three pairs of bronze doors for the main entrance. Thus a signal array of the ablest contemporary artists were brought into the service of the library to join their talents with McKim's in creating a harmony of the arts that had never previously been attempted in the United States upon such a scale.

The contributions of these painters and sculptors only enhanced, rather than created, the beauty of the building, for one cannot praise too highly McKim's feeling for space, his sense of proportion, and his uncanny flair for texture. Royal Cortissoz rightly said that to McKim

> building materials were what pigments are to the painter; he handled them with the same intensely personal feeling for their essential qualities that a great technician brings to the manipulation of his colors, and he left upon his productions the same autographic stamp.

The extraordinary beauty of the *rouge antique* marble of the doorways in the Delivery Room was due to no happy accident of a contractor, while anyone who studies with care the subtle gradations of color in the Siena marble of the great staircase will detect in them the same "autographic stamp." Augustus Saint-Gaudens, who first saw the staircase finished in November 1894, in company with his brother, expressed a feeling that has been echoed for more than sixty years when he wrote McKim:

> We were completely bowled over by it; it is a splendid piece of work and even as it is, without the paintings of Puvis, I know nothing to equal it.

Perhaps today one might say that even *with* the paintings of Puvis there is nothing to equal it, for the subtlety of Charles Follen McKim's design and textures has outlived the appeal of his coadjutor's contribution.

Many of these decorative projects required years for their completion; some never materialized. Negotiations with Whistler went so badly that by the spring of 1895 the offer of a contract was withdrawn, to his considerable disgust. Although Saint-Gaudens held the groups of figures for the main entrance more at heart than any other work he had undertaken, he was never able to complete them. His first plan was for a male personification of Labor, between female figures signifying Science and Art on one pedestal, with a male likeness of Law between female Religion and Force (or Power) on the other. He went about his commission so conscientiously as to set up painted reproductions of the figures in front of the library façade to determine the scale. Eventually the design changed to Law, flanked respectively by Executive Power and by two figures personifying Love for one pedestal, with the other devoted to Science, with Labor and Art (in the guise of Music) as the subsidiary figures. Although Saint-Gaudens—when he returned to Paris a sick man in 1897—continued to work in his rue de Bagneux studio upon these plaster models, they proved too exacting an assignment. He did, however, carve in pink Knoxville marble and install over the three arches of the main entrance, panels depicting the seals of the Library, the City, and the Commonwealth. The library device, originally suggested by Kenyon Cox, consists of two nude boys, holding the torches of learning, and acting as supporters to a shield which bears an open book and the dates of founding and incorporation of the library. Above is the motto OMNIUM LUX CIVIUM, while in the background are dolphins and laurel branches. This attractive composition, although of the most idyllic and high-minded nature, was presently denounced as a major indecency. Reporters, who since the discovery of the acrostic had given the library façade their most devoted attention, were immediately scandalized by the innocent nakedness of the small boys. The *Boston Evening Record* of 10 February 1894, under the headline "WIPE OUT THE BLOT! The Women and Children of Boston Have Rights Even at the Public Library," told the sad tale of a "well known business man," whose sixteen-year-old son, "a pure-minded lad, who has seen statues of antique casts in the Art Museum," cried in anguish as he observed that Saint-Gaudens's boys lacked fig-leaves, "See that thing they have put up there, papa, isn't it horrible? I should think they would be ashamed to put such a thing on the Public Library." Because of the acute eyesight of this "bright, clean Boston boy," the *Record* clamored: "*This indecency must not remain to affront people who wish to enter the building.*" Although the *Record* continued to denounce "the thing on the Public Library," called for workmen with chisels, and even went so far as to describe the entire building as a "stench and an eye-sore," its crusade was too ridiculous to succeed even in Boston, Saint-Gaudens's seal remained, with its boys neither clothed nor castrated.

After the autumn of 1892 construction progressed without further interruption, and in two years' time the building was completed. Some small collections were moved there during the fall of 1894; the transfer of the bulk of the library began on 14 December 1894, and was completed on 27 January 1895. The Boylston Street library finally closed its doors to the public on 24 January.

Externally in design, and internally so far as the placing of the courtyard, staircase, Bates Hall and the Delivery Room were concerned, the library occupied in 1895 was substantially as Charles McKim had designed it in 1888. During the long years of construction, however, important modifications had been made in the use of the remaining space. The great book stack, originally designed to occupy the rear half of the building, was reduced practically in half and concentrated in the southwesterly quarter to provide space for the bindery and newspaper room. These were accessible either from the northwest corner of the courtyard, or by a separate entrance from the Boylston Street façade, in the center of which was an enclosed driveway by which carriages might deposit their passengers dry-shod either at this stairway or at arched doors giving upon the courtyard arcade. The ordering and catalogue departments remained on the first floor, to the left of the entrance, as originally planned, but the corresponding rooms on the right were reassigned to bound and current periodicals. The monumental oval Trustees' Room opening out of the Delivery Room had given place to a Librarian's Office and a working area which contained the terminus of an ingenious miniature railway, whose cable cars brought from the adjacent stacks the books requested by slips whisked through pneumatic tubes. In an entresol overhead the Trustees were pleasantly accommodated with a meeting room having green velvet walls over Empire wainscoting, an ante-room, and an open loggia, occupying the center of the Blagden Street façade. On the third floor, opening out of the sandstone gallery to be decorated by Sargent, were rooms for music, fine arts, and the Barton-Ticknor libraries, while around the three sides of the court were high, well-lighted students' rooms with alcoves for the housing of special collections.

The building of the library had been a long struggle. It had involved battles with public indifference, municipal economy, political maneuvering, bad taste, the temperament of artists, the fixed ideas of artisans, the criticism of professional librarians, the unsympathetic and often unfair tirades of journalists, and, above all, with a lack of popular understanding of the purposes of the Trustees. One might more accurately say, with the purposes of Samuel A. B. Abbott, who was, as President, the sole survivor of the board charged with the task of construction by the 1887 Legislature. He was an irascible, domineering man who wanted his own way, bitterly resented criticism, and, when replying to it, put himself in the worst possible light. Yet it was Abbott who chose McKim, who worked intimately with him through all the myriad details, upheld his vision consistently, and was rewarded by the masterpiece of a great architect that, after more than sixty years, does honor to Boston. Now that the antagonisms of the movement have been forgotten, one can only be grateful to Abbott, to whom the tribute paid the Trustees by the 1894 Examining Committee is uniquely applicable.

> The Trustees are to be congratulated that they are reaching a termination of long, arduous, and varied services connected with the new building, and that such a noble end crowns their work. Thanks are due to them, not only from Boston, but from all who esteem truth and propriety in design, for their choice of style. It is difficult to avoid following a fashion in architecture as well as in other matters, but they have not yielded to a passing fancy for the unusual, and for styles not of the greatest ages of art and history.
>
> They have spared us an essay in archaeology, and have given us, especially in the interior, grace and dignity, in a style associated with one of the grand eras of human progress. It is the majestic and beautiful style of Italy, in the great period of the revival of learning, as well as of art, and of the foremost artists and discoverers in our modern world. They would feel at home in such an edifice, and the best of them seldom walked through a better vestibule and up a better staircase. The august and venerable prelate in the Vatican of our time could hardly find a courtyard so noble for the solace of his meditative promenades. Every person who enters the delivery-room visits one of the exquisite library rooms of the world, and reaches it without a stormy voyage.
>
> In a variety of departments, in value and completeness as well as in size, we have here one of the great libraries of the world. Honorable public service and distinguished achievement have, for more than forty years, characterized the Board of Trustees, and to-day, amid immense failures sadly marking our country, we can offer congratulations, with full hope and confidence in the future, for a grand success, secured for civilization as well as for Boston.

More than fifty years later David McCord expressed the same view with a poet's succinctness when he wrote of the library:

> Meanwhile, like St. Paul's in London it continues to dominate the square that bears an artist's name and its immortality seems assured.

SOURCES

In addition to the annual reports of the Trustees there are several separate pamphlets relating to the planning of the new library, such as *The Public Library of Boston, Report of a hearing before the Legislative Committee on Harbor and Lands on the petition of the City of Boston for a lot of new land on the Back Bay for a site for the Public Library* (Boston, 1880); *Report by the Trustees of the Public Library on the fitness of the English High and Latin School Building for the uses of the Public Library* (Boston, 1882); and the *Minority Report of William H. Whitmore (One of the Trustees of the Public Library) on the fitness of the English High and Latin School Building for the uses of the Public Library* (Boston, 1882).

The Trustees' votes concerning a new library from 1879 to 1895 are conveniently abstracted in a volume in the Trustees' Room labelled *New Library Building Extracts* (T.R. 25.15).

The McKim, Mead and White drawings for the Copley Square building are to be found in a *Supplement to Thirty-Seventh Annual Report of the Trustees of the Public Library, 1889*. Charles Moore, *The Life and Times of Charles Follen McKim* (Boston: Houghton Mifflin Company, 1929), pp. 62–94, deals with the building, while Ralph Adams Cram, *My Life in Architecture* (Boston: Little, Brown and Company, 1936), pp. 32–35, indicates its effect upon a young architect of the time. Herbert Small, *Handbook of the New Public Library in Boston* (Boston, 1895) describes the building in detail.

CHAPTER VIII

The New Library under Herbert Putnam

The dominant purpose in the administration of a library is to have the books used, and used as freely as possible, consistent with their safety.

—HERBERT PUTNAM

The fine thing about Boston is that when a matter of this sort comes up, it always proves to be a burning question.

—CHARLES FOLLEN McKIM

DURING the first week of February 1895 the doors of the new library—fortified by placards requesting all who entered to wipe their feet—were open to allow Bostonians to come in from the slush of Copley Square and inspect the building. Although the mural decorations were not in place and carpenters' hammers were still heard, the books had been moved from Boylston Street and visitors, during these days, had a foretaste of the conveniences that would soon be available. Instead of seats for 200 readers, there was place for 900. In the old library 300 reference volumes had been on open shelves. Here there were six thousand in Bates Hall that might be taken down and read, as if at home, without the intervention of an attendant, and 5,800 that might similarly be consulted in the Patent Library. With only the simple formality of signing a register, 91,540 volumes were available for direct consultation on the Special Libraries floor, while in addition, a Children's Room— dreamed of by Justin Winsor, but never achieved for want of space —placed three thousand books within the unhampered reach of young readers. It offered an extraordinary contrast to Boylston

Street, and suggested that an institution whose 628,297 volumes—exceeded only by the Library of Congress—gave it the second place in the country at last had a dignified and commodious home. Moreover the use of this admirable building was to be directed by a skilful and inventive Librarian.

More than seventeen years had passed since the *Sunday Herald* had published its biting little fable about the ship that went to sea without any captain. During fourteen of those years two learned and conscientious men had held the nominal title of Librarian without either the responsibilities or the prerogatives of command. When Herbert Putnam took over on 11 February 1895 the ship had its first real captain since the departure of Justin Winsor. Few appointments have caused so much general satisfaction, for the lack of competent direction had caused grave misgivings in past years. The *Transcript,* on 6 February, summed up popular feeling in an editorial beginning:

> A chorus of praise fills the cold air of Boston, and the morning papers sing together. The new librarian, Mr. Putnam, is hailed with good wishes on every hand. It was a fortunate, a dramatic moment for the appointment of a librarian, and both he and the trustees who have appointed him deserve congratulation on the time and place chosen.

Herbert Putnam, a son of the New York publisher, was a member of the Harvard class of 1883, and, at the time of his appointment, practicing law in Boston. But seven of his thirty-three years had been spent as a librarian in Minneapolis, first in charge of the local Athenæum and later as head of the newly established Minneapolis Public Library. He was a man of imagination, energy, and executive ability, who had, moreover—as a friend of his once observed to C. K. Bolton—a "clever way of keeping a guarding and controlling hand over men without offending them." In addition, he entered office under different circumstances than his predecessors, for the Trustees had come to a realization—made public in their 1895 report—that "the responsibility for the proper administration of the Library in all its various departments must rest practically upon the Librarian, to whom the success or failure of the Library to meet the just wants of the public must really be due."

Changes were also taking place in the board, for Professor Henry W. Haynes had resigned the previous year and had been replaced by Josiah H. Benton, Jr., a New Hampshireman practicing law in Boston, who was intimately associated with the affairs of the Old Colony Railroad. Phineas Pierce, a Trustee since 1888, found Benton's company so uncongenial that he resigned almost immediately upon the appointment, and was replaced in the autumn of 1894 by Dr. Henry P. Bowditch. In April 1895 Herbert Putnam was made Clerk of the Corporation, and as William R. Richards did not wish to serve another term as Trustee, the Reverend James DeNormandie of the First Church in Roxbury was appointed in his place.

The new building was opened for public use on 11 March 1895, except for the Newspaper Reading Room and the Special Libraries floor, which were not ready until 3 May and 4 November respectively. Although work on the electric light plant occasioned some irregularity in early months, the closing hour was extended from nine to ten o'clock, while all departments of the library were regularly open on Sundays from two to ten. Books could thus, for the first time, be withdrawn on Sundays as well as on weekdays, for in the old building Bates Hall alone had been open, for reading on the premises. The *Transcript,* in describing the 11 March opening, spoke with pleasure of the "air of eagerness wherewith readers found their places" and the manner in which the arts of architecture, sculpture and painting became "but a frame for the figure of the humblest citizen seeking and securing the use of a book." As a subtle testimony to the refining influences of environment, it added a little anecdote of

> . . . a reader, seeking the registration room, [who] asked one of the stately policemen adorning the opening day, "Which way shall I go to the desk where we are to take out books?" He replied affably, "I ain't had no instructions yet." Then the academic atmosphere of the place swept over his spirit and he stood corrected before himself. "I haven't had no instructions yet," he called softly after the vanishing reader, with an accent of exquisite content.

Gears necessarily ground somewhat in the first weeks of operation, for books classified with a view to the alcoves of the old building did not always fall in convenient locations in the new stacks. The book railway kept breaking down; call slips jammed in the pneumatic tubes, and other mechanical devices needed adjustment. All these problems causing delays in service were soluble, and Putnam was constantly seeking means for their solution. It was characteristic that he begged readers to report delays of more than fifteen minutes in delivery with the words, "Such a complaint will not be deemed an intrusive grievance, but a service." This was entirely in keeping with Putnam's order to the staff, issued the day after opening.

> Any person, who for any reason cannot be properly attended to or have his wants supplied in the ordinary routine, or expresses a dissatisfaction which cannot be allayed by explanation from the attendants, is to have an opportunity to confer with the librarian.

> The librarian will depend upon the attendants to bear this instruction in mind and see to it that every such person having complaint or grievance, whether just or unjust, or unable to get the material he desires in the ordinary course, shall be conducted to him.

During April 1895 Edwin A. Abbey and John Singer Sargent brought to Boston the first of their paintings for the library. When these were installed, McKim, Mead and White, with the permission of the Trustees, invited a group of friends to inspect them, after the usual closing hour, on 25 April. The effect of the decorations is best described in the journal of Thomas Russell Sullivan.

> *April 25.* The architects, McKim, Mead and White, gave a reception this evening in their beautiful Public Library to Abbey and Sargent, the painters, whose decorative work was unveiled for the first time. There were two hundred guests, men and women, forty of whom came over from New York for the night. It was a splendid affair of brilliant jewels and costumes which can never be repeated, for the building now becomes the People's Palace, making further fashionable exclusion there impossible. An orchestra played on the landing of the marble staircase, up and down which the pretty women strolled in all their glory of satin, lace and diamonds. It happened to be a very warm night, and through the open windows of the court the fountain flashed and sparkled, throwing its tallest jet almost to the roof. The Abbey and

Sargent pictures overwhelmed us all. Five of the former's Holy
Grail series are finished, covering half the wall-space. They are
brilliant dramatic scenes, well composed, glowing with color.
Sargent chose for his subject "The World's Religions," and has put
up one niched end of the Hall leading to the Special Libraries, a
confusion of pagan symbolisms in arch and lunette, with a frieze
of prophets below. In the centre of the lunette the children of
Israel, in a strong group, plead for help under the rod of Egypt
and the Assyrian yoke. Assyria raises his sword to strike them
down, but the hand of God arrests his arm. To right and left are
pagan attributes and idols; above, the seraphs's crimson wings. To
Moloch and Astarte the vaulted arch is given, with Nut, the Vault
of Heaven Goddess above and behind them, dominating all. The
scheme is tremendously ambitious, and to be understood must be
studied carefully. It is a powerful and most original work, which
will hold its own with any decorative masterpiece of modern times.
The prophets are superb figures, wonderfully painted, with great
folds of drapery, white, black, and brown. Moses stands in the
centre, worked out in high relief, holding the tablets. The group
on the left despairs; that on the right looks toward the light with
outstretched arms, and these figures are incomparable. After the
reception, some of us were invited to a supper at the Algonquin
Club, toastmaster Judge Howland of New York, who brought out
speeches from Sargent, Governor Russell, and Henry Higginson.
Bed at 3:30 a.m.

Sullivan's enthusiasm was so widely shared that within a few months
Edward Robinson of the Museum of Fine Arts was successful in
raising among local admirers of the decorations a subscription of
$15,000 that would permit Sargent to continue his work along the
lateral walls of the third floor gallery. For sheer artistic excitement
and enthusiasm there had never been anything in Boston quite to
equal this unveiling of Abbey's and Sargent's work; it was not to be
matched until New Year's night 1903 when Mrs. John L. Gardner
first threw open the beauties of Fenway Court. The *Transcript* and
Herald were warm in their praises, but the *Journal* and *Traveler*
undertook to snipe at the architects for having given the reception,
and at President Abbott for having permitted it. This latest hue and
cry, under the headline "WHO OWNS LIBRARY?" was one too
much, and on 1 May 1895 Abbott resigned. The vision of the building was his; he had seen it through to completion; it was in working

order, and there was no longer any reason why he should, to the detriment of his own affairs, give endless time and thought only to receive the brickbats of sensational journalists by way of thanks. The more sober newspapers expressed regret at his decision and genuine appreciation of his services. Boston saw little of him thereafter, for in January 1897 Abbott became the first Director of the American Academy in Rome, and although continuing in that post only to 1903, lived chiefly in Italy until his death in 1931. The record of his accomplishment remains in Copley Square, although few Bostonians now recognize it as such. Former Mayor Prince was elected President in October 1895, while Samuel Carr was appointed a Trustee for the remainder of Abbott's unexpired term.

The prospect of the new library had attracted important gifts during the years that the building was under construction. In January 1893 Judge Chamberlain announced the intention of bequeathing his extensive collection of historical documents, manuscripts and autographs on the condition that a special room be furnished for their safe lodging, and his willingness immediately to transfer the larger part of the material on deposit. As this offer was accepted with enthusiasm, space was at once provided and the collection installed in the new building during 1894. In the winter of 1893–1894 steps were taken to secure the deposit of certain books of President John Adams, who had, in his eighty-seventh year, presented the town of Quincy with "the fragments of my Library, which still remain in my possession, excepting a few that I shall reserve for my consolation in the few days that remain to me." The 2,756 volumes thus given batted from pillar to post in Quincy for sixty years, with considerable loss, theft and mutilation, until in 1882 the remnants were placed in the new Thomas Crane Public Library. The phenomenal range of John Adams's intellectual interests made his library of peculiar interest, and, although many of the books had been mutilated by autograph thieves, others contained marginal annotations of singular value in tracing the evolution of their owner's ideas. President Abbott subsequently proposed to Charles Francis Adams, in November 1893, that the books be deposited in a special alcove in the new Boston Public Library, on the theory that they would be more accessible to historical students than in Quincy. As this met with approval in Quincy, John Adams's library was transferred to Copley Square, and a catalogue prepared by Lindsay Swift, who had since 1878 been at work under James L. Whitney in the Catalogue Department of the Public Library. Thus, as with the Prince Library a quarter of a century before, the deposit of an extremely valuable collection had been secured chiefly because adequate space was available for its suitable lodging.

Although both the Chamberlain collection and the John Adams library ranked as trophies, increasing the prestige of the institution but really of value only to an occasional scholar, major gifts by William C. Todd of Atkinson, New Hampshire, and Allen A. Brown of Boston, greatly broadened the scope and increased the popular usefulness of the Public Library. Notwithstanding the practice of many of the early proprietary and mercantile libraries of furnishing numerous current newspapers in their reading rooms, the Boston Public Library had intentionally avoided such a development. Justin Winsor in his 1868 report had stated flatly, "a newsroom our hall was not intended to be, and we offer no comparison with other reading rooms in that respect," pointing out that while the Boston Athenæum subscribed to 115 magazines and 82 newspapers, the Public Library took 287 magazines and only four newspapers, all foreign. Even the Athenæum's number of papers was small beside the 200 of the New York and Philadelphia Mercantile Libraries and the 300 provided in the comparable institution in San Francisco. Although the number gradually increased, to the satisfaction of the Lower Hall's chair warmers, who wished to enjoy the comfort of the room without taxing their intellects, the Public Library never attempted a broad and representative collection until 1893 when William C. Todd offered an annual gift of $2,000 for the purpose. His letter of 16 June clearly explains his motives.

> Boston is a city of rare privileges, but it lacks one possessed by many others, viz., a place where all—citizens and strangers—can enter freely, and read the leading papers of the day; some such place as the Cooper Institute of New York affords. The Boston Public Library is well supplied with magazines, but not with newspapers. It is too late to discuss the value of newspapers—they have become a necessity. The business man, the student in every depart-

ment, the politician anxious to feel the public pulse, the men who, like the Athenians of old, "spent their time either to tell or hear some new thing,"—all, of every pursuit and condition, must read the newspapers to learn what has transpired the world over. The press has become the great agency by which information is diffused, leading opinions discussed, and public opinion moulded. . . . It is not enough to read one paper, and that partisan, if any one would be correctly informed and judge clearly; yet many newspapers are too expensive for ordinary readers, and a large part are desired only for occasional use.

Accordingly, if the Trustees would provide a suitable room in the new building, Mr. Todd promised an adequate annual gift, and, eventually, a fund of $50,000 "to secure forever the annual payment." This generous offer was gratefully accepted, and the lecture hall (occupying nearly half of the Boylston Street façade on the second floor) redesignated as a Newspaper Room. The gift was extremely welcome, for as the Trustees pointed out in their letter to Mr. Todd:

> The free Public Library—"open to all"—was not established for the sole use of students and scholars, but for the enjoyment of the people of all classes and professions, especially the "plain people," to quote the language of our martyred President. These latter will greatly appreciate your benefaction.

When this Newspaper Room was opened on 3 May 1895, some two months after the building as a whole, 125 papers were available on the racks, with the intention announced of increasing the number to two hundred. By 1896 there were 318, of which 111 were foreign. In October 1897 Mr. Todd carried out his promise of giving $50,000 to place the newspaper collection on a permanent basis.

Allen A. Brown's gift in 1894 of his collection of music and musical literature extended the usefulness of the Public Library in still another direction. While the individual musician accumulates, and wears out, the texts necessary for his own performance, he is unlikely to go far beyond that. The collection of a musical library involves very peculiar problems, for full orchestral scores when published are expensive, while some are available only in manuscript copies that are rented rather than sold, and then under rigid proprietary restrictions. Thus such collecting requires not only specialized knowledge but a degree of patience and bibliographical enthusiasm that is beyond the range of the average musician. The works of Bach, Mozart, Haydn and Beethoven do not find their way to his shelves with the ease by which a poet may arm himself with Chaucer, Donne and Keats. Mr. Brown's gift therefore had peculiar significance to a city that, since the foundation of the New England Conservatory of Music in 1867 and the establishment of the Boston Symphony Orchestra in the eighties, was becoming increasingly conscious of the art of music. His collection was designed for study rather than performance, and consequently he provided that no volumes were to circulate, and no instruments were to be allowed in the room set apart for the books. The Allen A. Brown Music Library was installed in the handsome room directly over the main staircase, and opening out of the Sargent Gallery on the third floor.

The commodious provision of space for special libraries on the third floor attracted the gift of smaller collections upon particular themes. In 1896 Colonel Thomas Wentworth Higginson presented a thousand-volume "Galatea Collection of Books relating to the History of Women," while Miss Victorine Thomas Artz of Chicago established the "Longfellow Memorial Collection," by the gift of $10,000, the income of which was to be spent for the purchase of "valuable rare editions of the writings, either in verse or prose, of American and foreign authors." In the same year, the Twentieth Regiment Association of Massachusetts Volunteer Infantry—which had already given one of the lions on the main staircase—took steps toward providing an endowment of $5,000, received the following April, for books of a military and patriotic character, while Mr. and Mrs. James M. Codman began a collection of landscape architecture in memory of two members of that profession, Henry Sargent Codman and Philip Codman. These private gifts were particularly welcome, for it was recognized that, with the greatly increased expense of operating the new building, additions to the trust funds were highly necessary if books were to be purchased on a proper scale. The Trustees, in their 1896 report, reminded friends of the Library that, out of a $225,000 city appropriation, but $25,000 was available for books, and that this barely sufficed for the more popular departments.

> The city has erected for the library a noble building; but the moneys it provides for its maintenance must be directed to the educational needs of the great mass of citizens. The funds required to enable the institution to render the service which a great reference library can perform for the higher scholarship must be contributed, as we have said, by individuals.

There was a proper concern, however, lest collecting in such specialties, even by private generosity, run away with itself. The 1895 Examining Committee, reiterating that the Library's chief function was popular—that is "placing at the disposal of the general public of books which, in the broadest sense, the general public may find either useful or wholesomely interesting"—urged that the Trustees decide, in relation to the other resources of the neighborhood, upon "a definitely announced policy as to what special subjects shall be kept up by the Public Library and what shall be disregarded." This committee realized, earlier than some enthusiastic collectors, that "to make any single library totally comprehensive is manifestly impossible." The Trustees wisely adopted a policy of uniting the "four great libraries of Boston and Cambridge and the several special libraries of Boston to avoid unnecessary duplication" and to "develop certain lines of subjects in which each should endeavor to be exhaustive."

Such a policy became increasingly important with the expense involved in an orderly development of the branches. The beginning of the system was, like so many other things, due to Justin Winsor, but without his guiding hand there was little central control in the following years. An Inspector of Branches was mentioned in the 1894 report as a desirable innovation, but it remained for Herbert Putnam, who went about matters with the effectiveness of Winsor, to place the system on a properly planned basis. He created the office of Supervisor of Branches and Stations, in 1896, "to unify the outlying system, to strengthen the collection of books, to improve the equipment, and to introduce uniform and modern methods of administration." The open shelf system and children's sections were rapidly extended to the branches, while reclassification of their books by a common method was undertaken. With the opening of the remodelled West Church as the West End Branch, on 3 February 1896, the somewhat dubious North End Branch was eliminated. Thus the system comprised, in 1896, ten branch libraries, four branch reading rooms (Lower Mills, Mattapan, Mt. Bowdoin and North Brighton), and twelve delivery stations. Two libraries (Brighton and West End) were in separate buildings devoted exclusively to their use, and owned by the city; six (Charlestown, Dorchester, East Boston, Jamaica Plain, South End and West Roxbury) were in city buildings devoted in part to other municipal uses. The Roxbury Branch was in the library building leased from the Trustees of the Fellowes Athenæum, while the South Boston Branch occupied rented rooms in a commercial building.

In reading Putnam's reports one inevitably feels that, almost by his very arrival, he brought the Public Library back to the heights of the great Winsor decade, when important things had been happening in every direction at once. A Special Libraries Department was established under the care of Otto Fleischner. Francis W. Lee was transferred from the Catalogue Department to the charge of the Printing Department, where linotype machines were installed for the composition of catalogue cards and other library printing.

In March 1895 a new system of graded service was put into effect whereby both appointment to the library service and promotion from grade to grade within was by examination. The adoption of the system "created both hope and despondency," as Putnam drily observed, "hope in the minds of the younger employés, more fresh from school or college, and despondency in employés who lack an academic training, or whose academic knowledge has lapsed from disuse." Five grades, each with a minimum and maximum salary, were established. Once the maximum was reached, no further increase in pay was possible, save by promotion to a higher grade, which was dependent both upon examination and the capacity demonstrated by previous service.

The *Bulletin*, which had appeared quarterly since its foundation, was published each month beginning in 1896, when Lindsay Swift was appointed Editor of Library Publications. The old quarterly had been printed in an edition of 1800 and sold—at five cents per copy for residents of Boston and twenty-five cents for non-residents —but 5,000 copies of the new monthly, which listed accessions of the previous month, were issued and distributed free. A system of inter-library loans within Massachusetts was instituted in May 1896; lectures and exhibitions were provided on the Special Libraries floor, and in many ways the boundaries of the library were enlarged by Putnam's imagination and energy. In 1898 he brought Worthington C. Ford, formerly Chief of the Bureau of Statistics of the Treasury Department, from Washington to take charge of a newly created Department of Documents and Statistics.

Even the most cursory review of Putnam's accomplishments compels agreement with the *Boston Herald's* editorial comment of 6 April 1896, after the completion of his first year of administration.

> Mr. Putnam has not lost himself in the routine work of library management. Without neglecting any duty, he has risen to the conception of what the Public Library should be to the people of Boston. He has administered it in a liberal spirit, showing a willingness to accommodate the people wherever it was possible, and granting to scholars more and more the privileges which they desire. At the same time, he has kept the expenses of running the institution below the limit of expenditure provided by the city. How this could be done it is not easy to see, but it shows a control of details which will give the public the confidence that whatever may be asked for by the trustees of the Public Library will be worthily expended for its needs. The conclusion reached by most readers of this report will be that the administration of the library is in safe hands, and that it is destined in the near future to be far more influential in the best directions than it is today.

Herbert Putnam's administration was, incidentally, a kind of shakedown cruise for the new building, during which its virtues and defects were carefully studied with a view to future improvement. Inevitably there were difficulties to working in a palace, even when it was conceived as a "palace for the people." H. Carrington Bolton, who had come from New York for a few weeks' work in Bates Hall soon after its opening in 1895, found that

> The introduction of the much-lauded decorations by eminent artists is a great drawback to the undisturbed enjoyment of the privileges for which the building is primarily erected. The throngs

of people who crowd the grand staircase to visit the splendid building are not content with gazing at the wall decorations by Abbey, Sargent and others, but must needs tramp through Bates Hall as well, clicking their heels on the stone floor throughout its entire length. One morning, as I sat at a table in the reading-room, I noted, within the space of one hour, a troop of eleven women tourists, two bands of school-girls personally conducted by their mistresses, besides scores of individual sight-seers of all ages, alone or in group of varying numbers.

Although Mr. Bolton and others had misgivings about conducting "their researches amid the social surroundings of a public art museum," the die was cast. In an article in *The Forum,* Herbert Putnam observed:

> In the new building for the Boston Public Library there has been a definite and pronounced design to produce a work of art. Such a structure has in itself undoubted educational value; but its erection cannot of course augment the functions of the library which is to inhabit it. It represents chiefly a sort of apotheosis of the confidence which the American people have come to feel in the public library as a branch of education.

During 1895 the largest of the Puvis de Chavannes panels—the Muses welcoming Genius, the Messenger of Light—had been installed on the main staircase, and in October 1896 the last of his panels arrived from Paris. The completion of this great composition attracted less than suitable attention because of a ludicrous tempest in a teapot arising from a generous gesture of Charles Follen McKim. As early as April 1890 McKim had expressed the desire to give a fountain for the library courtyard as a memorial to his wife. As his offer was both gratefully and promptly accepted by the Trustees, McKim devoted especial care and thought to a decoration that was at once to be the final adornment of his beautiful court and a fitting tribute to Julia Appleton McKim. H. T. Parker, writing from New York to the *Boston Transcript* for 23 May 1895, gave the first public news of the promised gift, telling how McKim

> . . . chose as his especial care the fountain in the interior court, designing it in the fashion of an impluvium of a Roman house—a shallow, quadrangular basin, framed in a broad rim of marble, and reflecting in its water, as in a mirror, the surrounding

walls and the open sky above. At first only a jet of water was to spout upward from the centre of the basin; but subsequently he decided to adorn the fountain with sculpture. Delays of various sorts then arose, and it was not until Mr. MacMonnies's visit, some months since, to New York, that a final decision was made. The sculptor then proffered to Mr. McKim his bronze "Bacchante and Child," and in spite of many suggestions that it remain in this city, it will become the chief part of the fountain in the court of the Boston Library.

Frederic Macmonnies, who was still working upon his Bacchante in Paris, had sent to New York only a study on a greatly reduced scale, but it was fine enough to convince McKim that his quest was over. His appreciation was shared in Paris, for, on finding that the original bronze was destined for Boston, the French government ordered a replica for the Luxembourg. H. T. P. thus described the bronze, which was slightly larger than life:

> The nude Bacchante is in vigorous and joyous motion, poised on the toes of her left foot, her springy weight falling altogether on her left leg, her right uplifted and her bended knee thrust forward, as, half-dancing, she pursues her way. In her left hand she raises a bunch of grapes high above her head. With her right arm bent about him as though to make a seat of her elbow, she carries a naked child, that presses its head eagerly against her throat and cheek, and gazes with wide-eyed and open mouthed eagerness at the quivering grapes.

He found in the vitality of the work great charm and the "mingled suggestion of felicitous imagination and easy executive skill." It would be highly decorative in the courtyard.

> With its vitality and gaiety, and its suggestion of the joy of life, it promises to gain by contrast with the austere dignity of its surroundings. In giving it, Mr. McKim and Mr. MacMonnies will give Boston one of the few admirable examples of imaginative sculpture in public places in America.

Alas for H. T. P.'s prophecy, they gave Boston instead a *cause célèbre!*

In July 1896, the reduced model of Bacchante was submitted to the Boston Art Commission so that their approval might be obtained before the full scale statue was shipped from New York. The Commission invited a "Committee of Experts" to report their individual opinions upon the artistic merits of the statue. This group took more than two months to consider the matter, but finally came up with five pro and four contra. Augustus Saint-Gaudens and Daniel Chester French were among those in favor, but, alas, the supposedly

BACCHANTE

infallible Charles Eliot Norton was on the other side. After considerable debate a vote to approve the acceptance of Bacchante was defeated four to one, the only favorable vote being cast by F. O. Prince, who was both a Trustee of the Public Library and a member of the Art Commission. The Secretary was then "instructed to inform the Trustees of the Public Library that, while recognizing the remarkable technical merits of Mr. Macmonnies' statue . . . as a work of art, this Commission does not regard it as suited to the Public Library building." Unfortunately, former Mayor Prince, in talking to an *Advertiser* reporter after the meeting, admitted that no questions of artistic merit or nudity had troubled the Commission, but only the appropriateness of placing "a monument to inebriety" in the library. This comment immediately caused poor Bacchante, who was simply on trial as a work of art, to be placed in triple jeopardy on grounds of intemperance and immorality. It also caused other cities to laugh. The *New York Herald* reported the affair under the headline "Too naughty for Boston Library" while the *Springfield Republican* described it as "a fine example of the continuing Puritanism of Boston." Although the *Boston Post* shrieked: "No Tipsy Statue for the Public Library, Messrs. Trustees" and campaigned militantly, other local papers joined New York in amusement. The *Advertiser* proposed placing the statue of a policeman near Bacchante "in order that the Boston idea may be fully represented," while the *Globe* offered Mr. McKim the suggestion that he substitute "a nice moral statue—of a Sunday school teacher, say." Thomas Russell Sullivan, outraged by the decision, wrote in his journal:

> Considering that the Commission has never taken the pains to see the group, the discourtesy of this proceeding passes belief. Their verdict of inappropriateness was based entirely upon photographs and a reduction of the bronze eighteen inches high. The wording of their refusal is hopelessly provincial, and the tone of the press in commenting favorably upon their course is equally so. McKim and Saint-Gaudens, our foremost sculptor, wrote strong letters recommending the group—in vain. The depressing little incident seems to drop us back a century or two towards the dark ages.

Two of the Public Library Trustees, Dr. Henry P. Bowditch, an eminent professor in the Harvard Medical School, and the Reverend James De Normandie, so successfully taxed the Art Commission with decision upon insufficient knowledge that "in the course of justice and official courtesy" (as Sullivan put it) the Commission agreed to have Bacchante temporarily installed in the library courtyard so that she might be seen *in situ* with the fountain playing. Although the moment for dispassionate criticism had passed, if one may judge by the *Boston Post*'s reticently subtle headline of 11 November: "BACCHANTE COMING. Art Commission Will Set Up Naked Drunken Woman for Inspection," a private view was held on 15 November. T. R. Sullivan considered it "an amusing day," and noted

This Sunday morning, McKim's gift, the rejected Bacchante, was set up in the Library court with the fountain playing about it, and the solemn Art Commission with its experts in tow assembled there for deliberate inspection. When about noon, the august conclave retired into secret session, a hundred or more invited guests were turned loose in the court for their private satisfaction, discussion and argument. The scene had its comic side, although a strong, virulent minority, finding the group inappropriate as well as indecent, conducted itself with portentous earnestness. The majority, however, including many intelligent women, thought it singularly fine and beautiful, and frankly hoped it would remain. One important fact was made clear at once. So far as scale goes, the group is in perfect harmony with the surrounding arcade. In this particular, at least, it stands as if in obedience to the laws of predestination.

McKim, who had come on from New York to see the show, discreetly looked down on the court from an upper window. The suppressed excitement of the crowd, he told Sullivan, surprised and pleased him. "The fine thing about Boston," he remarked, "is that when a matter of this sort comes up, it proves always to be a burning question. The crowd was like a French one in its movement and gesticulation." Some of the old reticences still survived, for the Rector of Trinity Church, wishing to see without being seen, was, through the tactful consideration of Dr. De Normandie, specially admitted at 11 p.m. for a most private of private views!

After seeing the statue, the Art Commission's "Experts" wavered, seven approving and two (one of whom was Norton) continuing in absolute opposition. In view of this change of heart, the Art Commission reversed its former decision and, on 17 November, approved the statue by a vote of four to one. The statue thus remained on public view during the rest of November.

Although now officially blessed, Bacchante was still the target of violent abuse. The Reverend James B. Brady, preaching Sunday night, the 15th, denounced such an infernal representation of "strumpetry" and shouted:

Erect a memorial, if you will, to Benedict Arnold, to John Wilkes Booth, to Guiteau, or to Josephine Mansfield, but for the sake of virtue, God, the country, the commonwealth and the city, don't set up a memorial to the worst type of harlotry with which the earth was ever afflicted.

Away with the horrid thing, and bury it where the Bostonians buried the tea in 1773.

Bacchante was removed to winter quarters in the library basement, while a permanent pedestal was being prepared. During her absence petitions and counter-petitions circulated. Congregational and Baptist groups denounced the statue while T. R. Sullivan begged the Trustees to disregard interference. On 14 December he wrote:

> Both cats have their backs well up, and the fur is likely to fly before spring comes. I have several volunteers who are carrying my paper about, and we hope to overwhelm the howling dervishes by our numbers if not by rational arguments. Against the group are arrayed President Eliot, Professor Norton, Robert Grant, Barrett Wendell, and others, who regard it as "a menace to the Commonwealth." Their allies, the sensational clergy, go a few steps further, and declare that this begins a righteous crusade against the intolerable indecencies of the antique in the Art Museum. Verily, impropriety makes strange bedfellows!

Criticism descended to a personal plane. It was asserted that the original of Bacchante was none other than the Parisian artists' model Sarah Brown, the reputed daughter of an English peer and a beautiful Jewish circus rider. In support of this identification, a drawing by Charles Dana Gibson of Sarah (very fully clothed) and Macmonnies, taking a friendly glass at a café table, was reproduced. This was hotly denied by those who claimed that the virtuous Mlle. Beatrice W—— was Macmonnies model! Such inanities continued until the following May when McKim withdrew his gift. "This," according to T. R. Sullivan, "at the instigation of the Public Library Trustees, who decided that they did not care to face the music. The Philistines be upon us, and they have conquered!" J. T. Trowbridge, who thought no better of this "apotheosis of Philistia," drew a sketch of a liberally clothed "bicycle goddess" as an acceptable substitute. The Metropolitan Museum promptly accepted Bacchante from McKim, who wrote Macmonnies in Paris: "Removed from Puritan surroundings to this Metropolis, where she belongs, I think we may regard the question of her virtue as settled for all time." George R. White promptly made his feelings clear by purchasing from Macmonnies the second bronze replica—the first having gone to the Luxembourg—and presenting it to the Museum of Fine Arts! Thus Macmonnies' Bacchante, having been banished from one side of Copley Square, settled on the other, remaining there happily and without scandal until the Museum moved to its present building in 1909. Although she adorns the courtyard enclosed by the Decorative Arts wing on Huntington Avenue, not a few Bostonians still hope that she may some day return to the fountain in the Public Library, where *they*—if not McKim—think she belongs.

While citizens of Boston were making a national laughing stock of themselves over the Bacchante "scandal," Herbert Putnam quietly continued his efforts to fit the new building to the needs of the library. Thanks largely to his skill in increasing the public usefulness of the institution, it soon appeared that the building was, if anything, too small rather than too large. Bates Hall, which had seemed vast, was by the end of 1896 so overcrowded that some wiseacres proposed glassing over the courtyard and converting it to a reading room! The building had, after all, been planned in 1888, after a decade of professional stagnation, without even the nominal advice of Judge Chamberlain. It was small wonder that the result, handsome as it was, did not in every respect meet the needs of an institution that, after dozing peacefully under a tree for eighteen years, had not only rejoined the race but rapidly returned to the lead. By 1898 the changes required for more efficient administration, more rapid delivery of books, better accommodation of readers, and improved ventilating arrangements were so imperative that an Act of the Legislature, and subsequent action of the City Council, provided a special appropriation of $100,000 to make them possible. The heating and ventilating system was enlarged. In order to double the Children's Room in size, space was fitted up beyond the court for the Patent Library. The Newspaper Room was moved to its present location on the first floor, thus becoming more accessible and freeing for use as a Lecture Hall space originally intended for that purpose. The Librarian's Office was thrown into the working area of the Delivery Room, where improved tubes and carriers to speed up the issuing of books were concentrated, while a section of stack was rebuilt to provide a new set of administrative offices. On the first floor the Ordering Department was doubled in size, and the new Branch Division accommodated in a former stack area. Offices for the Editor, the Chiefs of the Issue and the Ordering Departments, and staff luncheon and locker rooms were provided in Entresol A. The courtyard remained unspoiled, but its carriage entrance from Boylston Street was sacrificed to make space for a periodical room. The loss of this architectural feature is the more to be regretted because the 1898 abandonment of the Boylston Street entrance made possible, a few years hence, the planting of a subway exit squarely in the middle of that façade. Thus today, as A. Kingsley Porter sadly remarked in 1918, "this entire monumental composition leads up impressively to a hole in the ground." Upon the completion of the work, Putnam observed:

> The improvements above described do not, indeed, absolutely perfect the building for present uses. The issue of the books from the stacks for reference readers, and the issue for borrowers, are still dependent upon one set of attendants, one system of mechanism and one channel of issue. The books required from the stacks by the reference reader in Bates Hall must still be forwarded to him from the issue desk by hand, through a public room at times crowded with sightseers. And, ample as is the general space provided for readers, and sufficient (for a few years) as is the shelving, there is very great need of rooms set off for special collections for the use of classes and for specialized research. But most embarrassing difficulties have been overcome, and the most pressing needs of the moment have been met; and what has been done will add greatly to the comfort of the public, and greatly to convenience in administration.

In the fifty-five years that have followed, the chess game of shifting space to meet "the most pressing needs of the moment" has become perennial. This playing of the gambit was Herbert Putnam's last major contribution to the Boston Public Library, for on 13 March 1899 President McKinley appointed him Librarian of Congress. For the good of the country and the library profession there could have been no finer choice, but the accomplishments of Herbert Putnam's forty years of distinguished service in Washington inevitably cause regret that he had so brief a time in Boston. In comparing the Boston Public Library as he found it and as he left it, one may well imagine what he would have done in a term of office no longer than Justin Winsor's ten years.

SOURCES

For Herbert Putnam's administration, see Charles F. D. Belden, "The Library Service of Herbert Putnam in Boston," and R. R. Bowker, "The Appointment of Herbert Putnam as Librarian of Congress," in *Essays offered to Herbert Putnam* (New Haven: Yale University Press, 1929), pp. 10–21.

Passages from the *Journal of Thomas Russell Sullivan 1891–1903* (Boston: Houghton Mifflin Company, 1917) tell of the opening of the building, and of the enlightened side of the Bacchante controversy. Judge Robert Grant in *Fourscore, An Autobiography* (Boston: Houghton Mifflin Company, 1934), pp. 292–293, recalled after almost forty years his activity on the other side. Nearer the event he had introduced the commotion into his novel *The Chippendales* (New York: Charles Scribner's Sons, 1909). The story of the Reverend E. Winchester Donald's midnight private view of Bacchante was told by the Reverend James De Normandie at a dinner given in 1909 by J. H. Benton to my predecessor at the Athenæum, Charles Knowles Bolton, who recorded it in his diary. I am grateful to Mr. Robert Peabody Bellows for allowing me to examine the records of the Art Commission of the City of Boston in regard to Bacchante. *Boston Public Library Newspaper Clippings Jan. 3, 1895 to Jan. 25, 1897* (T.R. 27.21) contain some delightful bits of journalistic nonsense. I treated the subject in somewhat more detail than is possible here in a paper "The Vicissitudes of Bacchante in Boston" that was read at the 19 May 1954 meeting of the Club of Odd Volumes, and printed in the *New England Quarterly*, xxvii (December 1954), 435–454.

CHAPTER IX

The Administrations of Whitney and Wadlin

> The problem of working the Public Library,
> therefore, is the problem of bringing its books and
> other materials into the most general and extensive
> public use within the limit of the amount of money
> which the taxpayers are willing to pay for that use.
> —JOSIAH H. BENTON

UPON Herbert Putnam's departure for Washington, James L. Whitney, Chief of the Catalogue Department, was appointed Acting Librarian. This modest and painstaking bibliographer had entered the service of the Public Library in 1869, thirteen years after his graduation from Yale. By 1872 he had become not only Deputy in the Catalogue Department, but Principal Assistant (or a kind of second mate) to Justin Winsor, while two years later, upon the death of William A. Wheeler, Whitney was promoted to the dual post of Assistant Superintendent (later called Principal Assistant Librarian) and Chief of the Catalogue Department. Although his executive functions became obscured in the early nineties during the unacknowledged quasi-librarianship of President Abbott, and were not reaffirmed during Putnam's administration, Whitney's quarter century of meticulous supervision of the Catalogue Department represented unique continuity. Save for two female clerks who had come to work in 1868, no one had been longer employed in the library than he. Herbert Putnam's departure was shortly followed by the resignation and death of former Mayor Frederick O. Prince, President of the Trustees, who was succeeded by Solomon Lincoln, a lawyer of the Harvard class of 1857. The old Boylston

Street library, which had been leased in October 1896 to the management of the Bowdoin Square Theater for unlearned use as a pop concert hall and beer garden, was in February 1899 sold for $850,000 to the Frederick L. Ames estate, which demolished it and erected the present Colonial Building on the site. As the proceeds were turned back into the City Sinking Fund, the library was deprived of rents that had been of material assistance during the previous two and a half years.

Thus 1899 was a disoriented year so far as future planning was concerned. Several unemployed politicians—invariably referred to as "the Hon." X. Y. Snodgrass—were "prominently mentioned" by their friends as suitable candidates for the librarianship, but in the end, only three days before Christmas, the Trustees reached the welcome decision of appointing Whitney Librarian. The sudden death in June 1899 of Philip Henry Savage, who had served as Putnam's secretary, caused general consternation in Boston. As the loss of this promising young man, "rich in love, if not in fame,"— to quote Bliss Carman's elegy upon him—left a void in the library administration, Otto Fleischner, a native of Bohemia who was Custodian of Special Libraries, was in January 1900 appointed Assistant Librarian.

Whitney's interest in historical matters was reflected in the prompt establishment of a Department of Manuscripts under the charge of Worthington C. Ford, the energetic Chief of the Department of Documents and Statistics, who, in collaboration with Lindsay Swift, promoted the publication in the *Bulletin* of many of the more important historical documents owned by the Library. Ford's activities in assembling public documents and squeezing from them statistical data concerning commerce, transportation, labor, production and finance amounted, among other things, to a forerunner of a business reference service. The Manuscript Department's enthusiastic accumulation of papers and broadsides relating to the early history of Massachusetts and Boston represented, however, an opportunistic collection of material that lay more properly within the province of the Massachusetts Historical Society. The early years of the new century were, however, so full of dreams of expansion in every direction that in 1901 the Trustees purchased, through the knowledgeable assistance of Sydney C. Cockerell in London, some thirty-five examples of illuminated manuscripts, ranging from the twelfth to the sixteenth centuries. It is not easy to reconcile all this with the theories of popular education that brought the Public Library into being, particularly when so little money was available for the purchase of books. In 1899 the City appropriation, used for maintenance and operating expenses, was $255,000, while books had to be bought from the $12,337 received as income from trust funds. As the appropriation during the last year in the Boylston Street building had been only $175,000, the higher cost of maintaining the Copley Square library represented a sufficient drain on public funds to make it evident that more endowment must be secured. On this point, Putnam had spoken plainly in his last report.

> There is a general impression among citizens of Boston that the general and even development of the Library is amply assured by endowment and appropriation. This is an error which ought by every means to be corrected. On its popular side the Library is developing normally. The scholarly side is *not* developing in proper proportion. On this side the Library is relatively losing rank. It will not, cannot, regain this rank until the citizens of Boston come to its aid with further endowment.

In spite of frequent reminders, they did not jostle each other to do so. The first really substantial increase came only in May 1903 with the receipt of Robert Charles Billings's $100,000 bequest, while that remained in solitary splendor for rather a long time.

After three years as Librarian, and thirty-three in the service of the library, James L. Whitney resigned. A scholar by temperament, he had found the heavy responsibilities of administrative work uncongenial and taxing after a lifetime devoted to the minutiae of bibliography. As he was in his sixty-eighth year, the constant pressures of office may have weighed more heavily upon Whitney than they would have a decade or two earlier; in any event he turned over his duties as Librarian to Horace G. Wadlin on 1 February 1903, and thereafter became Chief of the Department of Documents and Statistics, with additional responsibility for the Department of Manuscripts, succeeding Worthington C. Ford who had resigned the previous September. In this subordinate niche, which was perhaps better suited to his temperament and strength, Whitney continued to serve the Library until his death on 25 September 1910.

The appointment of Horace G. Wadlin, Chief of the Massachusetts Bureau of Statistics of Labor, represented a new departure, for he was chosen on the theory that executive ability rather than knowledge of books or previous library experience was the qualification to be sought in a librarian. Born in Reading in 1851, he had entered an architect's office upon leaving school. In this profession he was responsible for building certain schools, fire stations, and various shingled and heavily-gabled private houses before entering the Massachusetts Legislature and becoming involved in census affairs. An unnamed Trustee of the Public Library explained to the Boston newspapers that his colleagues felt that the appointment of a Librarian "who has demonstrated his ability as a business man" was "in direct line with the wishes of Mayor Collins, who has indicated his desire for business administration of the city's functions by appointing business men to the board." Consequently it is in no way surprising that the emphasis of the next fourteen years in the life of the Public Library was upon orderly housekeeping, with little attempt to revive the energetic and imaginative experiments of Justin Winsor and Herbert Putnam.

There were many problems in reconciling limitations of funds and space with the demands of readers throughout the city. By moving the Binding and Printing Departments to rented quarters in Stanhope Street in 1902, space was created in the Copley Square Library for enlarging the accommodation of the Patent and Statistical Departments. In spite of constant worries about theft and damage, an increased number of books was placed upon open shelves, until by 1905 nearly 200,000 volumes were thus available between the central library and the branches. In the same year Wadlin noted the increasing responsibilities placed upon the Public Library by the tides of immigration.

> It is comparatively easy to attract the children of foreign-born parents, and to lead them by progressive stages into the world of English literature, particularly since the elementary schools are also opening the way; but many of the adults never master the new

language so as to read it easily. If the Public Library is to serve all classes, these must not be overlooked. Another phase of this demand is reflected in the remark of a young Bulgarian to the custodian of one of our reading rooms: "I read French and German, and am learning English; but unless I can read a Bulgarian book once in a while, I forget my native tongue." . . . There is a duty resting upon us of extending the influence of the library, as a civic institution, toward enlarging the life and broadening the intellectual outlook of those who have recently entered the ranks of American citizenship without preliminary training in the English tongue.

While recognizing these urgent calls, the preoccupation with the national standing of the library continued. Also in 1905, while expressing their regret that no important bequests or gifts of money had been received during the year, the Trustees noted:

> It is from such sources that the Library must provide the rare volumes and larger publications which it must possess in order to retain its high rank among the libraries of the world.

To compensate for the lack of gifts the Trustees reverted to the often tried and much debated practice of reducing purchases of fiction. Cutting down the number of novels always pleasingly increases the sense of self-righteousness from which certain Bostonians perennially suffer. It was in this vein, so unlike that of George Ticknor, that the Trustees wrote in May 1906:

> In reference to the purchases of books of fiction, the Trustees have continued to confine such purchases to works of authors of recognized distinction or of deserved popularity, and to works of obvious intrinsic merit. It is quite impossible, with the funds at the disposal of the Trustees, to purchase any large portion of the current fiction of the day, or the number of copies required to meet a popular demand; nor is it in the judgment of the Trustees desirable. The collections of the Library must be of more permanent value. It is not difficult for those who seek lighter literature to obtain it elsewhere.

These constantly recurring problems were attacked with fresh energy in May 1908 when Josiah H. Benton became President of the Trustees, succeeding the Reverend James De Normandie who had filled the office in the months following the death on 15 October

1907 of Solomon Lincoln. Benton had been a member of the board since 1894, but as a younger man had necessarily been obliged to devote the greater part of his time to his own legal and railroad interests. These had prospered so satisfactorily that, upon becoming President, he was able to spend many hours of each week in the library, enthroned in the Trustees' Room, dealing energetically, and often in a highly personal manner, with matters not only of major policy but of minor routine administration. Although a man of action who had made his way in a competitive world, Benton's enthusiasm for the local history of New England led to several studies, privately printed by the Merrymount Press. As an avid book collector, who was also a parishioner of Trinity Church, he assembled an outstanding series of editions of the Book of Common Prayer, beginning with the 1549 First Prayer Book of Edward VI. Moreover he sincerely loved the Public Library, and made it his major interest during the remaining nine years of his life.

The City appropriation for the support of the library had been increased from $302,000 in 1901 to $325,000 in 1907. In 1908, when the Trustees' estimates called for $332,800, the City Council had instead cut the sum back to $310,000. Faced with diminution of service, Benton undertook to explain to the taxpayers in simple terms what the library involved and what it did for them. Consequently the Fifty-seventh Annual Report, for 1908–1909, was cast in a wholly new form. The detailed statistics that had been published annually since the time of Justin Winsor were entirely omitted. The typography was altered, although one could hardly say improved, while the report itself was translated into popular terms intended to drive home the magnitude of the Library's operations. There were six acres of rooms to be "kept in repair, cleaned, policed, heated, lighted and maintained in proper condition for library use," between nineteen and twenty miles of shelves, holding nearly a million books, nearly three and a half million catalogue cards, and about $8,000,000 worth of real and personal property.

> The property and plant of the library system is of value only as it is worked. The books, manuscripts, and other materials are useless except when they are being read and examined. And the public library plant, like every other, should be worked, if it is

worth working at all, to the limit of its capacity. It would be as absurd to work the public library plant to half its capacity for profitable use as to work only half the spindles in a mill, or half the locomotives upon a railroad. The problem of working the Public Library, therefore, is the problem of bringing its books and other materials into the most general and extensive public use within the limit of the amount of money which the taxpayers are willing to pay for that use.

The library cannot be worked without proper catalogues and a competent staff. Two hundred and nineteen persons were required, but these 85 men and 134 women were scarcely enjoying handsome salaries, for the average compensation—including that of the Librarian and heads of departments—was $670.45 a year. Excluding the dozen heads of departments, the average annual salary was $585.34, which amounted to an average of $610.12 for 75 men and $575.22 for 132 women. The highest salary paid to any branch librarian was $910.00. Nevertheless 77 of these employees were in the third, and highest, grade of educational qualification—determined by competitive examination—which required the equivalent of a college course and familiarity with two foreign languages. The library's cooperation with schools, its assistance to readers, its exhibitions and lectures were described in justification of an annual appropriation of not less than $350,000 if the institution were to be worked to the limit of its capacity.

The argument had its effect, for the following year the City appropriated very nearly the sum requested. Thus a salary increase brought the average compensation of the regular library staff to $719.43, being $903.66 for men and $630.45 for women employees. The summary of library operations contained in the 1908–1909 report was used by Benton as the basis of an address on "The Working of the Boston Public Library" given before the Beacon Society of Boston on 2 January 1909. Subsequently printed separately, this paper was revised for a widely distributed second edition in 1914. With a similar view to spreading popular information regarding the library, Horace G. Wadlin prepared a 236-page history of the library that was published by the Trustees in December 1911.

Only in 1916 were the last of the major decorative elements of the Copley Square library completed. Edwin A. Abbey's final work on the Holy Grail series was installed in January 1902. A year later Sargent's Dogma of the Redemption was unveiled, although he did not finally decorate the ceiling and side walls of the third floor gallery until 1916. The most obviously unfinished element was the main entrance, where great pedestals awaited the bronze groups that Augustus Saint-Gaudens found it so difficult to complete. As his death in 1907 brought to an end all hopes for his participation in the decoration of the library, the Trustees finally, in May 1910, commissioned Bela L. Pratt to execute the seated bronze figures that have since the summer of 1912 occupied the pedestals on either side of the central doorways. Upon the payment to Pratt of $30,000 for these, the total cost of the construction and decoration of the building amounted to $2,558,559. Reserving $10,000 for the final payment upon Sargent's work, the building account was closed and $14,640.44 that remained from the appropriations transferred to the sinking fund.

The practical-minded had grumbled their fill about McKim's building, yet over the years it profoundly affected the lives of many who came to it looking only for books, and found as well a peace and beauty that was lacking in the crowded tenements where they lived. The concept of a "palace for the people" had seemed far-fetched in the late eighties, yet to many young people it proved to be exactly that. The testimony of Mary Antin, whose autobiograpical *The Promised Land* was published in 1912, is too eloquent to require comment:

> Off towards the northwest, in the direction of Harvard Bridge, which some day I should cross on my way to Radcliffe College, was one of my favorite palaces, whither I resorted every day after school.
>
> A low, wide-spreading building with a dignified granite front it was, flanked on all sides by noble old churches, museums, and school-houses, harmoniously disposed around a spacious triangle, called Copley Square. Two thoroughfares that came straight from the green suburbs swept by my palace, one on either side, converged at the apex of the triangle, and pointed off, past the Public Garden, across the historic Common, to the domed State House sitting on a height.

It was my habit to go very slowly up the low, broad steps to the palace entrance, pleasing my eyes with the majestic lines of the building, and lingering to read again the carved inscriptions: *Public Library—Built by the People—Free to All.*

Did I not say it was my palace? Mine, because I was a citizen; mine, though I was born an alien; mine, though I lived on Dover Street. My palace—*mine!*

I loved to lean against a pillar in the entrance hall, watching the people go in and out. Groups of children hushed their chatter at the entrance, and skipped, whispering and giggling in their fists, up the grand stairway, patting the great stone lions at the top . . . Spectacled scholars came slowly down the stairs, loaded with books, heedless of the lofty arches that echoed their steps. Visitors from out of town lingered long in the entrance hall, studying the inscriptions and symbols on the marble floor. And I loved to stand in the midst of all this, and remind myself that I was there, that I had a right to be there, that I was at home there. All these eager children, all these fine-browed women, all these scholars going home to write learned books—I and they had this glorious thing in common, this noble treasure house of learning. It was wonderful to say, *This is mine;* it was thrilling to say, *This is ours.*

I visited every part of the building that was open to the public. I spent rapt hours studying the Abbey pictures. I repeated to myself lines from Tennyson's poem before the glowing scenes of the Holy Grail. Before the "Prophets" in the gallery above I was mute, but echoes of the Hebrew Psalms I had long forgotten throbbed somewhere in the depths of my consciousness. . . .

Bates Hall was the place where I spent my longest hours in the library. I chose a seat far at one end, so that looking up from my books I would get the full effect of the vast arched reading-room. I felt the grand spaces under the soaring arches as a personal attribute of my being.

The courtyard was my sky-roofed chamber of dreams. Slowly strolling past the endless pillars of the colonnade, the fountain murmured in my ear of all the beautiful things in all the beautiful world. I imagined that I was a Greek of the classic days, treading on sandalled feet the glistening marble porticoes of Athens. I expected to see, if I looked over my shoulder, a bearded philosopher in a drooping mantle, surrounded by beautiful youths with wreathed locks. Everything I read in school, in Latin or Greek, everything in my history books, was real to me here, in this court-yard set about with stately columns.

Here is where I liked to remind myself of Polotzk, the better to bring out the wonder of my life. That I who was born in the prison of the Pale should roam at will in the land of freedom was a marvel that it did me good to realize. That I who was brought up

COURTYARD

to my teens almost without a book should be set down in the midst of all the books that ever were written was a miracle as great as any on record. That an outcast should become a privileged citizen, that a beggar should dwell in a palace—this was a romance more thrilling than poet ever sung. Surely I was rocked in an en-chanted cradle.

Mary Antin expressed vividly what many less gifted and less articulate young readers felt about the Public Library in the early years of this century. Although the Copley Square building minis-tered to the eye as well as the mind, that happy situation did not pre-vail in the branches, which were obsoletely, if not squalidly, housed.

In 1899 there were ten branches with large permanent collections of books, five reading rooms, thirteen delivery stations, twenty-two engine-houses, a post office, five public schools and five other public institutions receiving books on deposit—a total of sixty-one outlying agencies of varying degrees of importance. In the early years of this century each annual report proudly raised the number over the preceding year. There were eighty-seven, then one hundred and seventeen, one hundred and fifty-six, one hundred and eighty-five, and finally, in 1905, two hundred and one. This somewhat boastful statistical trend was checked in 1906, when the number came down to 199 and fires were reported in the South End and Charlestown Branches. It was also admitted that the new Reading Room at Codman Square, Dorchester, opened on 6 March 1905, was unique in being the "only one of the buildings under the control of the Trustees" in the branch system that had been designed chiefly for library purposes. As an example of the general practice, the South End Branch, formerly in the basement of the English High School, was shifted in 1904 to quarters improvised in the building of the Every-Day Church on Shawmut Avenue.

Benton brought the matter out squarely in the 1909–1910 report when he wrote:

> Boston should have the best equipped library system in the United States. Our citizens are proud of its Central Library building, and we believe are satisfied with the administration and working of the Library Department as a whole. But in respect to the branch system, which comes most directly in contact with those of our people who most need the Library, we are, on the whole, behind any other important city in the Union. We have no branch library building so constructed as to be operated with the utmost efficiency and economy and with the best service for the public.

He described the reading room stations as "inadequate and inconvenient, badly situated for convenient use, ill-ventilated, and in general not creditable to a city of the wealth and population of Boston." The Examining Committee of the same year commented acidly:

> The burning of the municipal building in Jamaica Plain is to lead to the construction of a small but adequate independent branch li-

brary building. Without waiting for a fire, the City should provide such other buildings where the need is greatest.

A year later the 1910–1911 Examining Committee said of the branches, "We would hide them from visitors to our City." Its report described children flattening their noses against the windows of the City Point Reading Room to see if there were room inside. With seats for fifty there would usually be a hundred children within, half of whom stood, leaning against the bookcases. The Committee spoke eloquently of the "book hunger" of the children in Ward 6.

> Let any warm-hearted student of social conditions go to the North Bennet Street Reading Room at the hour when the boxes of books come in from the Central Library. Let the visitor stand for a half hour at the delivery desk, and watch the eager faces and outstretched hands of the children. The bright-eyed Italian boy, the keen-faced Jewish girl, the Greek or Portuguese is often ragged and ill-fed, and bears the marks of the home where severe poverty cramps and dwarfs the life; but if the boxes contained sweetmeats or toys, they would hardly be more joyously greeted than are these piles of rusty books. Among the children whom we call happier than those who fill North Bennet Street there are too many who must be coaxed or driven to taste the joy of reading. But in North Bennet Street, the worn, shabby book is the key to a palace of delight, and the crowded rooms are positively ablaze with the sheer happiness which radiates from the faces of the scores of reading boys and girls. There is surely no part of our City where the hunger for books is so keen and so universal as among the crowded tenements in the North End, where the children of twenty different nations are being made,—well made or ill made,—into American men and women. . . .

> It is difficult to state the conditions, the need, the opportunity too strongly. The Chairman of this sub-committee [Miss Heloise E. Hersey] will not soon forget a single incident which she witnessed in the squalid North Street Reading Room. The books were being distributed from the big wooden chest, while the children crowded about as at the unearthing of hid treasure. One little chap on crutches waited impatiently in the background. It seemed as if the last book had been taken out when his thin voice cried, "Oh, teacher, aint my Brownie book come?" There was a whole world of bitter disappointment in his tone. Then from the very bottom

of the box his Brownie book was brought forth. He snatched it, tucked it under his arm, swung bravely off on his crutches to a corner of a table, seated himself, buttressed his elbows on the table and his head on his hands, and in two minutes had left behind him lameness and poverty and ignorance, and had become one who might well be the envy of a king.

Such references to miserable conditions gradually had their effect upon the City Government. In July 1911 a new Jamaica Plain Branch—the first independent building apart from the central library built by the City exclusively for library purposes—was completed, at a cost of $33,000. On 1 January 1912, by the annexation of the town of Hyde Park to the city of Boston, the Hyde Park Public Library, occupying a respectable building completed in 1899, became a branch of the Boston Public Library system. The 1911–1912 Examining Committee reminded the City Government "that he gives twice who gives quickly," pointing out that

> The wistful throng of boys and girls who stand outside the closed doors of a crowded library in 1912 will not be there in 1913, and by so much as the City fails in its duty to those particular children do they become a reproach to both the generosity and wisdom of the City.

The problem was complicated by "adults who come to be warm and not to read, some of whom are not free from the influence of liquor" and who spat rather freely; but even so, new quarters were urgently needed. In 1913 conditions began to change for the better. A fine new North End Branch costing $86,000 was opened in February of that year, and a new building for the Charlestown Branch, costing $71,400, in November. The City Point Reading Room moved to decent quarters in January 1914 and a new building for the East Boston Branch, provided at an expense to the City of $93,600, was ready for occupancy in April. The new buildings had their effect, for as a Branch Custodian reported in 1914:

> The adults' room is used by intelligent and ambitious men (women are in the minority), mechanics, carpenters, clerks, laborers, and students; and students come night after night. Loafers do not come, the room is too light and clean and open to view to attract them.

It is fair to observe that these serious people came at least in part because of the sympathetic and intelligent attitude of the library staff. The custodian quoted above reported the following conversation recorded by one of the attendants in that branch.

> A young man, a student who comes here, brought a friend to the library the other evening. This friend was a young Russian Jew, a student of electrical engineering, who had arrived in America that day. Our young friend introduced him to me and said: "I brought him to the Library first, because I wanted to show him what advantages American libraries offer to the student." I addressed the young man in Yiddish, using the universal Jewish welcome: "Peace be unto you. From whence cometh a Jew?" I never saw a more surprised person. For a moment he couldn't answer me. Then he said, "Is it possible that in America they even employ Jews in public places and that these same Jews are neither afraid nor ashamed to speak Yiddish?" I then explained to him that in America, officials worked for and with the public rather than as in Russia, the public for the officials.

Eager arrivals of this kind quickly found their way to the central library as well, for it was noted in 1915 that the cards referring to Shakespeare, Browning, Dumas, Arithmetic, Polish and Russian literature in the Bates Hall catalogue were so soiled and damaged by constant use that they required more frequent renewal than any others.

In 1915, when one looked back over the twenty years that had passed since the opening of the Copley Square library, striking changes were to be noted. In 1894 the Library consisted of 457,740 volumes in Boylston Street and 152,635 in the branches. Three hundred books were on open shelves in the old Bates Hall and none elsewhere. In 1915 there were 828,342 volumes in Copley Square, 30,000 of which were on open shelves, as were the greater part of th 270,360 volumes in the branches. The total expense of the branch system in 1894 was $42,355; in 1915 it had reached $140,000. This was entirely proper, considering the popular character of the library, but it went far to explain why the Trustees' estimates for the current year totalled $417,688, with an additional $10,000 requested for increase in wages. It also answered the question of whether to plough the library field of the city wider and deeper, by showing that any increase in the number of reading rooms, without commensurate increase of financial resources, would simply place burdens upon the existing system. The Trustees wisely concluded:

> What the Library needs for the present, and from the point of economy and efficient administration, is enlarged equipment to make more effective the operation of its present agencies of public service, rather than the establishment of new agencies.

Incidentally, it brought into perspective the library's policy on the purchase of scholarly books in relation to the other institutions of the neighborhood. The phenomenal growth of the Public Library in its early decades had lent plausibility to aspirations toward "completeness," but with the equally phenomenal increase in the output of printing presses completeness became, in the twentieth century, a steadily less attainable—or even desirable—ideal. Moreover the Harvard College Library, although for a time outstripped by the Public Library, grew in steady relation to the expansion of Harvard University during President Eliot's administration. When Professor Archibald Cary Coolidge was appointed Director in 1910 by President Lowell, the University Library soon became beyond question one of the great scholarly libraries of the world, with prospects of future growth enhanced by the completion, in 1915, of the new building given in memory of Harry Elkins Widener. With Harvard just across the river, and with a recently enlarged and rejuvenated Athenæum even nearer at hand, the folly of useless duplication became evident. Wadlin, in his 1914–1915 report, recognized this when considering that after buying replacements for worn-out books and providing for the continuation of serial publications, only $11,-840 was left, on the average annually, for the purchase of other new books of every kind.

> It will be seen at once, that little money remains to establish and maintain in completeness special collections which otherwise might be perfected, especially in belles lettres, collections which a rich public library ought to possess, but which, if used at all, are used only by specialists or by small groups of scholars. It is inevitable that all branches of literature cannot be completely covered on the limited amount which we have at our disposal, and that choice must be made within rather narrow limits. . . .

A library, limited in this way, although it may deplore the necessity, must leave to other and more richly endowed institutions,—more richly endowed, at least, in proportion to the demand, the establishment of exhaustive collections in fields alien to its larger constituency. It must leave to libraries which have specialized in certain departments of literature and which aim to make such departments complete, the responsibility and the satisfaction of continuing these distinctive collections; and confine its own purchases to the representative volumes in largest demand in its own territory, so far as that demand can be gauged. This can be done with less heart burning now than ever before, since the inter-library method of lending often enables a library to obtain for the use of its borrowers a book which it has not been able to buy, or which it has refrained from buying because some other accessible library has it. Every library thus limited must also conserve its resources in co-operation with other libraries in its vicinity, and thus avoid extensive duplications of purchases by institutions only a short distance removed from one another.

A year later, Wadlin summed up the situation by stating that the library—notwithstanding the fact that its founders, "scholarly men, mindful of the needs of scholars, placed upon its shelves many volumes, which, in the course of time, have become rare, and can be found in few public collections"—must now "buy with the purpose of meeting proportionately, so far as possible, the requirements of a cosmopolitan population." This involved buying "not always the books of highest literary merit, but the books which are best adapted to meet the needs of readers of varying attainments and sometimes of untrained literary taste."

By 1913 the stacks of the Copley Square library, which had seemed so spacious in 1895, were already overcrowded. Passageways were lined with extra bookcases; makeshift sections were tucked hither and yon, while books, boilers and bunkers were mixed confusedly together in the cellar. Finally in October 1915 the Trustees asked the City to take the three houses on Blagden Street, adjoining the library, as the site for a future addition. Mayor James M. Curley responded promptly, recommending an appropriation of $130,000 for land and $170,000 for the building. The Street Commissioners took the land equally promptly, at a cost of $122,500; demolition began in May 1916 and the building erected on the site was occupied in the autumn of 1918. This addition provided more stack space, working quarters for the Branch Department, and permitted the return to the library roof of the Printing and Binding Departments, which had been from 1902 to 1912 in rented quarters in Stanhope Street, and since 1912 in Columbus Avenue.

As early as 1910 the problem of pensioning and retiring employees was concerning the Trustees. Mayor John F. Fitzgerald had called the board's attention to Chapter 619 of the Acts of 1910, which authorized cities and towns to establish retirement systems for their employees, and asked for an opinion as to the possible net gain or loss to the City both in terms of money and of efficiency, if such a system were applied to the Public Library. The terms of this act provided such meagre return as to discourage voluntary retirement before 70, "while the comparatively small weekly allowances accruing in numerous cases at that advanced age would hardly overcome the disinclination of the Trustees to force the retirement of faithful employees." Thus the Trustees felt that the act would be of no practical value to the library. As Chapter 113 of the Acts of 1911 allowed the retirement on half-pay of Civil War veterans, incapacitated for further service, after at least ten years' employment, Dennis McCarthy, a night watchman since 1888, was retired on 2 November 1911, thus becoming the first library employee ever to receive a pension.

In 1912 the Trustees urged special legislation allowing them to contribute "to the support of employees who become worn out in the service of the Library." This was only fair in view of the small salaries paid, which left so little margin above actual living expenses. The need was borne out by a branch custodian in Charlestown who died in the harness at 76, and an 84-year-old janitor who was still employed because he could not afford to quit. Such recommendations were repeated annually without success, and as late as 1917 nothing had been accomplished. Not even the modest proposal that library fines be allotted for a retirement fund met with any municipal support.

Further disquietude was caused early in 1916 by the City's request that the Trustees itemize all salaries in their budget for the year. As this smelled suspiciously like the political maneuver of

1877 that had led to the loss of Justin Winsor, the Trustees reminded the City Council that, since their incorporation in 1878, salary appropriations had invariably been made in a lump sum, leaving the individual salaries to be increased or decreased at the discretion of the board. Although the salaries were, in the end, appropriated in a lump sum, the City Council undertook to break down the $112,405 required for other expenses into 39 different items, varying in amount from one of $5.00, a premium on a bond, to $33,500 for "library." This required no less than 27 separate transfers or reappropriations during the year. Although this represented to the Trustees an entirely unwarranted and unnecessary infringement upon their rights under the 1878 Act of Incorporation, they were even more concerned by a proposal made late in 1916 to place library employees under the rules of the Massachusetts Civil Service Commission. This would have involved the destruction of the carefully planned system, established under Putnam in 1895, by which many employees were working toward graded promotions. In their 1916–1917 report, the Trustees stated their views bluntly:

> This would in our judgment be a most serious blow to the efficiency of the Library. It would practically remove the appointment of these employees from the control of the Trustees. The power to appoint and to remove its employees which is given to the Corporation of the Library Trustees necessarily comprehends the power to fix the standard of qualification of the person or persons to be appointed. The power to fix the standard is the essence of the power to appoint. Without it the power of appointment is nothing. The Trustees are to say what qualifications the persons whom they desire to appoint are to have for the duties which the Trustees wish them to perform. Take away the power to provide the standard of qualification and you take away the essential power of appointment. It would be absurd to say that the Trustees may appoint their employees, and remove them, but that they shall only appoint such persons as are found to fill the standard of qualification established by somebody else upon an examination by somebody else, and yet that is precisely what the civil service rules accomplish. It is wholly abroad of the question whether such inclusion of the Library staff in the civil services rules is expedient, as we are clearly of the opinion it is not.

While this matter was still unresolved, Wadlin, on 10 November 1916, presented his resignation. The Trustees, after an unavailing attempt to induce him to reconsider, reluctantly voted on 22 December to accept it as of 1 July 1917, or at any earlier date when his successor might be appointed and qualify. On 26 January 1917 the Trustees elected to succeed him Charles F. D. Belden, State Librarian of Massachusetts since 1909, who assumed his new duties on 15 June.

CHAPTER X

Belden's Fourteen Years

The service of the public library begins in the
work with children. For them it is the chief gate-
way to the world of books. Similarly the public library of today can do much to increase the earning power of the community and its members.
Recent immigrants may be aided in becoming better Americans; the stranger may be made at home;
the scholar, the inventor, the poet, the artist, can
be helped toward creative work by the public library. It is all things to all men.

—CHARLES F. D. BELDEN

JOSIAH H. BENTON, President of the Public Library, died unexpectedly on 6 February 1917, only eleven days after Charles F. D.
Belden had been designated to succeed Horace G. Wadlin as Librarian. Benton's devotion to the Library could not have been shown
more clearly than by the generous provision made for various phases
of its welfare in his will. First of all he made immediate bequests
of his great collections of the Book of Common Prayer and of books
printed by John Baskerville, as well as of a sum of $100,000 to be
held as "The Children's Fund," the income to be applied to the purchase of books for the young. The remainder of his property, after
payment of specific bequests, was to be held by two trustees—one of
whom was Wadlin—who were, after the death of Mrs. Benton, to
turn it over to the Public Library. Half the income of this residuary
bequest was to be used "for the purchase of books, maps, and other
library material of permanent value and benefit for said library;
meaning and intending hereby that such income shall be applied
for books desirable for scholarly research and use." The other half
was to be added to principal and reinvested as an accumulating

fund until a total of two million dollars had been reached, which was then "to be applied to the enlargement of the present central library building in Boston or to the construction of another central library building in such part of the City as may be then most desirable for the accommodation of the people of said City."

Benton knew the shortcomings of the Boylston Street library, built by a group of inexperienced, though well-intentioned, commissioners, and of the Copley Square building, which had been nominally the responsibility of the library Trustees but actually the personal creation of their President. He therefore provided that any building erected under his will was "to be constructed under the advice of the Librarian of the Library at that time in such manner as may be most desirable for efficient practical working of a library therein." To prevent the City Council from resting on their oars and failing to make suitable appropriations for the library because of his gift, Benton provided that the income from the Children's Fund and for the scholarly books should "be applied for those purposes only in years when the City appropriates for the maintenance of the Boston Public Library at least three per cent (3%) of the amount available for department expenses from taxes and income in said City." In any year when the City did not appropriate the amount specified, the income was instead to "be paid to the Rector of Trinity Church in the City of Boston to be by him dispensed in relieving the necessities of the poor." Although the hundred thousand dollars for the Children's Fund was paid by the Benton estate in March 1919 to the Trustees of the Boston Public Library, the income has had to be paid over to the Rector of Trinity Church for the relief of the poor ever since, for at no time since the establishment of the fund have the City appropriations for the library fulfilled the three per cent requirement of Benton's will. Thus in spite of Benton's generous intentions the library was no better off in the years immediately following his death than it had been previously.

Early in Belden's administration, the Trustees, with his hearty concurrence, determined to ask disinterested competent librarians from other parts of the country to look into the library's methods. In January 1918 Edwin H. Anderson, Director of the New York Public Library, and Arthur E. Bostwick, Librarian of the St. Louis

Public Library, were invited to undertake this survey, with a third person of their own designation. Thus in May these gentlemen, with William H. Brett of the Cleveland Public Library, came to Boston for a week's intimate study of the library system. Although requested to consider questions of collections, classification, catalogues, serv- ice, buildings and equipment, they were sufficiently disturbed by the personal shortcomings of both the Trustees and the staff to de- vote most of their attention to the fundamental problems of human relations involved in the library system. They found the Trustees encroaching upon the duties of the Librarian, an ingrown and largely self-trained staff, poorly paid, suspicious of methods evolved elsewhere, and resentful of anyone brought in from without. While Belden was quite able to bring about useful changes in detail, the fundamental personal relations in the library required correction on a higher level. The conclusions in their report submitted on 18 September 1918 were:

1. The Boston Board of Trustees controls directly a large amount of administrative detail that in other libraries is under the charge of the librarian. It meets weekly, approves all book purchases by title and authorizes expenditures for supplies by itemized lists. It does not necessarily approve the Librarian's recommendations for appointments and promotions; and it, or its individual members receive and act upon applications and complaints from members of the staff, independently of action thereon by the Librarian. These things are done, so far as we know, in no other American library. The usual custom is for the Board to convene not oftener than once a month, and then either directly or through commit- tees to act on recommendations of the librarian in such a way as to give him large discretion, so that separate items need not neces- sarily be discussed or acted upon by the Board. This course seems to us most likely to develop a strong executive with initiative, such as is needed in every large institution, public or private.

The Board of course, is the ultimate authority in the Library. The Librarian, however, is not only its executive, subject to its orders, but also its professional expert and adviser. If the Board is not willing to place matters of administrative detail in his hands and to follow his advice in all important professional matters, he should be replaced by an executive who does have the confidence of the Board.

We believe that a lack of this confidential relation between the Board and its Librarian has been an injury to the Library in the past and is so at the present time.

2. We find that the Library staff, although in the main composed of intelligent and interested assistants, and with some notable instances of professional skill and knowledge, is somewhat out of touch with the trend of the library movement in other cities throughout the country. Few members of it have ever worked in any other library or have any familiarity with methods outside of their own institution. Few have been trained in library schools where the teaching of comparative methods gives a broad view. Although there is in Boston a library school of the first grade— that at Simmons College—there seems to have been no effort to make use of it in training material for the Public Library work.

The feeling among a large number of the staff is distinctly hostile to the employment of persons outside of Boston. This under the conditions noted means very largely the employment of untrained persons, often of limited education, receiving these in the lower grades of the staff and promoting them from time to time. This works well in some instances, but it is not a desirable general policy. A large public library should receive new blood from without continually and it should itself act as a feeder to other libraries. By continual exchange of assistants, some entering from without and others leaving, promotion is on the whole facilitated, contact with the library world is secured and stagnation due to inbreeding is prevented. Lack of such contact is particularly apt to foster an idea that an institution is operated, not for the benefit of the public, but for that of the employees themselves, that length of service is in itself a sufficient reason for promotion, and that an appointment from without is primarily an act of injustice to the staff.

The committee suggested, as point three, either an affiliation with Simmons College or the establishment of a training agency within the library to improve the professional competence of the staff. In the fourth place, they made clear their awareness that some of the changes they recommended were in part dependent upon provision of adquate funds by the City.

Professional librarians of training and experience cannot be attracted from other fields without the offer of adequate salaries. . . . But we would point out that adequate support is itself to a considerable extent dependent on popular appreciation of the Library's services. Public opinion has often forced, from a city government, reluctant support of a public institution. Now there is a general opinion among librarians, whether well-founded or not, that the Boston Public Library has not of late years retained its relative standing among American libraries. Its position was once one of preëminence, but it is so no longer. We find that this opinion is shared to a greater or less degree by many citizens of Boston whose influence should count heavily in such matters as these. It is possible that indications of a change of policy, together with a clear demonstration that further change must be dependent on increased income, might be effective in placing the public opinion of the city so solidly behind the Library that adequate support would follow as a matter of course.

The committee's five specific recommendations were the following:

1. That the by-laws of the Board be amended so as to admit of monthly meetings and that the routine of these meetings be so changed as not to require approval of all purchases or appointments in detail by the entire Board.

2. That the Board discourage, by formal resolution, the reception of complaints or requests from members of the staff, singly or collectively, either by the whole Board, or by individual members.

3. That effort be made to develop in the staff a feeling of professional *esprit de corps* as librarians and to discourage the attitude that consideration is due its members as a local body of municipal office holders; that high-grade positions be filled freely where necessary by appointments from without, and that long service in one grade be not regarded as *prima facie* evidence of fitness for promotion to a higher grade.

4. That for all library positions, other than those of messengers and the clerical and janitorial force, preliminary training or experience be a *sine qua non,* and that steps should be taken to give inexperienced persons an opportunity for training, either in direct connection with the Library or through some school in affiliation with it.

5. That an effort be made through well-considered publicity to inform the public with regard to the benefits of these changes of policy and of the fact that these require, for their complete realization, an increased income.

In January 1919 arrangements were completed with Simmons College for the organization and supervision by the college of a course in reference service at the library, for the admission without charge of designated library employees to any regular Simmons course in library training, and for the sending of college students to the library for instruction in work with children and for unpaid practical work to be given by the head of the Children's Department of the Public Library. The need for such opportunity was indicated by the fact that within the ten years from 1908 to 1918, 156 persons, only four of whom had a college education, had been promoted within the library service, while only 36 had been appointed from outside. Fourteen of the 36 had had a college education, and two of them library school training as well. During the first year of the cooperative arrangement with Simmons College, 87 members of the library staff took advantage of the opportunities offered. Somewhat later, in 1927, the library established a training class of its own for applicants for positions. In view of the fact that no tuition was charged, it was expected that graduates, if appointed to a position, would remain in the service of the library for at least two years.

Low salaries remained a perennial problem. Indeed most of the library's difficulties in the first quarter of the present century had arisen from the need of spreading too little money over too large an area, with consequent skimping sometimes on books, sometimes on buildings, but more often on people. The total city appropriation for the library in 1907 had been $325,000. In 1909 Benton's estimated minimum of $350,000 was almost reached, and from that point onward, although there was no retrogression, advances came slowly. In 1916 $409,080 was appropriated and $424,476 the following year. Even so, with wartime prices, many of the library staff were forced to work nights and Sundays in order to earn living wages. In 1918 the Trustees consequently requested an increase to improve the situation. That raised the total appropriation to $491,940. Successive efforts in this direction, combined with the higher cost of all commodities during the post-war inflation, brought appropriations in 1919 to $546,594, in 1920 to $667,936 and in 1921 to $747,120. Belden in 1920 pointed out that the library employees found themselves "in far too many cases, literally stranded, in an amazed and wondering frame of mind," asking not so much "What am I worth?" but "What shall I do?" As a provision against actual want, it was imperative to increase the worst paid in a higher ratio than the more skilled, even though this involved a basic unfairness to the able, better educated, and more energetic, who were "justly entitled to recognition in proportion to the value of their services." The often repeated pleas for some equitable pension plan finally resulted in the library staff benefitting under the Pension Bill relative to the retirement of certain city employees, passed by the Massachusetts Legislature in 1922. The world was so far out of joint in these days of Harding-Coolidge prosperity that, even when the annual library appropriations passed the million mark, as they did in 1926, the library employees were still inadequately paid. In 1928 the Trustees complained that "it becomes more and more difficult to fill vacancies in the library staff at the salaries now paid" and that if the library "is to maintain its standing and to carry on to higher levels the quality of its service, the salary scale must be advanced to keep pace with that current in other American libraries of the first rank." A year later, the Examining Committee pointed out that "ill paid work is poor economy" in recommending careful consideration of the whole question of salaries.

An adequate supply of books proved an equally pressing problem. As Belden wrote in 1919:

> The demand for more books is continuous and insistent. Replacements must constantly be made of the worn-out but worthy volumes both of non-fiction and fiction; many collections, already noteworthy, must be enlarged whenever opportunity serves; serial continuations, ever increasing in number, must be kept up; books for the student and scholar in all intellectual fields must be added as published. All this implies a careful selection in order that a wise distribution may be made to the various departments and that a proper perspective be maintained. An altogether too meagre balance of available funds is thus left for the purchase of children's books and popular fiction.

Although Benton's bequests promised some eventual relief so far as scholarly and children's books were concerned, the income from trust funds amounted only to a little over $20,000 at this time.

Therefore not only salaries and maintenance, but a large share of the book purchases—if they were to be made—had to be squeezed out of the City appropriations. For 1921 the Trustees asked for $100,000 for the purchase of books, an increase of $40,000 over the previous year. They got it, and the additional sum expended caused an increase in circulation of over 233,000 during the year. In 1922 a similar sum was again provided, but its buying power was sadly reduced by the steadily increasing prices of books. Even in 1926, when the book appropriation first reached $125,000, Belden wrote:

> The increasing appropriations for the purchase of books have scarcely kept pace with the advancing demands upon the library; the failure of a corresponding increase in the endowment of the Library from private sources has caused it to lose ground in the effort to maintain its foremost place among the scholarly public libraries in the country.

The Trustees in 1927, while sadly comparing their endowment of $755,000 with the $22,647,000 of the Reference Department of the New York Public Library, pointed out the inevitable relation between the circulation and acquisition of books. During the year they had purchased 98,487 volumes, while the Cleveland Public Library had acquired 201,174. In the same period, Boston's circulation increased by 206,250 while Cleveland's jumped by 807,005. Such arguments eventually proved so effective that in 1931 the city appropriated for books over $190,000, $145,000 of which was spent upon those needed for the branch libraries. Added to the $20,-547.23 available from trust funds, the 1931 total book expenditure of $211,103.24 represented a record in the history of the library to that time.

During the twenties and early thirties, the city provided not only more books for the branches but appropriated substantial sums toward the improvement of their buildings. Belden's report for 1920–1921 called attention to the needs of the system by a substantial appendix that provided details of the history and character of each of the sixteen branches and fourteen reading rooms. The highest circulation of all—124,139—was in the West End Branch, which served a population of twenty-two different nationalities. The balconies of this fine old church were converted into a Children's Room, while on the floor adults crowded in to read books in Yiddish, Russian and Italian, as well as English. The East Boston, South Boston, South End, Uphams Corner and Warren Street Branches all had annual circulation in excess of 100,000 volumes.

Although the use of the branch libraries was highly satisfactory, their quarters often left much to be desired. An attractive new West Roxbury Branch, dedicated on 17 April 1922, made the accommodations in other regions seem even less suitable. The West Roxbury Branch, designed in a simple Georgian style by Oscar O. Thayer, with most of its activities concentrated on one floor, save for a lecture hall and related staff quarters in the basement, represented a considerable advance in convenience and appearance over the branches of the previous decade. The Charlestown Branch, opened in 1913, and the East Boston Branch, opened in 1914, had been two-story and basement buildings of rectangular form, oddly resembling packing cases. There was nothing of striking interest in their designs; moreover their plan required constant staff coverage on at least two of the three levels, and sometimes in the basement as well. The West Roxbury Branch which is still, over thirty years after completion, a good library building, opened a new stage in the planning of Boston Public Library branches. The 1921–1922 Examining Committee, in commending this improvement, remarked that "as some seven-eighths of the circulation originates in the branches and reading rooms, it is clear that the question of a satisfactory model for the branch buildings is one of primary importance." Six years later the proportion was even higher, for the Trustees' report for 1927 stated: "The Branches are the channels through which nine-tenths of the circulation of the Library is carried on; they must not be allowed to become clogged." The 1929 Examining Committee, of which Boston's perennial Mayor, James Michael Curley, was (while between terms in City Hall) a member, considered the inadequacies of branch library buildings. Mr. Curley spoke up vigorously concerning this unfortunate situation; he considered it unfortunate and said that something should be done about it. Shortly thereafter he became Mayor again. Through his personal initiative, a special appropriation of $200,000 was received in March 1930 as the first installment on a construction program. With this aid modern buildings were provided for the Parker Hill and Mattapan Branches to replace wholly inadequate rented quarters. When these were nearing completion in the spring of 1931, a second appropriation of $200,000 permitted the construction of new buildings in the Faneuil district of Brighton, the Boylston district of Jamaica Plain, and the Jeffries Point district of East Boston. In 1932 Mayor Curley proposed a third appropriation of similar size, but because of the economic depression no further action was taken for almost two decades. The five branches built with Mayor Curley's 1930 and 1931 appropriations have, like the West Roxbury Branch of 1922, continued to be serviceable buildings. As they were the work of different architects, they were in a variety of styles. With the exception of Thomas Williams's Jeffries Point Branch, they were one story and basement buildings. The Parker Hill Branch was designed in the Gothic manner of Cram and Ferguson; the Boylston (now Connolly) Branch by Maginnis and Walsh was a mixture of Tudor and Jacobean; the Mattapan Branch by Putnam and Cox was of Georgian inspiration, while the Faneuil Branch was designed by Kilham, Hopkins and Greeley in what was considered "modern" at the time. In the Mattapan and Faneuil Branches all public areas were placed on one floor level.

As early as 1918 the Trustees urged an appropriation to establish a business branch in the downtown area, but a dozen years passed before this desirable addition to the library's service became possible. Since 1898 when Herbert Putnam brought Worthington C. Ford to Boston to create the Department of Documents and Statistics, the needs of the business man in the Public Library had been recognized as of equal validity with those of the scholar, the general reader, or the immigrant seeking adjustment to his new home. The establishment in 1919 of an experimental *current* Federal Document Information Service, which brought Belden the hearty congratulations of Governor Coolidge, was another step in making the Public Library of use to those concerned in public and private business. An even more significant event was the agreement reached with Harvard University in 1927 for the consolidation of the material relating to business in the Public Library and in the George F. Baker Library of the Harvard Graduate School of Business Administration. The Business School had recently occupied new and ample quarters near Soldiers Field in Brighton, across the Charles from the remainder of the university. As the Baker Library was within the city limits of Boston, the idea of designating it a branch of the Boston Public Library and transferring to it material relating to the past history of business, retaining in Copley Square only "live books" on the practical aspects of business, had obvious advantages for both parties to the agreement. Through an arrangement with the Boston Medical Library in 1906, technical books of slight interest to the general reader had been placed where their usefulness would be enhanced by association with others of their kind, under the care of an expert and specialized staff. The cooperative tie with the Baker Library similarly placed certain infrequently consulted books of purely historical interest in the location where they were most likely to be used. An important feature of the agreement was the pledge of Harvard University to "cooperate in the establishment, as a branch of the Boston Public Library, of a business reference library in the down town section of Boston, to be established, operated and maintained by and in cooperation with the two Libraries." The following year Louis E. Kirstein, a Trustee of the Public Library since 1919, who was elected its President in June 1928, offered to give a building for use as a downtown business branch as a memorial to his father, Edward Kirstein. The location proposed—the site of the abandoned Police Station 2 on City Hall Avenue—was not only city property but convenient to the centers of business activity. Mr. Kirstein's generous offer was accepted by the Trustees on 21 December 1928, and on 7 May 1930 the new building, whose façade echoed the central pavilion of Charles Bulfinch's destroyed Crescent on Franklin Street, was opened for public use. The Business Branch, furnishing magazines, business services, trade and city directories, and statistical yearbooks, occupied the first two floors of the Kirstein Memorial Library, while the third floor was devoted to a general branch library for adults. The response was immediate, for during the first months of operation the attendance averaged 438 readers a day. The load was made even heavier than had been anticipated by the presence, in addition to the business man for whom it had been designed, of unemployed victims of the October 1929 crash who were sensibly studying to prepare themselves for a better job when one came along.

During Belden's administration the Copley Square building, having passed the quarter century mark, proved a frequent cause of

KIRSTEIN BRANCH

concern, both because of its state of repair and of its restricted adaptability to the changing needs of the Library. In 1920 an Open Shelf Room, containing some 2,500 volumes of nonfiction, selected for the special convenience of "those persons who wish to find with the least trouble something good to read," was established as an experiment. It met with a good response, but as the only space available for it was unfortunately a dingy little first-floor room to the right of the main staircase, originally intended by McKim for the location of a public toilet, its proper development was well nigh impossible. The 1921–1922 Examining Committee thought that it was "not too early to begin considering plans for the new Library building that must inevitably be erected in a few years." They wrote:

> We have observed with some apprehension the inadequacy of the Central Library building and many of the quarters provided for the branches and reading rooms. In the Central Library the Newspaper and Periodical Rooms are at times uncomfortably crowded. There is already evidence of pressure on the Informa-

tion Bureau, the Document Service Room and the new Open Shelf Room. On the second floor the Children's Room is unequal to the demands made upon it in busy hours. The book stacks, even with the relief afforded by the annex, will not provide for the probable accessions of more than a very limited period. The catalogue space in Bates Hall is almost exhausted. The Statistical Department is hidden away in cramped and somewhat inaccessible quarters and the Industrial Arts Collection is housed on the top floor with the Fine Arts Collection and made subsidiary to it, although of an essentially different character. The Lecture Hall, unattractive, badly ventilated and poorly equipped, is inferior to the halls in many high schools and municipal buildings. All of these are growing departments or features of the Library and the future is likely to see much greater congestion in all of them, to say nothing of the creation of new departments.

One solution would be, they felt, the use of the Copley Square library for special collections and exhibitions, thus setting aside "the whole interior of this beautiful structure . . . for serious research in an atmosphere of artistic distinction," and the addition of an adjacent and connected new building for "the collections which are of more general service and those departments that are frequented by the general public." A year later the Examining Committee was considering a suggestion for "book storage building, planned purely for utility at some point within a reasonable distance of the Central Library, where land values are low, but sufficiently central for convenience, to which little-used books for special uses could be transferred, and to which readers could be directed." At the same time Belden urged the addition of two floors to the Blagden Street annex in order to transfer the Catalogue and Ordering Departments to new quarters and thus release valuable space on the ground floor for public purposes.

In an article on "The Function of the Public Library," Belden had observed:

> The service of the public library begins today, as it has for years past, in the work with children. For them it is the chief gateway to the world of books. . . . Similarly the public library of today can do much to increase the earning power of the community and its members. . . . Recent immigrants may be aided in becoming better Americans; the stranger may be made at home; the scholar,

the inventor, the poet, the artist can be helped toward creative work by the public library. It is all things to all men.

The success of this inclusive ideal was not aided by a building that besides being too small was falling into disrepair. It was overcrowded in 1922; by 1925 there were leaks in the roof, the main ventilating system had long since been abandoned, the heating was only thirty per cent efficient, the elevators were shaky, and the book railway and pneumatic tube system had so completely broken down that it was necessary to hire additional messengers to do their work. The 1924–1925 Examining Committee recommended an annual appropriation of $50,000 for extraordinary repairs "until the property is built up to a standard that can be maintained" on the ground that constant pruning of appropriations had produced cumulative neglect until the time had come "when money must be spent in larger amounts upon this part of the City's property, or paralysis of its function will result." Moreover the building was not just shabby and in disrepair; it had, in addition, become a singularly uncomfortable place for quiet work.

In Boylston Street there had been a marked division between circulating and reference functions. The Lower Hall was given over to circulation, while Bates Hall, upstairs, was a reference library. The constantly growing demand for books for home use tended to wipe out the distinction between the two, and in Copley Square it wholly disappeared, so that there was simply one great circulating library, containing, however, many volumes restricted to "hall use." The new Bates Hall, after initial respect for its magnificence had been diminished by familiarity, drew more than its share of winter readers who chiefly wished to keep warm and had no other place to do so, just as the charming arcades of the courtyard were in summer too often preempted by unsavory characters who paused at length to refresh themselves in the shade after visiting the library's public toilets. Joshua Bates in 1852 had expressed the belief that "when it is desired to know something of a young man, the question will be asked, 'Does he frequent the library?'" Seventy or eighty years later, an affirmative answer would not necessarily have implied what Joshua Bates anticipated. In addition, there were in Bates Hall a steadily increasing number of students who used no other library facilities than the chairs and tables. Many of them were quiet enough, but, as Belden pointed out in 1925, "the law students often become so boisterous in discussing the cases which they are studying that strong measures are sometimes necessary to muffle them." Then there were the puzzle and contest fiends. During the second week in January 1925 there was, Belden wrote, standing room only in Bates Hall.

> The reference books proved to be such a magnet to those who were seeking the solution to prize crossword puzzles that at one time 432 persons were counted in the room, although it has chairs for only 310. Those who could not find seats, all converted for the moment into earnest students, were clustered in swarms about the walls like bees in a flower-garden. There was a quiet buzzing, but no disorder. This earnestness was very destructive to the reference books and cost the Library three copies of Webster's "International Dictionary," to say nothing of extensive bindery repairs.

This nuisance proved far from temporary, for two decades later historical puzzles were causing equally useless theft, mutilation and damage to local histories that were less easily replaced than Webster's dictionaries. All this tended to drive quiet readers to the Special Libraries on the third floor. Even there they were not left in peace, for, as the contents of the special collections were included in the general card catalogue, readers wanting ordinary books would rush to the third floor when circulating copies were not available. Thus a school child, wishing to take a copy of *Hamlet* home, might appear in the Barton Library and demand a quarto, to his own frustration, the annoyance of the staff and the disturbance of those readers who had fled from the budding lawyers of Bates Hall.

The Special Libraries staff were thus confronted with uncommon difficulties in preventing both general readers and undergraduate students from promiscuously invading areas designed for specialized use. As originally planned, the third floor had been designed for the safe and spacious accommodation of the Barton, Ticknor, Prince, and Bowditch libraries and other equally valuable books and manuscripts. The exigencies of space had, however, diluted the original plan so far as to place there all books dealing with fine arts, music, technology, many classes of government documents, all maps and oversize books of every class. There was consequently a pressing need for a large closed room, in which to bring together and give adequate protection to the rarer books from various parts of the library. The most reasonable solution involved refitting the North Gallery to accommodate the special collections, shifting the music library into the existing Barton-Ticknor room, and turning the Music Room into a Treasure Room with cases designed for the fire-proof housing and ready exhibition of the greatest rarities.

Major repairs during 1925 and 1926 placed boilers, elevators, ventilating system and the book railway in proper working order, while in December 1927 the City Council appropriated $250,000 for the improvements contemplated on the third floor. This reconstruction was completed during 1929 in spite of the necessity of spending some $200,000 additional during that year to explore and repair weakened piles that were jeopardizing the foundations of the library. The new Treasure Room, equipped with cases that harmonized with the dignified architectural character of the room, naturally lent itself to exhibitions that brought the varied rarities of the library to popular notice.

Increased attention was also given to making the resources of the library known through popular publications. In the fourth series of the *Quarterly Bulletin,* beginning in 1919, news of the library and information not purely bibliographical was introduced, while manuscripts and broadsides of historical interest were reproduced. Beginning in January 1924 it was replaced by a *Monthly Bulletin of Recent Books,* which was in turn superseded in March 1926 by a monthly entitled *More Books,* which in addition to the selected list of new books carried in each issue several articles relating to the book treasures and manuscripts of the library. Lindsay Swift, who as Editor of Library Publications had been responsible for the *Bulletin* since 1896, died in 1921 after more than forty-three years service in the Library. With the first issue of *More Books,* Dr. Zoltán Haraszti, previously an assistant in the Special Libraries Department, became Editor. The new publication, which was given considerably wider distribution than the earlier *Bulletin,* was characterized by articles—frequently by the Editor—which, although scholarly in content, were aimed to excite the interest of the frequenters of the library rather than to inform the specialist. Accounts of the library's manuscripts and incunabula, designed to explain the literary significance of the contents, proved highly useful in attracting interest to the exhibitions in the newly constituted Treasure Room.

Charles F. D. Belden died on 24 October 1931 while still in his fifties. The fourteen years of his administration, producing, as they had, steady progress along established lines rather than any outstanding innovations, had done credit to the institution. In 1925 he had been elected President of the American Library Association— the first Librarian of the Boston Public Library to hold that office since Justin Winsor half a century before—and in 1926 Harvard University gave him the honorary degree of Master of Arts. Perhaps the most significant aspect of his fourteen years is the steadily increasing support given the Public Library by the City Government during bad years as well as good. In 1917 the total appropriations were $424,476; in 1929 they were $1,171,544 and in 1930 $1,-173,144. In 1931, notwithstanding the depression, they reached $1,262,504, plus special appropriations of $480,750. This was singularly fortunate, for the widespread unemployment of the early thirties was to throw even heavier burdens than before upon the library.

CHAPTER XI

Depression and Consolidation

It has been truly said that "the rediscovery of
the Public Library is a by-product of the depression."

—1934 EXAMINING COMMITTEE

THE UNEXPECTED and much regretted vacancy created by
the sudden death of Charles F. D. Belden was filled within the
month by the appointment as Director of Milton Edward Lord, Director of Libraries at the State University of Iowa. A member of the
Harvard class of 1919, whose undergraduate studies had been interrupted by military service during World War I, Mr. Lord had
worked in the reference department of the Harvard College Library
before going to Rome in 1926 as Librarian of the American Academy. From this post he had become a member of the group of
American librarians charged by Pope Pius XI with the beginnings
of the reorganization of the Vatican Library. When he took office as
Director of the Boston Public Library on 1 February 1932, he assumed problems and responsibilities of bewildering complexity. The
administration of a great library rarely permits its director to enjoy
a peaceful and leisurely acquaintance with the books in his custody,
but this was more than usually true of the Boston Public Library
at the close of its eighth decade. The Copley Square building was
overcrowded, inconvenient, and in doubtful repair. The condition
of many of the branches, through which the greater part of the library's work was accomplished, left much to be desired. The 1918
survey by Messrs. Anderson, Bostwick and Brett had, without minc-
ing words, indicated the deficiencies of the library in organization
and professional competence. Substantial progress had been made
during Belden's administration. Under Capen and Jewett the aver-

age annual growth of the book collection had been 9,006 volumes, a figure that mounted strikingly to 17,692 during the decade of Justin Winsor's superintendency. From 1878 to 1894 the average increase was 17,021, while during Herbert Putnam's administration it rose to 26,419. Under Whitney and Wadlin (1899–1917) it relapsed to 23,535, but during Belden's fourteen years the book collections grew by an annual average of 28,875 volumes. The city government had nobly done its part by more than doubling the library appropriations during these fourteen years, and more than tripling those for the purchase of books. Against $50,000 provided by the city for this purpose in 1917, the 1931 appropriation amounted to $175,000. This happy situation was rudely altered in 1932, when the backwash of the 1929 crash brought simultaneously the need for stringent economy in municipal government and a vastly increased use of the library by victims of the depression who had no other means of passing their days.

Those who love to measure and judge in purely quantitative terms might well reflect upon the meaning of the Boston Public Library circulation statistics over ten years of depression and gradual recovery.

YEAR	Number of books lent to borrowers	Percentage of increase or decrease over preceding years	Percentage of increase over 1929	Appropriations for purchase of books
1929	3,930,068			$140,000
1930	4,133,459	+ 5	+ 5	160,000
1931	4,702,932	+ 13	+ 20	175,000
1932	5,567,681	+ 18	+ 42	160,000
1933	5,548,283	− 0.3	+ 41	75,000
1934	5,194,351	− 6	+ 32	100,000
1935	4,949,701	− 5	+ 26	100,000
1936	4,806,737	− 3	+ 22	55,000
1937	4,531,378	− 6	+ 15	75,000
1938	4,354,044	− 4	+ 11	73,875

The peak of increasing use reached in 1932–1933 suggests not so much a widening taste for literature or a growing appreciation of the library's services as the stark fact that in a period of widespread unemployment large numbers of men and women turned to the library because they had no other way of using their time. In 1929 45% of the users of the branch libraries were adults and 55% children. In 1932 the figures were exactly reversed. Although city appropriations inevitably declined—the 1931 figure of $1,239,257 was not reached again until 1941—the library stoutly sought to meet larger demands with smaller resources. When it became apparent in the autumn of 1932 that some 78,000 individuals—many of them children—had lost their library cards because of non-payment of fines, a temporary moratorium was declared. During Fine Cancellation Week, from 17 to 22 October 1932, 30,922 borrowers cards were renewed, 3,642 seemingly lost books were recovered, and 2,219 cards were issued to those who had not previously been borrowers. The Examining Committees from 1932 to 1934 strongly urged "that the facilities of the Library be at least maintained, if not increased; and certainly not contracted," for "the rediscovery of the Public Library is a by-product of the depression."

A second point to be derived from the circulation statistics of the thirties is that one cannot greatly increase the reading of books without constant and generous replacement of one's stock. The steady decline in circulation from 1934 onward may be attributed quite as much to the smaller appropriations for buying books as to the expanding employment and gradually increasing economic health of the community. Books, when used, wear out. Unlike people, they do not benefit from wide and varied human contacts. Even Dante, Sterne, Keats and Thoreau appear more beguiling—at least to those who have not previously been honored by their friendship—in clean suits than spotted. In 1932 the book stock of the Boston Public Library amounted to 1,631,422 volumes. Therefore, acting on the logic of the young woman who refused to consider giving her father a book for Christmas *because he already had one,* economy-minded city authorities cut the library's 1933 appropriations for the purchase of books from $160,000 to $75,000. Their reasoning was unfortunate, for the reduction came at the moment when thousands of books were literally being worn out from greatly increased use, and replacements were more urgently needed than ever. Moreover, the imposing collections of the central library in Copley Square obscured the fact that in the branches, which accounted for nine tenths of the library's circulation, books were being discarded faster than new ones were added. Upon this point Mr. Lord wrote in his 1937 report:

It seems so self-evident that a library must have books that one wonders what further can be said in support of such an axiom. Yet one frequently hears the query as to why more books are needed anyway. The Library has enough volumes in its system already. In the central library, for instance, there are 1,195,704 volumes as compared with the 504,977 volumes in the branch libraries. Why should not some of those in the central library be turned over to the branch libraries?

But who wants to choose his reading from the sermons of the Reverend Cotton Mather or the Bay Psalm Book or the First Folio of Shakespeare? Who wants to read volume after volume of specifications of German patents or of the *Sessional Papers of the House of Commons* in the nineteenth century or of the *Atti dell' Accademia dei Lincei* of fifty years ago? Who wants to read Boston, Worcester and Springfield city directories for 1875 or the *Boston Transcript* for 1833 or *Who's Who in America* for 1903? Who wants to read Andreas Vesalius *De humani corporis fabrica libri septem* (Basle, 1555) or François Appert's *L'art du conserver, pendant plusieurs années, toutes les substances animales et vegetales* (Paris, 1810) or Friedrich Engel's *Die Lage der Arbeitenden Klasse in England* (Leipzig, 1845)?

It is of items of the above sort—in single copies only, for the most part—that the excellent book collections of the central library are made up. They do not contain, available for use in multiple branch libraries, multiple copies of books of the sort which the average citizens of Boston frequenting the branch libraries wish and need for their regular reading. What the central library has is the vast accumulation of materials which are needed by the students or the scholar engaged in serious research and investigation. And for the upkeep and further development of its collections of this sort it has special support in the form of trust funds which have been given for the purpose and for no other.

On the other hand, it is on the branch libraries that there falls the brunt of the book demands of the citizens of Boston at large. *Ninety per cent of the books borrowed from the entire library system are asked for and obtained from the branch libraries.* Yet to meet this demand the branch libraries have book collections which total only thirty per cent of the book holdings of the entire library system. And the discouraging feature is that the number of volumes in the branch libraries is decreasing rather than increasing. In 1935 the branch libraries had to discard as worn out 4,257 volumes more than they could add; in 1936 they fell short by 9,091 volumes; in 1937, by 3,930 volumes. In other words, in 1935 they discarded 53,996 books and added only 49,739; in 1936 they discarded 41,859 volumes and added only 32,768; in 1937, they discarded 44,346 books and added only 40,416.

This eminently reasonable statement concluded with a plea for an annual book appropriation of $150,000 as "the minimum amount with which the Library can function to advantage" on the basis of past experience. It was not heeded, for the book appropriations dropped to $73,875 in 1938, to $55,000 in 1939, and only reached $90,000 in 1946. For the years 1947 to 1949 they amounted to $125,000—the level of the 1926–1928 period. In 1950 they rose to $150,000, in 1951 to $230,000, and they were in 1953, through the enlightened activity of Mayor John B. Hynes, to rise to $277,-500. Alas, the fantastic increases in the price of books have made the gain to the Library more apparent than real, as anyone who tries to balance his own checkbook these days can readily understand. Because of this, the average annual rate of growth during the first twenty years of Mr. Lord's administration declined to 17,592 volumes—a figure lower than that of Justin Winsor's day, and only slightly higher than that which prevailed during the doldrums of the eighties. It should be noted in passing that the portion allocated for the purchase of books from the total amount of City funds appropriated for the library had declined markedly from 15 per cent in 1931 to 8 per cent in 1951. Even when supplemented with the income of trust funds, the percentage available for the purchase of books slipped from 17 in 1931 to 9 in 1951. At the end of 1951 the book stock totalled 1,924,640 volumes, of which 1,291,934 were in the reference and research division at Copley Square, while 632,-706 volumes (mostly in the branches) were designed for home reading. As is suitable, the greater part of the city appropriation went to the purchase of books for the branches, while the income of the trust funds was used almost entirely for the development of the reference and research collections. The expenditures for books in 1951 were divided thus:

	Home Reading	Reference	Total
City Funds	$188,960.79	$37,667.62	$226,628.41
Trust Funds	870.49	37,879.45	38,749.94
	$189,831.28	$75,547.07	$265,378.35

During the depression years much was accomplished in reforming and modernizing the library administration. The 1918 survey had sharply criticized the amount of administrative detail directly under the control of the Board of Trustees, and particularly the fact that "its individual members receive and act upon applications and complaints from members of the staff, independently of action thereon by the Librarian." "These things are done," wrote Messrs. Anderson, Bostwick, and Brett, "so far as we know, in no other American library." There was indeed grave need for a change, as anyone who reads Josiah H. Benton's pamphlet *The Working of the Boston Public Library,* or chapter VII of Wadlin's history, will readily see. The following sample will suffice to show the bottleneck that existed through excessive centralization of administration:

> No supplies are purchased or repairs made without a vote of the Trustees. At each weekly meeting the Librarian submits a list of these which, upon examination and revision, is voted by the Trustees, and then transmitted to the Library Auditor as authority for the purchase and repairs. All orders for such supplies and repairs are in writing, signed by the Librarian, and numbered to correspond with the stub record, upon which is minuted the date of the list authorized by the Trustees upon which the item appears, and the number of the item on that list. Bills rendered are checked up from the stub record, and the receipt of the goods and the completion of the repairs is certified by the head of the department to which the goods are delivered, or in which the work is done, or if the receipt is for supplies to be kept in stock their receipt is certified by the custodian of the stock room. The bill then goes to the Library Auditor, who certifies it as correctly figured. It is then endorsed by the Librarian, presented to the Trustees, and its payment voted by them.

As similar procedures applied to all processes, including the purchase of books, one is left to wonder how the Trustees, solemnly deliberating over every triviality, and the Librarian, meticulously putting numbers on stub records, ever had time to attend to the proper duties of their offices. Altogether the Boston Public Library suffered from a curious blending of personal autocracy and bureaucratic rectitude. In the high-handed years when Samuel A. B. Abbott was planning the Copley Square building to conform to his personal taste, the Trustees' records show numerous votes of such world-shaking importance as one of 15 November 1892 "that *Sanitas* be the form of water-closet bowl to be adopted for use in the new Public Library building." The same spirit persisted long after Abbott's departure, for from 1908 until his death in 1917 Josiah H. Benton would hold court many times a week in the Trustees' Room, hearing petitions and giving arbitrary judgments on points of minor library detail, with a lordly disregard of any principles of orderly administration. When such an attitude at the top of an institution is screened by an elaborate system of vouchers, stubs, and rubber stamps, initiative and imagination inevitably suffer. H. M. Tomlinson, vexed with the petty regulations governing travel in the modern world, summed the whole matter up recently in the single sentence: "Rubber stamps are for the rumps of sheep."

Moreover, during the course of World War I, there was an unhappy period when certain appointments were made to the Board of Trustees which were not of the type to be expected for an institution such as the Boston Public Library. In consequence, a certain number of typical office-holders, lacking in professional qualifications, found their way to employment by the library. Fortunately this situation was only temporary, for from 1919 onward the Mayors of Boston made a succession of very suitable appointments to the Board of Trustees, including such widely respected citizens as Louis E. Kirstein (Vice-president and general manager of William Filene's Sons Company), Frank W. Buxton (Editor of the *Boston Herald*), Ellery Sedgwick (Editor of the *Atlantic Monthly*), John L. Hall (a leading lawyer in Boston), William Cardinal O'Connell (Archbishop of Boston), Monsignor Robert H. Lord (formerly Professor of History at Harvard College and Vice-Rector of St. John's Ecclesiastical Seminary), Richard J. Cushing (Archbishop of Boston), and others. As all of these Trustees were of a type that commanded the respect of the community and of the members of the City Government, there was in consequence no attempt on the part of anyone in the Mayor's Office, in the City Council, or in other political areas to attempt to interfere politically in the administration of the library. Perhaps the best tribute to the independence and standing of the Public Library, and the respect in which it has been held, is to be found in the tale of the two politicians who, during the depression, were discussing possible jobs for their constituents. One, having heard that the Public Library had a large WPA project, allowed that he was going there to force the appointment of an unemployed constituent. The other looked at him in horror and exclaimed, "My God, man! Don't you know you can't do that? The Library is holy!"

Fortunately the theory of "the indispensable man," nurtured during the long presidencies of Greenough, Abbott, and Benton, did not survive Benton's death. In the past three decades, the presidency of the Library has usually been rotated, on the basis of terms of a single year, thus giving greater scope to the varied abilities of the competent citizens that have served the City as Trustees. While the yearly change of presidents afforded a prospect of refreshing stimulation to the Director (as the Librarian had been redesignated in 1923), that devoted official still staggered under the weight of an inherited excess of detail. Although the operations of the branch libraries were highly centralized, with a Supervisor of Branches who alone reported straight to the Director, the central library was organized in exactly the opposite manner. There, some twenty entirely separate and unrelated department heads had no common superior short of the Director, who was thus unreasonably burdened with minor chores that might better have been dealt with lower on the ladder. Moreover, in the business operations of the institution there was room for improvement in method. With the greatly increased use of the library during the depression the need of more effective administration became apparent, particularly as appropriations were shrinking. Consequently in September 1932—seven months after Mr. Lord's arrival—the Trustees adopted a revised plan of organization based upon the functional lines along which the major activities of the library fell, that is:

1. circulation of books (centered largely in the branch libraries)
2. reference use of books (centered chiefly in the central library)
3. business operations (the business management of the entire library system)

The plan called for the creation of a Circulation Division, a Reference Division, and a Division of Business Operations, each headed by an officer who would be responsible to the Director for the entire functioning of his division. Thus by logical decentralization, the Director would become the general administrator of the entire library system, while the division heads—the second ranking officers of the library—would be the active executives for their respective divisions. In August 1933, when the three divisions were established, Mr. Lord wrote:

> The Boston Public Library is an unusual institution. It is not only a large active public library in the usual sense of the term; it is also a great scholarly reference and research library, possessing many of the marks of the university library. Both of these characteristics require recognition.
>
> The Circulation Division is therefore conceived as a unit combining all of those activities that belong to the public library as it has been developed generally throughout the United States. The American public library is essentially a popular institution. Dedicated to the spread of general reading among all classes and at all age levels, it has long attempted to provide books in as many copies as popular demand requires and to circulate them widely for use in the home as well as in the library. In the Boston Public Library system most activity of this sort takes place naturally in the branch libraries. In them there is centered, in large part, also the specialized work for children, the general work with the schools, and extension activities in general. The Circulation Division was therefore established to combine, coördinate, and develop the popular library activities of the Boston Public Library system.
>
> The Reference Division, on the other hand, is conceived as a unit made up primarily of the highly specialized subject and related departments that are centered around the scholarly book collections of the main library, and which make it one of the ranking scholarly and research libraries of the United States. As a division it is to be responsible for the maintenance, use, and development of these scholarly reference collections.

Finally, to the Division of Business Operations is given the immediate responsibility for the business management of the library system as a whole. The intent has been thereby to afford relief, as far as possible, from non-bibliothecal activity for those individuals in the Circulation and the Reference Division who are engaged in duties that are primarily bibliothecal.

The financial stringencies of the times prevented the immediate carrying out of the entire plan, but in 1934 the appointments of the division heads were made, Orlando C. Davis becoming Chief Librarian of the Circulation Division, Richard G. Hensley, Chief Librarian of the Reference Division, and James W. Kennedy Comptroller, at the head of the Division of Business Operations. The title of Mr. Lord, the general administrator, was changed to Director, and Librarian. In the Reference Division recognition was given to the great rare book collections by the establishment of the post of Keeper of Rare Books, to which Dr. Zoltán Haraszti, the Editor of Publications, was appointed.

The Boston Public Library is essentially two institutions in one, being both a popular public library in the usual sense and a major research institution. Each of these areas requires quite a difference of approach—a fact recognized for the first time in the administrative reorganization of the thirties. When fully developed, this change provided finally a fourfold division. In the General Administrative Offices were grouped the Director and two assistants (one serving also as Chief Executive Officer and the other as Secretary of the Trustees); the Personnel, Information and Exhibits Offices; the Editor of Publications; and a section of Records, Files and Statistics. The Division of Home Reading and Community Services (originally and less mouth-fillingly called the Circulation Division), administered by a Chief Librarian, was managed by Chiefs of Book Selection and of Cataloging and Classification, a Supervisor, three Deputy Supervisors (in charge of work with adults, young adults and children respectively), a Chief of Open Shelf for Home Reading at the central library, thirty-three Branch Librarians, two Bookmobile Librarians, and three Readers' Advisors. In the Division of Reference and Research Services—called in a more laconic and less precise world the Reference Division—were grouped a similar galaxy of Chief Librarian, Supervisors and Deputy Supervisors, plus thirteen Chiefs of Departments, Keepers of Rare Books and of Prints, and two Curators. An Assistant to the Director, in charge of Business Operations, whose hands were upheld by two Deputy Assistants, became responsible for the Business Office, the Accounting, Book Purchasing, Book Preparation, Printing, and Binding Departments, as well as the province of the Superintendent of Buildings with his regiment of carpenters, painters, electricians, cleaners, watchmen, and the like. Dull as all this sounds on paper, it accomplished the highly useful purpose of lowering from thirty to three the number of persons bothering the Director with minutiae of daily problems, thus giving him, for the first time, an opportunity to concern himself with the larger aspects of the library. Furthermore, by concentrating business operations in a single division, it allowed the persons engaged in purely library matters to put their full minds upon their proper business without irrelevant distractions, and provided for desirable autonomy of the groups dealing with the dissemination of popular reading on the one hand, and with the care of reference books on the other.

As any plan of organization, however neat and logical it may appear on paper, stands or falls upon the character and the abilities of the people who carry it out, immediate attention was given to enlarging the opportunities for training the library staff. When promotion is based chiefly upon length of service, and advancement depends largely upon the next man above one being gathered to his eternal reward, initiative suffers, and an office-holding philosophy results. In many institutions, including the armed forces, down to relatively recent times one unfortunately reached, or did not reach, the head of one's profession chiefly because of the accident of longevity. The United States Navy in 1916 introduced the more reasonable system of promotion by selection on the basis of demonstrated abilities. Two decades later the Boston Public Library applied similar principles to its own service. In 1933 Mr. Lord wrote, in reference to the administrative reorganization:

> The chief implication in the above plans is that extensive training of personnel is necessary for full success in carrying out the proposed developments. An appreciably large number of individ-

uals within the library staff must be constantly in training for higher responsibilities, and there must be an ample number of intermediate positions in which they can gain experience and recognition.

With this in mind, the Library Training Class, established in 1927 for a limited number of students, was in 1932, at the end of its fifth academic year, expanded to offer courses to all full-time members of the library staff. Although entirely voluntary, and carried on outside library hours in the staff members' own free time, the response was gratifying, for during the first three years 405 different staff members enrolled. The courses were designed both to supplement formal library training obtained elsewhere and to provide a substitute for such opportunities in the case of those who had not previously had them.

The next step, taken on 1 January 1938, was to carry to full development previously incomplete arrangements (dating from the eighteen nineties) for the classification of personnel and for staff examinations. These were based, as the Director's report for 1937 explained, on two fundamental assumptions.

> The first of these is that individuals are not naturally equal in their respective capacities and accomplishments, that some can and will progress faster and farther than others, that there must therefore be provided a ladder with easily recognizable steps up which individuals may climb, thus achieving a classifying and grading of themselves largely through their own efforts. In other words, the belief is that in general the personal qualifications of an individual are likely to afford a better basis for financial recognition than does the relative standing of a particular position in which the individual happens to find himself and to which a particular rate of pay happens to be attached at the moment.

> The second fundamental assumption is that, beyond the possession of the common background which all librarians ought to have of the ordinary tools and technique of their work, they ought also to be possessed of specific excellence in some particular direction or directions. The discovery of such competence or excellence in the members of the library staff is of the highest importance in the further development of a staff adequate to the needs and standing of the Boston Public Library.

Acting upon these assumptions, a framework of ten steps was established—five in the Probationary Service and five in the Permanent Service, each with its appropriate examination which must be passed to qualify for promotion and increased pay. The qualifying examinations for the Probationary Assistant were designed to test his knowledge of General Book Selection, Cataloging and Classification, General Reference Work, and the work of the Boston Public Library system, both in the central library and in the branches. The passing of each examination carried with it a small raise in pay; the completion of all five made one eligible for appointment as an Assistant in the Permanent Service. The first of the promotional examinations in the Permanent Service, which was common to all departments, attempted to test the employee's knowledge of the nature of the public library as an institution. In the second and third examinations the subjects varied according to the nature of the employee's duties. For members of branch library staffs they were set in the fields of the Social Sciences and History, and Literature; for workers in the central library the second examination would test an advanced knowledge of the French and German languages, and the third would deal with general knowledge of a subject field, such as Fine Arts, Music, Science and Technology, Social Sciences, History, or of Literature. The fourth and fifth steps concerned a special field to be selected from within the subject chosen for the third, or with aspects of specialized library activity, such as Cataloging, Classification, Extension Work, Children's Work, or Library Administration. Increases in pay would automatically follow the completion of the first three promotional examinations; in the fourth and fifth levels they would be awarded whenever, after one passed the examinations, there were appropriate vacancies to be filled.

Exemption from examinations in technical library areas was provided for those trained in accredited library schools, and from examinations in subject areas for those who had shown equivalent competence at a recognized college or university. On the other hand, the examinations provided an accessible road to advancement for many able library employees whose formal education had stopped early, without the rigid insistence upon the letter of the academic law that clutters so many summer schools with unhappy schoolteachers in quest of the degree that stands between them and a much needed raise in pay. Furthermore, the examination system impartially protects the library from the importunities—common in any public institution—of incompetents whose only recommendation for employment is political in origin. In the average year some five hundred applicants take the entrance examinations, three hundred the qualifying examinations, and fifty the promotional.

Salaries in the Boston Public Library had long been low in relation both to library salaries paid elsewhere and to those paid in other parts of the City of Boston service for work of a more or less similar nature. In the spring of 1933 they had been further reduced in common with those of all city employees. In many instances high school graduates entered the library service at $11.00 or $12.00 a week. Particularly fortunate library school graduates might receive as much as $20.00, although they were more apt to start at $15.00, which was the normal beginning rate for college graduates. In 1937, $20.00 per week was established as the normal entering wage for a Probationary Assistant (Grade C), with each of the qualifying examinations adding one dollar weekly. In the Permanent Service (Grade B), the schedule adopted was as follows:

Assistant, Beginning	$25.00
Assistant, 1st Step	29.00
Assistant, 2nd Step	33.00
Assistant, 3rd Step	37.00
Second Assistant	44.00
First Assistant	45.00

In the Professional Library Service (Grade A), Chiefs of Departments and Branch Librarians received from $2610 to $3130 annually, while the salaries of other officers were to be fixed for each case individually.

From this beginning, such steady progress has been made for more than fifteen years that the Boston Public Library system salaries are now not only entirely adequate even for present-day costs of living, but are well above those generally paid in other libraries in the area, and comparable to those in the better paid public libraries of the entire country. Today a college or library school graduate generally begins, not at $15.00 per week, but at about $3,600 a year. Unclassified Assistants receive between $2,410 and $3,160, while Assistants, Fifth Step, are paid from $4,510 to $4,760, with Chiefs, Deputy Supervisors, Supervisors, and Chief Librarians at proportionately appropriate rates up to $9,060. Thus the librarians, who were formerly the worst paid employees of the City of Boston, now receive salaries exceeded only by those of the school teachers. This is a change of which the City may well be proud.

Thanks to the Personnel Office, which recruits, keeps records, conducts in-service-training, examination and counselling programs, and administers a staff library and hospital, and to the greatly improved physical facilities for the convenience of the staff—rest rooms, lounges, toilets, locker rooms and lunch rooms—the office-holding philosophy of early decades has gradually diminished. In 1932, 24 per cent of the library staff were college graduates; 22 per cent had attended college without receiving degrees; 52 per cent had stopped at the end of high school, and 2 per cent had only attended grammar school. Twenty years later the percentages for the same categories were 46, 17, 37 and 0. In 1932 only nine library school graduates (2 per cent) were employed in the Boston Public Library, as opposed to sixty-four (10 per cent) in 1952. This change in the character of the staff led to the formation in 1946 of the Boston Public Library Professional Staff Association, to which over 90 per cent of the eligible employees belong. In addition, the Trustees have established four annual scholarships for study at library schools, and give five annual grants toward the cost of attending annual meetings of the American Library Association. Thus a substantial beginning has been made in breaking down the ingrowing character of the Boston Public Library staff.

In 1936 the Library received the first payments under the will of Josiah H. Benton. It will be recalled from Chapter X that that document contained a far from lucid provision requiring the payment of income to the Rector of Trinity Church for "relieving the necessities of the poor" in any year when the City failed to appropriate for the library "at least three per cent of the amount available for department expenses." Although the library Trustees felt that the provision was solely designed to guard against reduction in municipal appropriations for the library because of Benton's generosity, the will was sufficiently ambiguous to give lawyers a field day in the courts. It was not clear, for example, whether three per cent of "department expenses" was intended to include or exclude the very large expenditures for public schools. There was a difference of opinion as to whether Benton intended to benefit the poor of Boston, or simply seized upon the Rector of Trinity Church as a reliable recipient for funds in years when the City Council became stingy to the library. Litigation became prolonged, and the estate remained undistributed for many years until finally in January 1935 an agreement of compromise provided that sixty per cent of the income was to be paid to the library and forty per cent to the Rector of Trinity Church. The cash and securities constituting the bulk of the estate were received in 1936, and in 1938, after thorough auditing and accounting, the Benton Book Fund and the Benton Building Fund were set up. Had the residuary estate been divided in 1927, the date at which it became divisible under the terms of the will, each of these funds would have had a principal of $1,156,839.75. As the building fund was to accumulate until it reached the sum of $2,-000,000, the income received between 1927 and 1936 from that part of the estate was added to principal, so that the fund in 1938 amounted to $1,644,118.57. The principal of the book fund, after the deduction of certain losses arising from revaluation of securities, stood at $1,136,480.25, while the accumulated income for 1927–1938, after deducting the forty per cent payable to Trinity Church, totalled $306,279.55. A substantial part of this back income was very shortly spent for books "desirable for scholarly research and use," thus giving the Library an opportunity to fill some of the gaps, notably in its rare book collection, that was particularly welcome after the lean years of depression, when any funds available had been urgently required to meet the needs of popular reading. Today the Benton Building Fund has already passed the two-million-dollar mark, while the Benton Book Fund remains one of the Library's chief resources for the purchase of scholarly material.

In 1938 was received the Emily L. Ainsley Fund of $222,440, the income of which was to be used for the purchase of books. The generous gift was the second largest sum of money to come to the library up to that time.

As it is both inevitable and appropriate that the municipal appropriations should be spent only for the purchase and dissemination of books of wide popular interest and utility, it is fortunate that the Boston Public Library has on occasion aroused the imagination of private individuals who have, like Joshua Bates and Josiah H. Benton, made possible the development of great special collections. Although Thomas G. Appleton, one of the original Trustees, had given in 1869 some thousands of engravings collected by Cardinal Tosti, the library had, because of the extraordinarily rich resources of the neighboring Museum of Fine Arts, no valid reason for spreading book funds thinner by attempting to accumulate a print collection of its own. The development of a print department came about entirely by unanticipated private generosity. Albert H. Wiggin, a New York banker, had, from the early years of the present century, been an avid collector of prints. Although he particularly concentrated on the work of such British artists as Muirhead Bone, D. Y. Cameron, James McBey, Gerald Brockhurst, and Robert Austin, securing not only an impression of every plate they produced but, in addition, complete runs of trial proofs and "states," Mr. Wiggin made great efforts to include similar representations of French and American artists of the nineteenth and twentieth centuries, and to carry his collecting back into earlier eras of print making. The extraordinary completeness of the work of many of the artists represented made the Wiggin Collection particularly useful to students and scholars. While it would have been a valuable addition to the holdings of any of the American museums specializing in prints, Mr. Wiggin preferred rather to place it in an institution where it might stand by itself, bearing his name. Having approached the Boston Public Library through his friend John L. Hall—a member of the board from 1931 to 1946—the Trustees in 1935 voted to express their interest in the possibility of accepting the Albert H. Wiggin Collection. Friendly relations with the library developed so happily that late in 1940 Mr. Wiggin determined to deposit the collection within his lifetime. On 14 June 1941 it was formally inaugurated in quarters renovated for the purpose on the third floor, between the Sargent Gallery and the Fine Arts Reading Room. Having made the deposit, Mr. Wiggin then not only began the gradual gift of portions of the collection—completed in the course of five years—but continued until his death in 1951 to make extensive purchases to supplement its already rich holdings. During this decade major collections of prints by Alphonse Legros, Augustus John, Frank W. Benson, George C. Wales, John Copley, Goya, Daumier, Gavarni, and Frederick L. Griggs were added by Mr. Wiggin, while other donors generously followed his example. A

CHILDREN'S ROOM, ADAMS STREET BRANCH

collection of the work of the late Charles H. Woodbury was given in 1944 by Mrs. Charles Bruen Perkins and Mr. and Mrs. David O. Woodbury; Hiram C. Merrill started in 1945 the assembly of Thomas W. Nason's work; while in 1950 Edward C. Crossett gave some five hundred prints, states and drawings by Arthur W. Heintzelman.

The library was fortunate in being able to secure the services of Mr. Heintzelman as Keeper of Prints in 1941, for the usefulness of the Wiggin Collection has been greatly enhanced through placing it in the care of one of the most distinguished living artists in the field. Treated by ordinary library methods, Mr. Wiggin's gift would have become just another collection housed on the third floor; it required the presence of a skilled craftsman, fully versed in the technicalities of print-making, to interpret and derive full benefit from it. Through exhibitions shown in the library and lent to museums and colleges not only in this country but also in France and Italy, through lectures, and through generous technical counsel to students and visitors, Mr. Heintzelman has broadened the Wiggin Collection from an addition to the library's scholarly holdings to be also a valuable element in its task of popular education. His useful activities in this direction are comparable to those of Dr. Haraszti, the Keeper of Rare Books and Editor of Publications, who has done much through exhibitions and in the monthly pages of *More Books,* and in the *Boston Public Library Quarterly* that replaced it in 1949, to give the casual reader an appreciation of the nature and significance of the rare books and manuscripts owned by the library.

CHAPTER XII

Towards the Second Century

Cast your bread upon the waters: for thou shalt
find it after many days.
—ECCLESIASTES, XI, I.

D URING HIS American lecture tour of 1883 Matthew Arnold
was rarely aroused to unrestrained enthusiasm over New England habits. When courteously offered pie for breakfast in Andover,
he maintained an air of superior critical detachment. Nevertheless he
pronounced the Somerset Club, where he was lodged in Boston, as
"first rate" and "capital," and was profoundly impressed by the
democratic government of the Boston Public Library. An anonymous member of the library staff, in an interview with a *Herald* reporter concerning the cranks and eccentrics who frequented the
institution—reprinted in The *Library Journal* for June 1887—recalled the English critic's visit to the old building in Boylston Street.

> He came in here one day and saw a little barefooted newsboy sit-
> ting in one of the best chairs in the reading-room, enjoying himself
> apparently for dear life. The great essayist was completely as-
> tounded. "Do you let barefooted boys in this reading-room?" he
> asked. "You would never see such a sight as that in Europe. I do
> not believe there is a reading-room in all Europe in which that
> boy, dressed as he is, would enter." Then Mr. Arnold went over
> to the boy, engaged him in conversation, and found that he was
> reading the *Life of Washington,* and that he was a young gentle-
> man of decidedly anti-British tendencies, and, for his age, re-
> markably well informed. Mr. Arnold remained talking with the
> youngster for some time, and, as he came back to our desk, the
> great Englishman said: "I do not think I have been so impressed
> with anything else that I have seen since arriving in this country
> as I am now with meeting that barefooted boy in this reading-
> room. What a tribute to democratic institutions it is to say that,

instead of sending that boy out to wander along in the streets, they permit him to come in here and excite his youthful imagination by reading such a book as the *Life of Washington!* The reading of that one book may change the whole course of that boy's life, and may be the means of making him a useful, honorable, worthy citizen of this great country. It is, I tell you, a sight that impresses a European not accustomed to your democratic ways."

Although there is no clue to the identity of Matthew Arnold's barefoot newsboy, one may well assume that in the end he acquired not only shoes but a substantial place in the community, if the career of another unorthodox young reader of the same period may be considered as an example of what determination combined with "book-learning" may produce.

Of the second reader, whose name was John Deferrari, we know more, although none too much. The son of a Genoese fruit peddler, he was born during the Civil War in a North End tenement on Ferry Street. Leaving school at thirteen, he peddled fruit from a basket in State Street offices, where he saw, and resolved to emulate, prosperous citizens earning—so he was told—five thousand dollars a year. This beatific vision spurred him to acquire first a pushcart, then a horse and wagon, then a fruit store in Dock Square. The next step was to move his business to Boylston Street next to the then building of the Public Library, where travellers by the Boston and Providence Railroad, whose terminus was then in Park Square, might be tempted to buy, both day and night, from the Quality Fruit Store. This new location enabled John Deferrari to visit the Public Library next door regularly and devour books on real estate, law, business, economics, and statistics. Having an alchemist's yearning for gold, he studied with a passionate regard for detail any subject that might lead him to profitable investment. Gradually he converted the earnings of the Quality Fruit Store into stocks, bonds, and real estate. Having found the key to this new alchemy in the Public Library, John Deferrari left the fruit business at the age of 28, and devoted himself for the remainder of his life—more than half a century—to the accumulation and exchange of real estate and securities. Study and learning do not in themselves necessarily enlarge the human spirit. Lacking any human guidance,

John Deferrari resolutely ignored the poetic heritage of his race, and by his studies became a modern counterpart of the classic type of medieval miser, like to those who, in the fourth circle of the *Inferno,* join with the prodigal in rolling great dead weights against each other through eternity, to a chorus of mutual reproaches in which "Why chuck away?" alternates with "Why grab so tight?"

> Qui vidi gente più che altrove troppa,
> e d'una parte e d'altra, con grandi urli,
> voltando pesi per forza di poppa;
> percotevansi incontro, e poscia pur lì
> si rivolgea ciascun, voltando a retro,
> gridando: "Perchè tieni?" e "Perchè burli?"

He was an astute buyer, with a mortal distrust of banks, lawyers, and doctors. He paid cash for securities over the counter; had no office more private than the waiting rooms of railway stations; kept his files in his coat pockets secured by safety pins, and sought no advice more personal than the books of the Boston Public Library — and in later years those of the Kirstein Business Branch—could give. Like one of Mr. Dooley's characters, he made money "because he honestly loved it with an innocint affiction." His fortune increased, but his wants remained constant. He neither drank, smoked, nor swore, and rarely ate. Although he never married, he provided for his parents and sisters, and, as a single concession to sentiment, retained his father's double three story brick house in Wesley Place, off Hanover Street, as long as he lived, keeping his parents' tenement furnished and leaving the other five vacant. Living in Beacon Chambers on Myrtle Street under an assumed name, and having General Delivery as his only address, he would go to Wesley Place once a day and cook himself a meal.

As John Deferrari's holdings grew, he successfully weathered the increased responsibility of looking after them singlehanded even through the first two terms of the New Deal. Wartime regulations were the final straw, and early in the forties he reluctantly shuffled into the National Shawmut Bank to seek advice. He fell in with an officer of the Trust Department who was sufficiently alert and tactful to allay temporarily his lifelong distrust of bankers. In consequence, Deferrari returned to the bank now and then. He needed help, for he was approaching eighty and realized that he must eventually make a will and provide for the disposition of his lifelong accumulation of property. The result was a trust agreement establishing the John Deferrari Foundation, with himself and the National Shawmut as trustees, under which a jury consisting of the Mayor of Boston, the Chief Justice of the Municipal Court and other functionaries would make grants to deserving young men. This rather inchoate benefaction did not satisfy the old man, who feared political implications and wished to make his arrangements more precise.

During the summer of 1946, Mr. Lord received a telephone call from the National Shawmut Bank, asking whether the Boston Public Library would be interested in a bequest under which income would become available after the capital had accumulated to two million dollars. The only stipulation would be that a room should bear the name of the then anonymous intending testator, and should contain a framed photograph of him. Mr. Lord made the library's interest abundantly and immediately clear, but, as he realized that the Benton Building Fund was insufficient for an addition to the Copley Square library at post-war costs, suggested that, when the capital sum reached two million dollars, one million be taken from it for building purposes. He further proposed that an entire wing bear the donor's name, and that the framed photograph be improved to an oil portrait.

For nine months nothing happened. Then in April 1947 the bank called again. Mr. Lord for the first time learned John Deferrari's name. A meeting was arranged to such purpose that on 1 July 1947 a trust was established providing for the accumulation of the income of an initial gift of approximately one million dollars until the sum of two million was reached. At that point one million was to be paid to the Trustees of the Boston Public Library for the construction of a John Defarrari Wing to the Copley Square building, while the remaining million was to be allowed to double itself once again. When the sum of two million dollars has been reached for the second time, the income is to be paid quarterly to the Trustees for whatever use they may think appropriate.

John Deferrari felt that the Boston Public Library had made his career possible. He hoped in an obscure way to make his fortune useful to young men, and he recognized the parallelism of his gift to that of Joshua Bates nine decades earlier. The suggestion of a public announcement of his gift filled him with alarm, but by 6 September 1947 he had screwed his courage to the point of coming to the library and meeting both the Trustees and the press. Equipped with a new hat and a new suit, which was, however, disfigured by the customary safety-pins that guarded the integrity of his pocket-files, John Deferrari weathered his first press conference. He let it be known with modest pride that he "became a millionaire without benefit of a banker, a secretary, a bookkeeper, an automobile, or a telephone." As his wealth had come from intelligent use of the library, he was glad to return it to the source.

When Leopold Seyffert had completed painting John Defarrari's portrait, the subject came once more to the library for the unveiling. The ceremony was marred by the appearance of a process server who presented an attachment connected with a suit for damages rising out of a fire in a Bowdoin Street lodging house owned by Deferrari. After this regrettable unpleasantness he rarely went out of doors until after dark, and drew in upon himself so completely that four days passed after his death in the spring of 1950 before his body was discovered and identified.

One wishes that Matthew Arnold might have known the outcome of this curiously moral tale of virtue rewarded, for it would have startled him even more than the sight of the barefooted newsboy reading the *Life of Washington*. Certainly no library has ever been more richly or unexpectedly rewarded for doing its daily work simply and without affectation. Equally unanticipated was the bequest by Mrs. H. Sylvia A. H. G. Wilks of one unit (1/140th part) of the enormous estate that she had inherited from her New Bedford mother, Hetty Green. As with John Deferrari, the inspiration of this gift went back well into the nineteenth century, for it was designed to honor the memory of Mrs. Wilks's father's first cousin, Dr. Samuel A. Green, a Trustee of the Boston Public Library from 1868 to 1878, and its Acting Librarian during the year following Justin Winsor's resignation in the summer of 1877. Mrs. Wilks's estate amounting to more than ninety million dollars, the library received in 1952, without restriction as to use, $605,000, the bulk of which was appropriated by the Trustees to carry on the modernization of parts of the Copley Square building that had been undertaken in the mid forties.

Past chapters have alluded to the architectural merit and practical inconvenience of the great central library. When it was designed, there was little useful precedent to rely on, for the public library movement was only in its fourth decade. Moreover, President Abbott's conviction of his own omniscience discouraged any serious attempt to profit by the experience of other institutions. Charles McKim had consequently all too completely attained the palace ideal, even to the point of providing back stairs areas that were as grubby and inconvenient as anything at Versailles. Rebuilding to improve matters of vulgar utility, which began as early as 1898, became a perennial necessity. The results, even with the 1917 addition, actually amounted to lengthening a blanket by transferring a few inches from the head to the foot until 1942, when the completion of the New England Deposit Library made possible the physical removal of more than 100,000 rarely consulted volumes from Copley Square. This cooperative venture, planned by Keyes DeWitt Metcalf, Director of the Harvard University Library, and sponsored by a number of the overcrowded institutions of greater Boston, put up an economical building near Soldiers Field in Brighton, where participating libraries could store their less-used books at moderate cost. Thanks to this new resource the Boston Public Library at last gained room to maneuver.

For this particular game of chess, it proved singularly fortunate that each level of the Copley Square book stack was an independent structural unit with its own solid floor. In the 1898 rebuilding, when more working space was needed for the Delivery Room, the Librarian's Office had been moved into an area originally part of the book stack. This precedent suggested the possibility of rebuilding still other parts of the stack for administrative uses and internal work areas, but, even when space had been created by the transfer of books to the New England Deposit Library, the problem of using what was gained to the best advantage remained complex. Any changes made had to be logical not only in relation to the immediate

use of the building, but also to an eventual enlargement, of unde-
termined size and plan. In 1949 the Trustees bought the remainder
of the Dartmouth-Boylston-Exeter-Blagden block, although with the
provision that Boston University might occupy the buildings thus
acquired until 1959. With space for future expansion thus assured,
it remained to devise a plan that would respect the superb architectural qualities of the public rooms of the old building, while converting the working areas into forms that would be useful both before and after the construction of a new wing.

The first step was to assemble in the remodelled book stack the
various behind-the-scenes activities of the library, which had previously been scattered throughout the building in any available empty
corner. Working from plans prepared by the library's architectural
advisors, Messrs. Ames, Child and Graves of Boston, the library's
force of masons, carpenters, electricians, and painters was able to
accomplish this conversion, bit by bit, out of funds from the normal
annual operating budget of the library.

The personnel administration was centralized on one floor, with
attractive and convenient quarters for the Personnel Office, its In-
Service Training Course class rooms, a Staff Library and Staff Hospital, a Coffee Shop, as well as adequate rest, locker and toilet rooms
for the male and female members of the library staff and the building maintenance force. On another floor of the stack the Book Selection, Cataloging and Classification Departments, for both the Home
Reading Services and the Reference and Research Services, together
with the Book Purchasing Department, the Book Preparation Department, and the central Book Stock for the Branch Libraries were
brought together in well-planned offices. The administrative offices
were concentrated at a point near the Blagden Street entrance,
while in adjacent areas—conveniently accessible from the public
rooms at the front of the building—similarly consolidated offices
were provided for the Chief Librarians of the Division of Reference
and Research Services and the Division of Home Reading and Community Services and their assistants. The business offices were similarly centralized, with new quarters for the main Business Office
and the Accounting Department in a converted stack area, while in
the annex, where the Printing and the Binding Departments were

already located, improved space was provided for shipping and receiving, stock and supplies, as well as for the carpentry, electrical and paint shops.

Although these changes, spread over a period of years, were visible only to those who penetrated behind the scenes, they not only improved the working efficiency of the staff but also cleared areas that then became available for public use. In an effort to break down the old Boylston Street dichotomy between the Lower and Bates Hall, McKim had placed all book services on the second floor of the Copley Square library. Thus, to consult the card catalogue or to request or return a book, one had to travel a considerable distance through an impressive vestibule, climb the monumental stairway with its Siena marble walls and Puvis de Chavannes paintings, and, on the second floor, walk approximately to the corner of Dartmouth and Blagden Streets, either in the vaulted Bates Hall or in the imposing Delivery Room, where Abbey's Quest of the Holy Grail gleamed down above the oak panelling. It is to be assumed that this inconvenience was deliberately planned to expose the reader to the ennobling influence of the fine arts. This notion of culture by contagion still has its supporters, for the Harvard undergraduate bound for the main lecture room of the Fogg Art Museum (opened in 1927) must traverse a Renaissance courtyard and a great hall containing Romanesque sculpture before finding stairs that lead to his destination, while the budding engineer at M.I.T. using the Hayden Library (opened in 1950) cannot reach a spot where slide rules are permitted without following a circuitous course subject to the temptations of art exhibitions and recorded music. The theory is fine, but the practice leads chiefly to tired feet and loss of time. To the credit of McKim, it should be pointed out that the Harry Elkins Widener Memorial Library at Harvard College, opened two decades after the Boston Public Library, suffers from the same defects of plan without the agreeable decorative amenities, and with the addition of an extra monumental flight of steps leading from the Yard to the first floor. In the Sterling Memorial Library at Yale (1931) the card catalogue is at least on the ground floor near the door, although concealed by such a profusion of Gothic ornament that one instinctively fumbles for a holy water stoup on entering, and has consciously to resist the temptation to genuflect at the Delivery Desk.

The Cataloging, Classification, and Ordering Departments had occupied, from 1895, the southeast corner of the ground floor of the Copley Square library. When they were transferred to new quarters in the remodelled stacks, space thus became available for the development of an expanded Open Shelf Department for Home Reading, in which books offer themselves readily to the casual browser. The result, opened in 1952, is a revelation to anyone whose impression of the Boston Public Library is colored by memories of illiterate derelicts reading their own newspapers or catching up on sleep. Here there is no normal library furniture, but rather self-service shelves, containing an appealing selection of clean and attractive books, with chairs in which one can sit (but not sleep) comfortably at convenient intervals. The absence of tables emphasizes the fact that the room is designed for the choice of home reading rather than the detailed study of law cases. Separate attractive browsing areas, each with its own reader's advisor, have been set aside for adults, young adults, and children. In these, as in the rooms below that have been rescued from basement storage, are phonograph turntables by which as many as eight individuals may listen at one time with earphones to recorded music. On the lower floor, in addition to a poetry corner, with a soundproof room where poetry recordings may be heard without earphones, is a smoking area. The whole Open Shelf Department for Home Reading has an informal and pleasantly relaxed atmosphere, happily free from institutionalism. By means of pavilions containing book shelves, its services have also been extended in summer months to the courtyard, which has thus become something more than the lost opportunity that it has been for nearly sixty years. To redeem this delightful court from its former character of a haven for loafers and a passageway to public toilets is a major accomplishment.

Leading out of the basement section of the Open Shelf Department for Home Reading is an entirely new Audio-Visual Department, opened in January 1952. Here, with soundproof listening booths, one may select recordings for home use. Here also is an attractive little theater, for film showings and group presentation of recordings, as well as the library's film section. The creation of these agreeable quarters out of an unusually forbidding cellar, cluttered with conduits, pipes, and ventilating ducts, is testimony to the resourcefulness and imagination of the library staff and their architects. By the use of false ceiling equipped with fluorescent lights, one has no suggestion of being below ground in a converted basement. The effect of cheerful, well-lighted rooms is triumphantly and deceptively successful.

The completion of the Open Shelf and Audio-Visual Departments quarters, at a cost of approximately $150,000, derived from the library's annual operating budgets of three consecutive years, demonstrated what could be accomplished by judicious alterations within the fabric of the Copley Square library, without in any way doing violence to the architectural quality of the main public rooms. At the present time similar efforts in modernization are projected along the Boylston Street side of the building, and at the northwest corner of the courtyard. These changes, which are being undertaken with the Dr. Samuel A. Green Memorial Fund bequeathed by Mrs. Wilks, are designed to locate as many public areas as possible on the lower floors and to bring into being in nucleus form certain developments that will subsequently be expanded in the proposed enlargement of the building. At the back of the court
Newspaper Room, Current Periodical Room, a
bound files of both, are being located in the area to
by the old carpenter shop and the bound newspapers.
rent Periodical Room will be a Parent-Teachers Room fo
cation Department, above which will be located a Religi
phy-Psychology Department, in space previously given to t
cal Department. The present Patent Room, at the northwest
the courtyard, will be provided with a mezzanine floor for
commodation of the Patent Collection, while its main floor
rebuilt for the use of the Science and Technology Departmen
incongruously housed with the Fine Arts on the third floor.
ground floor rooms at the northeast corner of the building, now
cupied by the Newspaper and Periodical Rooms, will shortly hou
a Social Sciences Department (including a new Sports and Travel
Section) and a Government Documents Department (achieved by

breaking up the holdings of the old Statistical Department). Adjacent space will be devoted to the new Maps Department.

The Main Entrance Hall has acquired, without major detriment to its monumental appearance, Book Charging Desks and a central Book Return Desk, which obviate the long climb to the Abbey Room. Thus in the near future the Public Card Catalogue will be moved from the southern end of Bates Hall into the Abbey Room. The Bates Hall reading room will, as at present, house the History Department in the northern end and the General Reference Collection in its central portion. The southern end will be given over to a Literature and Languages Department. The Music Department will shortly move down to the second floor to the rooms formerly occupied by the old Children's Room and the Teachers Department, thus clearing additional space on the third floor for the expansion of the Rare Book Department. The removal of Science and Technology to new quarters will permit the Fine Arts Department to dig itself out from the present crowded confusion of the west gallery on the third floor. This game of musical chairs will require time for its completion, but the striking success achieved with the Open Shelf Department gives one a foretaste of what may be expected as the modernization continues.

Time has its curious revenges. For many decades, librarians devoted to the card catalogue smiled patronizingly as the British Museum continued to revise and publish its catalogue in book form. Today one goes with respect not only to the British Museum catalogue but to the bound volumes in which Library of Congress cards are now conveniently available in book form. Within the year the Lamont Library of Harvard College has issued its catalogue in book form. In 1882 the seemingly cantankerous William H. Whitmore saw no reason why the Boston Public Library could not economically accommodate itself in the English-High and Latin School buildings by housing its books in the numerous school rooms where, as in the Athenæum, they could be seen and used, rather than segregating them in a stack. The present plan toward subdividing the resources of the Division of Reference and Research Services into specialized departments, where the reader may consult books upon particular subjects with the aid of assistants familiar with the material, must, if these matters are of interest on the other side of the Styx, cause

Whitmore's shade to smile. In still another direction library technique has come full circle.

Since the acquisition of the land behind the library in 1949, the form of building to be placed upon it has exercised many minds. It must, by general agreement, respect McKim's façade. If it should fail to do so, it will not be for want of trying. Mr. Lord, for all the trouble he has had trying to make his institution work smoothly inside its walls, describes the central library unequivocally as "one of the chief architectural ornaments of the nation," and as "the most beautiful public library building in the world." The future extension must also be sufficiently functional and flexible to accommodate the library for many decades to come. For the observance of the centennial anniversary preliminary studies were made in which Alfred Morton Githens, as consulting architect, endeavored to translate into tentative plans the future needs of the library as now foreseen by the trustees and staff. These are to be widely circulated so that useful criticism and discussion may be brought to bear with ample time for consideration. The Boston Public Library has twice in its history moved into fine new buildings that did not work; it does not propose to do so a third time.

Simultaneously with the planning of the new Open Shelf Department for Home Reading in Copley Square, equally experimental steps were being taken with the evolution of a new form of branch library. These were long overdue, for at least half of the thirty-odd branch libraries needed new buildings. The West Roxbury Branch of 1922 represented almost the only respectable activity in that direction since 1900 until the spurt of municipal conscience that led to the completion in 1930–1932 of new branches at Mattapan, Parker Hill, Connolly (Boylston), Faneuil, and Jeffries Point to replace totally inadequate existing quarters. The depression, however, prevented any further improvement for another two decades. In the eighty-five years since the East Boston Branch—the first in any American city—was opened in 1871, it has been found more than once that requirements for library service alter radically with changes of population in given neighborhoods. In its current modernization plans, therefore, the Boston Public Library has experimented with the construction of simple, functional branch libraries, free from architectural pretension or elaborate decoration, that might, under changed circumstances, prove adaptable to other use if not needed for their original purpose. The branches at Adams Street, Dorchester (intended to replace the Neponset Branch Library) and at Egleston Square (an entirely new branch library area) completed in 1951 and 1953, are one-story buildings primarily of cinder block and glass, designed solely to make books available in the region under attractive conditions at minimum cost. In these latest experiments in branch library architecture, everything has been placed on one floor level. Such a plan not only reduces construction costs by eliminating the need for digging a cellar, but simplifies the problem of staff coverage. While designed for library use, such buildings are planned so that they could easily be converted to commercial purposes, if, through changes in the character of neighborhoods, they were no longer needed as branch libraries. The earlier ornamental type of branch library building lacked flexibility in its plan and could hardly have been adapted to any other use. The current type, having few permanent partitions and being planned so as to permit change of use of areas, simply by the moving of bookcases or similar dividing elements, achieves extreme flexibility. If one of these buildings were to be given up by the library, it could easily be converted into three or four stores by the installation of interior partitions and the cutting of additional doors through the façade.

From the point of view of attracting readers, a greater use of color and improved lighting make the recent branch library buildings considerably gayer than their predecessors, while the possibility of smoking attracts many readers. It is intended that the branch library buildings of today should serve as congenial community centers. To this end, space is provided for activities which can be library-centered, through library programs making use of recordings and films, which go considerably beyond the earlier concept of the branch library simply as a point for the lending of books. While this function retains its old importance, much has been added in the way of programs designed to stimulate the borrowing of books. Lectures, recitals of music, readers' advisory services, storytelling for children, book discussion groups for adults, and an increased quantity of audio-visual equipment, are all employed to lure readers to books. The Friends of the East Boston Branch Library, formed in 1948 following the seventy-fifth anniversary of the branch's establishment, has proved to be a genuine community development that has become a source of continued gifts of equipment—such as a motion-picture projector and screen, radio, phonograph, and tape-recorder—to the library. The Friends of the Phil-

ADAMS STREET BRANCH

lips Brooks Branch Library, established a year later on the example of East Boston, not only benefitted the library by gifts but has developed into a community organization for the entire Readville area. Similar organizations were formed immediately after the opening of the Adams Street and Eggleston Square Branch Libraries, and plans have been set under way for the development of such groups around other branch libraries. In addition to these efforts to attract general readers, the branch libraries have given increasing attention to the needs of special groups, developing closer relations with labor unions, public and parochial schools, and hospitals.

Even greater flexibility in circulation is attained by the use of two Bookmobiles which are on the go five days a week, taking books to areas not readily served by one of the thirty-two immobile branches. The first of these has been in operation since February 1950; the second since February 1952.

A new South Boston Branch, to replace the existing South Boston and City Point Branch Libraries, is scheduled for completion in 1956. It is to be hoped that the City Planning Board's recommendation that all branches in rented premises, and those inadequately accommodated in municipal buildings, be systematically re-established in new buildings at the rate of one each year, may be followed.

Such improvements in surroundings, and in the variety and attractiveness of the books offered, are bound to have an effect upon the future of the Library. The circulation figures of 1929 to 1938 quoted in Chapter XI showed a fantastic rise during the depths of the depression, and a consistent decline as employment gradually increased. From 4,354,044 volumes in 1938, circulation continued to drop through the war years to a 1945 low point of 2,661,741. While military service and increased employment unquestionably took away an appreciable number of library users, the book stock was becoming disreputable and uninviting at the very moment when paper-covered books and weekly periodicals were offering vastly increased cheap reading matter at newsstands and drugstores. Library books were wearing out and not being replaced just as long-playing phonograph records and the omnipresent television were increasing the competition with reading previously offered by Hollywood and the radio. It therefore became doubly necessary to provide fresh books and present them in convenient and pleasant surroundings. The results of the new Open Shelf Department for Home Reading in Copley Square, which includes films and recordings, and the effects of the new branches and of the Bookmobiles, are readily apparent in the post-war circulation figures:

1946	2,750,089
1947	2,770,841
1948	2,838,521
1949	2,912,146
1950	2,822,127
1951	3,055,607

During its first year of operation, the new Open Shelf Department distributed a number of books half as large again as had been previously lent from Copley Square for home reading. Similarly, the new Adams Street Branch, with agreeable surroundings and fresh books, moved to the head of all the branch libraries in its first year's circulation, while the first Bookmobile surpassed even the largest circulation in any of the branch libraries.

It cannot be too strongly emphasized that the steady rise in circulation since the war is directly attributable to the presence of fresh books in attractive surroundings. The obvious corollary is that still more books would lead to further use.

In appraising the usefulness of the Boston Public Library, however, one must not rely alone upon figures of gross circulation, for this would leave out of reckoning the extensive activities of the institution as a scholarly and reference library. Through the gifts of its founders and the energetic collecting of Jewett, Winsor and Chamberlain, the Boston Public Library had acquired in its early decades a collection of scholarly books far richer than is to be found in most public libraries. Constant purchasing within the limits of private endowment funds—greatly augmented when the income of J. H. Benton's bequest at last became available—and the receipt of such important special collections as the Brown music library and Albert H. Wiggins's prints, have so consistently maintained this interest that the Boston Public Library is (in company with the far larger New York Public Library) one of the only two public libraries in the United States admitted to membership in the Association of Research Libraries. At the end of the year 1951, with 1,924,640 volumes owned by the Boston Public Library, approximately one third (632,706) were in the Division of Home Reading and Community Services, while two thirds (1,291,934) were in the Division of Reference and Research Services.

Thus the library has an entire phase of its activity—clearly recognized in its present administrative organization—that is in no sense measured by statistics of circulation. One might note, for example, that the library staff has contributed to Jacob Blanck's *Bibliography of American Literature,* to the second edition of Lyle H. Wright's *American Fiction, 1774–1850: a bibliography,* and that it regularly checks descriptions of its materials for such bibliographers as W. W. Greg, Clifford K. Shipton, and R. W. G. Vail. The State Records Microfilm Project, carried on under the direction of the Library of Congress, in its early stages set up a microfilm camera in the Boston Public Library to reproduce printed and manuscript material relating to the Massachusetts Bay colony and province, while the Library's excellent set of the British House of Commons *Sessional Papers* was utilized in a microprint reproduction of that series a few years ago. Within recent months, the library has made available for first American performance manuscript copies of the chamber music of the eighteenth century Dublin composer, Philip Cogan; has supplied material to an old friend of Sibelius in Finland for a book on the influence of Sibelius in America, and sent photostats by air mail to Greece to aid in a production of Mozart's *Idomeneo* in the Athens Festival. Such biographers and historical novelists as Louise Hall Tharp, Janet Whitney, Catherine Drinker Bowen, Esther Forbes and Kenneth Roberts have drawn upon the manuscript collections of the Boston Public Library in the preparation of their books. Dr. Zoltán Haraszti, the Keeper of Rare Books and Editor of Publications, very largely based his *John Adams and the Prophets of Progress* upon the personal annotations in President Adams's books, which have been deposited in the Boston Public Library for sixty years, while the twenty-nine volumes of *More Books* and the seven volumes of its successor, the *Boston Public Library Quarterly* contain countless articles deriving from the library's holdings. Mr. Arthur W. Heintzelman, the Keeper of Prints and a distinguished etcher in his own right, organized in 1952 exchange exhibitions of contemporary prints between France and the United States, which are still travelling in the two countries. Mr. Heintzelman has also supervised a similar exchange exhibition between Italy and the United States at the request of the Calcografia Nazionale in Rome.

While such activities are taken for granted in research libraries, they do not as a rule occur in the majority of public libraries, and so merit mention in passing. On less scholarly and more practical (or curious) levels, the Boston Public Library constantly copes with requests for information on subjects as varied as zoning regulations, beavers' teeth, a delicacy that I have never encountered called "Boston Cream Pie," hook-up diagrams for converting an electric meter from 2-phase to 3-phase, the properties of bronze and brass alloys, the Ethiopian national anthem, and the operation of the Taft-Hartley law. All of this indicates that there is some possible use within the Copley Square building even for the most unlikely-looking volume in the million and a quarter books that do not help to increase the figures of circulation for home reading.

When one recalls George Ticknor's hopes for the Boston Public Library it is heartening to reflect that, at the beginning of its second century, its major concern is still with bringing the people of Boston to books and, on occasion, even bringing the books to them. The centenary observances that began in the autumn of 1953 rightly emphasized the highly varied aspects of the popular mission of the library, and forcibly brought home to many Bostonians the hitherto unrealized fact that the noble granite building in Copley Square is *not* the Boston Public Library—that it is, rather, the heart and nerve center of a great system that extends to all corners of the city and that has, for a century, lived up to Ticknor's hope for "an apparatus that shall carry the taste for reading as deep as possible into society."

SOURCES

For events of the nineteen forties and fifties, I have had to depend upon information furnished by officers of the Boston Public Library, due to the discontinuance of the older form of narrative reports and the substitution of a purely statistical annual pamphlet. The recent rebuilding of parts of the central library is described and illustrated in "Boston Modernizes—Plans for Enlargement" by Milton E. Lord in the *Library Journal,* LXXVII (15 December 1953). Mr. Githens's preliminary studies for the enlargement of the building are reproduced in a fund-raising pamphlet entitled *Building A Great Future upon A Glorious Past* issued by the Centennial Commission of the Boston Public Library in 1953. David McCord's *Reflections on the Centennial Anniversary of the Boston Public Library,* published by the Centennial Commission in the same year, is a delightful little book, full of information and free from the pompous solemnity that afflicts many commemorative publications of institutions.

I owe my knowledge of the Matthew Arnold anecdote to a reference in Mr. Collier's thesis, cited in my Preface.

Epilogue

THE hundred years covered in this history have seen momentous changes in the availability and distribution of books in the United States. At the beginning of the period, C. C. Jewett in his 1851 report found 694 libraries—accessible to the public on some basis although supported by private funds—with an aggregate of 2,201,-632 volumes. Of this number only five reached a total of fifty thousand volumes each. *Public Library Statistics, 1950,* issued as Bulletin 1953, No. 9 of the U.S. Department of Health, Education and Welfare, Office of Education, reported a total of 7,477 public library systems—receiving 87.4% of their income from local public funds—a century later. The 6,028 of these that returned the Department's statistical report owned a total of 142,931,000 volumes. These astronomical figures, it should be remembered, concern only public library systems in the modern sense, and exclude university libraries and those of numerous private and public institutions.

Of the five libraries reported by Jewett a century ago as possessing fifty thousand or more volumes, two—the Boston Athenæum and the Philadelphia Library Company—have grown only at a comfortable rate. The other three have become veritable giants. Harvard, with 84,000 volumes in 1851, reported 5,703,000 in 1953, standing second to the Library of Congress, whose 50,000 volumes of 1851 had multiplied to 9,847,000. Yale's 50,481 volumes had in the same period become 4,216,000.

In 1868 Justin Winsor found ten libraries in the United States containing upwards of 50,000 volumes, with the Boston Public Library (which was less than fifteen years old) in second place. In 1953, of 71 libraries participating in the Farmington Plan, belonging to the Association of Research Libraries, or to institutions belonging to the Association of American Universities (as listed in K. D. Metcalf's *Report on the Harvard University Library: A Study of Present and Prospective Problems*), plus five large public libraries (listed in Circular 393, revised June 1954 issue, of the Office of Education), no less than nineteen contained upwards of 1,500,000 volumes. In this list the Boston Public Library stands tenth.

1	Library of Congress	9,847,000
2	Harvard University	5,703,000
3	New York Public Library	5,511,000
4	Yale University	4,216,000
5	Cleveland Public Library	2,730,000
6	University of Illinois	2,656,000
7	Chicago Public Library	2,241,000
8	Los Angeles Public Library	2,036,000
9	Columbia University	2,026,000
10	Boston Public Library	1,961,000
11	University of Chicago	1,884,000
12	University of California, Berkeley	1,878,000
13	Brooklyn Public Library	1,803,000
14	University of Minnesota	1,689,000
15	Cincinnati Public Library	1,682,000
16	Philadelphia Public Library	1,651,000
17	Cornell University	1,613,000
18	Detroit Public Library	1,573,000
19	University of Michigan	1,551,000

Growth at such a pace, however inevitable, has not proved an unmixed blessing. Today those who are charged with the administration of great research libraries throughout the country are less apt to express pleasure in the richness and extent of their holdings than concern over means by which they are to be maintained. As books are added to libraries, problems increase by geometrical rather than arithmetical progression. On this point K. D. Metcalf has observed in his recent *Report on the Harvard University Library:*

> The most basic of all library problems is that library collections grow, which necessitates additional space and funds. It should be noted that the growth is different from the growth in most other parts of the University. The University admits students who in due course are replaced by others. The Library takes in books, but does not discard them. A new book does not replace an old book, and a basic factor in the growth of the Library is that it adds to its

collections and does not subtract. An older book in a research institution may be used infrequently, but experience indicates that it rarely becomes a dead book.

The dual nature of the Boston Public Library causes it to share in this inexorable problem of all research libraries, for while the third of its book stock that is devoted to popular circulation may—and indeed should—be subject to constant replacement and improvement without appreciable increase in size, the two-thirds devoted to reference and research must inevitably grow if it is to remain useful. By contrast with the university libraries which can, to some extent, predict the needs of the faculty and students that are its primary users, a public library has to try to foresee the wants of a body of readers in constant fluctuation who happen, at any period, whether permanently or temporarily, to require its services.

Boston of 1850 was a city of 136,881 inhabitants. In 1950 the number had increased to 801,444 within the city limits, which, with the 1,757,137 residents of eighty-two suburban cities and towns that naturally gravitate into Boston, makes a population of over two and a half million in Metropolitan Boston. Moreover, Boston University, Boston College, Simmons College, the Massachusetts Institute of Technology, the New England Conservatory of Music, and innumerable other colleges and schools—all founded within the past century—bring to Boston an immense temporary student population that inevitably and properly finds its way to the Boston Public Library, to supplement the resources of the libraries of those institutions. In addition to this constantly changing body of students living temporarily within the city, approximately 40% of the use of the Division of Reference and Research Services in the Boston Public Library is by Massachusetts citizens who are not resident in Boston. Furthermore, the Boston Public Library conducts an extensive inter-library loan program for the other libraries of the Commonwealth of Massachusetts, employing the full time of two individual workers solely for this purpose. Nevertheless, the City of Boston alone bears the cost.

At the beginning of its second century the Boston Public Library faces among its problems the need of strengthening community interest and of developing increased financial support. The Friends of the Library groups already established in certain branches indicate the usefulness of such organizations in the maintenance of community interest and in the support of individual Branch Libraries. It is hoped that similar groups may develop in support of the special subject departments of the Central Library, so that gifts from private sources may supplement the present endowment funds and the appropriations already made by the City of Boston. As much of the non-Boston use of the Central Library comes from the Greater Boston Metropolitan Area, it is apparent that nearby cities and towns may save money on their library collections because many important reference books are obtainable at the Boston Public Library. The financial implications of this should be explored to determine whether mutual help among the metropolitan libraries might be developed through contractual relationships in meeting certain costs. Similarly, a program of state aid for Massachusetts libraries needs exploration, for the present limited program of the Commonwealth for public libraries is designed to help small rural libraries only. Cities and towns receive no financial help whatever from the program, but have to depend entirely upon their own fiscal resources, which consist chiefly of the already over-burdened real estate tax. If imaginative answers are found to the problems of community interest and broader financial support, the further problems of improvement of the physical plant, the maintenance of the book collections, and new developments in the use of the Boston Public Library will be well on the road to solution.

In its approaches to the problems of the future, the Boston Public Library has the advantage of long-experienced guidance and of a continued tradition of generous and willing support by the City of Boston. The senior Trustee, Frank W. Buxton, has served continuously since 1928. The present Director, Milton E. Lord, having come to the Library in 1932, has guided its affairs longer than any of his predecessors. Like two others of them—Winsor and Belden—he has had the highest honor in his profession—the presidency of the American Library Association.

It is a good augury for the second century of the Library that its relations with the City Government have never been happier than at the present time. While it has been necessary to note in some detail the political interference that led to Justin Winsor's resignation in 1877, and the strains and stresses during the construction of the Copley Square building, it is pleasant to be able to observe in conclusion the happiness of association that has existed between the Trustees and the Director of the Library on the one side and the Mayor and City Council on the other during the past thirty years. The interest of the current Mayor of Boston, the Honorable John B. Hynes, has been particularly notable. Mayor Hynes, a long-time career official of the City, has had a deep respect and sympathy for the Public Library, dating from his boyhood acquaintance with it. He has supported the Library in every way in most understanding fashion, and has been the prime mover in making funds available for the construction of the new branch libraries at Adams Street, Egleston Square, and South Boston.

BOOKMOBILE

APPENDIX

Directors of the Library

From 1852 to 1858 the chief officer of the Library bore the title of Librarian; *from 1858 to 1877* Superintendent; *from 1877 to 1923* Librarian; *from 1923 to 1934* Director; *since 1934* Director, and Librarian.

Edward Capen, 1852–74
Charles Coffin Jewett, 1858–68
Justin Winsor, 1868–77
Samuel Abbott Green, 1877–78
Mellen Chamberlain, 1878–90
Theodore Frelinghuysen Dwight, 1892–94

Herbert Putnam, 1895–99
James Lyman Whitney, 1899–1903
Horace Greeley Wadlin, 1903–17
Charles Francis Dorr Belden, 1917–31
Milton Edward Lord, 1932–

Presidents of the Trustees

Edward Everett, 1852–64
George Ticknor, 1865
William Whitwell Greenough, 1866–88
Henry Williamson Haynes, 1888
Samuel Appleton Browne Abbott, 1888–95
Frederick Octavius Prince, 1895–99
Lincoln Solomon, 1899–1907
James De Normandie, 1908
Josiah Henry Benton, 1908–17
William Francis Kenney, 1917–20
Alexander Mann, 1920–23
Arthur Theodore Connolly, 1923–24
Louis Edward Kirstein, 1924–25
Michael Joseph Murray, 1925–26
Guy Wilbur Currier, 1926–27
Arthur Theodore Connolly, 1927–28
Louis Edward Kirstein, 1928–29
Gordon Abbott, 1929–30
Frank W. Buxton, 1930–31
Louis Edward Kirstein, 1931–32

Ellery Sedgwick, 1932–33
John Loomer Hall, 1933–34
William Cardinal O'Connell, 1934–35
Frank W. Buxton, 1935–36
Louis Edward Kirstein, 1936–37
Ellery Sedgwick, 1937–38
John Loomer Hall, 1938–39
Robert Howard Lord, 1939–40
Frank W. Buxton, 1940–41
Louis Edward Kirstein, 1941–42
Ellery Sedgwick, 1942–43
John Loomer Hall, 1943–44
Robert Howard Lord, 1944–45
Frank W. Buxton, 1945–46
Abraham Edward Pinanski, 1946–47
Francis Boyle Masterson, 1947–48
Robert Howard Lord, 1948–49
Frank W. Buxton, 1949–50
Frank Joseph Donahue, 1950–51
Lee Max Friedman, 1951–53
Patrick Francis McDonald, 1953–55
Richard James Cushing, 1955–

Trustees of the Library

INDEX

Abbey, Edwin A., mural paintings by, 148, 156, 158, 167–168, 176, 192, 193, 247

Abbott, Gordon, Trustee, President, 263, 264

Abbott, Samuel Appleton Browne, Trustee, President, 140, 263, 264; appointed Trustee, 118; elected President, 127, 146; assumes duties of Librarian, 127–128, 185; engages McKim, Mead and White, 141; in role of patron of the arts, 148ff; contracts with artists for decorative sculpture and painting, 158; his autocratic habits, 227, 228, 245; his unseemly interchange with W. F. Poole, 151–152; requests Adams Library, 169; his essential role in the building of the Copley Square library, 161–162; resigns in disgust, 168; his later life, 169

Abuses of library by readers, 66–67, 153–154, 170, 217–218

Acrostic on façade of Copley Square library, 156–157

Adams, Charles Francis, on committee to consider Vattemare's plan, 7, 9; engages Vattemare as ventriloquist, 7

Adams, Charles Francis (II), 169

Adams, Henry, 129

Adams, John, 169–170

Adams, William T. (Oliver Optic), delivers address, 88

Adams Library, 169–170

Adams Street Branch Library, 252, 253, 262

Administrative reorganization of 1932, 228

Agassiz, Louis, 9–10

Ainsley, Emily L., Fund, 236

Allen, James B., of City Council, appointed to first Board of Trustees, 27

American Academy of Arts and Sciences, 9, 16, 40, 72

American Antiquarian Society, 9, 77

American Baptist Missionary Society, gives books, 16

American Library Association, elects Justin Winsor President, 101; elects C.F.D. Belden President, 220; elects Milton E. Lord President, 261; meets in Boston in 1890, 151

American Library Journal, editorial on Justin Winsor, 108–109

Ames, Child and Graves, architects, 246

Anderson, Edwin H., surveys library in 1918, 205–208, 221

Andrews, William T., appointed by Boston Athenæum to consider merger with Boston Public Library, 8

Annual examination of books, 44, 69, 94–95

Antin, Mary, quoted, 192–194

Appleton, Samuel, gift from, 37

Appleton, Thomas Gold, Trustee, 27, 45, 93, 237, 264

Apthrop, William F., surveys musical department, 123

Arnold, Matthew, 240–241, 244

Artz, Victorine Thomas, gift from, 172

Association of Research Libraries, 255, 258

Astor Library, 15–16, 77

Audio-Visual Department, 248–249

Austin, Edward, gift from, 45

Bacchante, by Frederic Macmonnies, causes ludicrous controversy, 176–182; drawing of, 178

Baker Library, Harvard Business School, 213–214

Barlow, Samuel L. M., books bought at sale of his library, 123

Barton, Mrs. Thomas P., 92

Barton Library, 92–93, 121, 161, 218

Kirstein, Louis Edward, Trustee, President, 263, 264
Kirstein Memorial Library, 214; drawing of interior, 215

Labrouste, Henri, 143
Landscape architecture, Codman collection on, 172
Lawrence, Abbott, bequest from, 65
Lawrence, James, of City Council, appointed to first Board of Trustees, 27
Lecture Hall, 182
Lee, Francis W., placed in charge of Printing Department, 174
Lewis, Weston, Trustee, 96, 264
Library Company of Philadelphia, 2, 77, 298
Library of Congress, 2, 49, 77, 258
Library Training Class, 232
Light reading, pompous strictures upon, 51, 64, 88
Lincoln, Solomon, Trustee, President, 185, 190, 263, 264
Longfellow collection, 172
Lord, Milton Edward, Director, and Librarian, 263; appointed, 221; his administration, 221–239, 243–257, 258–262; quoted on need for more books, 224–225; negotiations with John Deferrari, 243–244; elected President of American Library Association, 261
Lord, Monsignor Robert H., Trustee, President, 227, 263, 264
Lowell Institute, 9
Lower Hall in Boylston Street library, 57–59, 70, 80–81, 102, 153–154
Lower Mills Reading Room, 174

McCarthy, Dennis, night watchman, the first employee to be pensioned, 201
McCord, David, quoted, 162
McDonald, Patrick Francis, Trustee, President, 263, 264
McKim, Charles Follen, architect of Copley Square library, 140–146, 148–150, 158–159, 161, 164, 192, 215, 251; his offer of Macmonnies' Bacchante, 176–177; the resulting commotion, 177–182; offer withdrawn, 182

McKim, Julia Amory Appleton, 141, 176
McKim, Mead and White, architects of Copley Square library, 140–146, 157, 167
McMahan, Rev. J. B., gift from, 19
Macmonnies, Frederic, statue of Sir Harry Vane by, 158; Bacchante by, causes ludicrous controversy, 176–182
Maginnis and Walsh, architects of Boylston (Connolly) Branch Library, 213
Mann, Rev. Alexander, Trustee, President, 263, 264
Mason Street Library, 34, 37, 41, 43–54, 57; drawing of façade of, 37
Massachusetts Acts: authorization to establish a public library (1848), 13; act to incorporate Trustees of Boston Public Library (1878), 110–111; grant of land in Copley Square (1880), 133–134; authorization to take additional land (1882), 133; amending act of incorporation of Trustees (1887), 139; authorization to issue bonds for new library building (1889), 149–150, 154; authorizing a further issue of bonds (1891), 151; authorizing alterations in Copley Square library (1892), 182
Massachusetts Historical Society, 9, 16, 40, 97, 112, 114
Massachusetts Sabbath School Society, gives books, 17
Masterson, Francis Boyle, Trustee, President, 263, 264
Mattapan Branch Library, 213, 251
Mattapan Library Association, 85
Mattapan Reading Room, 174
Matthews, Nathan, Mayor of Boston, 154–157
Mead, William Rutherford, 140
Mechanic Apprentices Library Association, enthusiastically endorses Vattemare's plan, 9
Mercantile Library Association, Boston, enthusiastically supports Vattemare's plan, 5–7, 9; gives its books for South End Branch, 112; slides to an inglorious end, 124–125

This book, designed by Rudolph Ruzicka, the text set in his Fairfield Medium type, was manufactured by the Plimpton Press, Norwood, Massachusetts.